Mastering Salesforce Reports and Dashboards

and Dashboards

Drive Business Decisions with Your CRM Data

David Carnes

Beijing · Boston · Farnham · Sebastopol · Tokyo

Mastering Salesforce Reports and Dashboards
by David Carnes

Published by O'Reilly Media, Inc., 1005 Gravenstein Highway North, Sebastopol, CA 95472.

O'Reilly books may be purchased for educational, business, or sales promotional use. Online editions are also available for most titles (*http://oreilly.com*). For more information, contact our corporate/institutional sales department: 800-998-9938 or *corporate@oreilly.com*.

Acquisitions Editor: Michelle Smith	**Indexer:** nSight, Inc.
Development Editor: Rita Fernando	**Interior Designer:** David Futato
Production Editor: Christopher Faucher	**Cover Designer:** Karen Montgomery
Copyeditor: Piper Editorial Consulting, LLC	**Illustrator:** Kate Dullea
Proofreader: Piper Editorial Consulting, LLC	

June 2023:   First Edition

Revision History for the First Edition
2023-06-14:   First Release

See *https://www.oreilly.com/catalog/errata.csp?isbn=9781098127848* for release details.

978-1-098-12784-8

[LSI]

Table of Contents

Preface

Year after year, Salesforce builds upon its offerings as a customer relationship management platform, enabling people to make informed business decisions and answer questions about the data in their systems. While Salesforce offers new and powerful add-ons for business intelligence capabilities, such as Tableau and CRM Analytics, it continues to innovate upon its core reporting features: reports and dashboards.

Salesforce reports and dashboards are incredibly useful. Whether they are run directly or embedded in page layouts, reports and dashboards answer user questions about their data, provide summary details, and show metrics graphically. Salesforce provides a set of formats to use in creating reports and a number of visual elements that can be used to build dashboards. The aim of this book is to step you through each of these reporting tools so that you can be successful in creating, using, and managing Salesforce reports and dashboards.

Who This Book Is For

This book will help everyday users, super users, managers, and executives alike make the most of Salesforce reports and dashboards with walkthroughs, best practices, and practical use cases. Everyday users will learn how to create reports and dashboards to make business decisions and answer questions about the data in the system. Report and dashboard super users will learn the range of features available, how to enable them, and when to use them. Executives will learn what is possible with reports and dashboards, and be empowered to be self-sufficient in analyzing their data. Managers will learn how to better oversee their team's data and lead their team confidently.

Navigating This Book

This book is organized roughly as follows:

- Chapter 1 provides an introduction to Salesforce reports and dashboards, including examples of use cases for various departments within an organization.

- Chapter 2 details reporting considerations related to Salesforce editions, permissions, data model, and data access.

- Chapters 3 and 4 describe capabilities of Salesforce reporting and walk you through the creation of reports.

- Chapter 5 documents the types of formulas that can be used to enhance the data calculated and displayed in reports.

- Chapters 6 and 7 step through the many dashboard features and how to use them to create effective dashboards.

- Chapter 8 focuses on the use of folders to store, organize, and grant access to reports and dashboards.

- Chapter 9 introduces the Analytics tab, which Salesforce is introducing as its Unified Experience for Analytics Home.

- Chapter 10 describes creating, using, and managing custom report types, which are the foundations that reports in Salesforce are built upon.

- Chapter 11 shows how a Salesforce administrator can embed report charts and dashboards into page layouts.

- Chapter 12 offers a tour of the range of report and dashboard features available in the Salesforce App for phones and tablets.

- Chapter 13 defines the value of leveraging trends in reporting and the various ways trending can be achieved using Salesforce reports and dashboards.

- Chapter 14 shares some final thoughts on how to continue your learning journey toward mastering Salesforce reports and dashboards.

Conventions Used in This Book

The following typographical conventions are used in this book:

Italic
> Indicates new terms, URLs, email addresses, filenames, and file extensions.

`Constant width`
> Used for program listings, as well as within paragraphs to refer to program elements such as variable or function names, databases, data types, environment variables, statements, and keywords.

 This element signifies a tip or suggestion.

 This element signifies a general note.

 This element indicates a warning or caution.

O'Reilly Online Learning

 For more than 40 years, *O'Reilly Media* has provided technology and business training, knowledge, and insight to help companies succeed.

Our unique network of experts and innovators share their knowledge and expertise through books, articles, and our online learning platform. O'Reilly's online learning platform gives you on-demand access to live training courses, in-depth learning paths, interactive coding environments, and a vast collection of text and video from O'Reilly and 200+ other publishers. For more information, visit *https://oreilly.com*.

How to Contact Us

Please address comments and questions concerning this book to the publisher:

O'Reilly Media, Inc.
1005 Gravenstein Highway North
Sebastopol, CA 95472
800-889-8969 (in the United States or Canada)
707-829-7019 (international or local)
707-829-0104 (fax)
support@oreilly.com
https://www.oreilly.com/about/contact.html

We have a web page for this book, where we list errata, examples, and any additional information. You can access this page at *https://oreil.ly/mastering-salesforce*.

For news and information about our books and courses, visit *https://oreilly.com*.

Find us on LinkedIn: *https://linkedin.com/company/oreilly-media*

Follow us on Twitter: *https://twitter.com/oreillymedia*

Watch us on YouTube: *https://youtube.com/oreillymedia*

Acknowledgments

There are so many people to thank for helping me along and inspiring me on my Salesforce reporting journey. These include my family and friends, the OpFocus team, participants in the Dashboard Dōjō, and the product management and engineering teams behind Salesforce's reports and dashboards.

This kind of writing project could not be successful without the endless support of my talented and patient editor, Rita Fernando, or my amazing crew of tech reviewers: Taylor Folt, Ezra Kenigsberg, Jesse Lingo, and Duncan Stewart. Thank you each for your time, consideration, and thoughtful input on the writing of this book.

CHAPTER 1

Introduction to Salesforce Reporting

Most Salesforce users start with the ability to create and run reports and to run dashboards, and can take advantage of both reports and dashboards via browser or on mobile devices. This leaves it up to your imagination and business savvy to determine what to build and for whom. In this chapter, I will introduce you to Salesforce's reporting tools and take you through department-specific use cases for reporting in Salesforce to help you get started.

Reports and Dashboards Overview

Within Salesforce there are three tabs that are useful in reporting. They are Reports, Dashboards, and Analytics, as seen in Figure 1-1. The Reports and Dashboards tabs are more commonly seen, each organizing their respective items in folders and giving users who have permission the ability to create and edit them. The Analytics tab is newer, and may be used in place of the other two to provide access to report and dashboard functionality.

Figure 1-1. Three reporting tabs

Reports Tab

The Reports tab shows you a list of all existing reports in your system that are shared with you. Each report has a name, a folder, and details such as who created the report and when. As you can see in Figure 1-2, the tab offers a simple filter mechanism by categories related to reports, folders, and favorites on the left. There is a report search across the top and buttons for creating new reports and folders on the right. To run a report, you click on its name. Each time you run a report, the data in the report is refreshed.

Figure 1-2. Reports tab

Dashboards Tab

The Dashboards tab shows you all dashboards in your system that are shared with you. These might be department-specific dashboards, ones created for individual users, or ones set up for your executive team. In Figure 1-3, you can see a list of dashboards, with information about each and the folder it is stored in. The list of dashboards you see may be very different than the list of dashboards a colleague sees, as access to them is controlled by the folders they are stored in. To run a dashboard, you click on its name. Unlike reports, when you run a dashboard, the data displayed will likely not be updated until you click the Refresh button. More on that in Chapter 6.

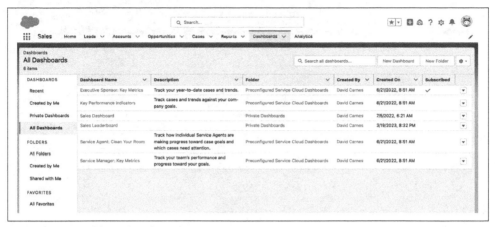

Figure 1-3. Dashboards tab

Analytics Tab

The Analytics tab provides consolidated access to reports and dashboards and their folders with a more user-friendly interface and powerful search capabilities. This tab is newer within Salesforce, and some organizations have yet to embrace using it. Figure 1-4 shows the default Home screen on the Analytics tab, with Browse, Favorites, and Collections categories in the lefthand menu, its powerful search in the top center, and more specific lists in the For You and My Analytics sections through the center. The search tool includes additional filters, allowing you to search for reports created by a particular user, or created or modified within a specific date range. Collections allow you to create and share curated sets of reports and dashboards such as "Year End Planning." To run a report or dashboard from the Analytics tab, click on its title.

You can simplify your system by offering users the Analytics tab instead of the Report and Dashboard tabs, especially for users who only run reports and dashboards, and don't create or manage them. Your system administrator controls which tabs users are able to see in Salesforce and which apps the tabs appear in by default.

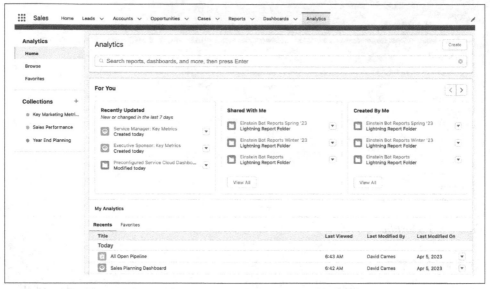

Figure 1-4. Analytics tab

Reports

Reports provide an easy way to query current data in your system and display the results in rows and columns, with optional groupings, summary columns, formulas, and charts. You choose the columns of information that you want to appear and whether you want to see the detail rows or a collapsed summary. You can use them to quickly see a list of all cases closed last month or look at the current state of your sales pipeline.

Reports can be used to answer a single question about your data, provide insights about an area of your business, or to run an entire team. They allow you to choose an area in your system to focus on, filter to see only specific records, and organize the resulting information to help drive understanding and decisions.

Let's say you are the director of sales and want to see how your team is doing. With a report, you can have that information at your fingertips. Figure 1-5 shows an example of a sales report on current quarter sales. At the top of the report, you see grand totals of the number of records and the sum of the amount of won opportunities. You can see that the data in this report is grouped by opportunity owner, with subtotals below each grouping. The report creator made this report a summary report by grouping the report on opportunity owner. They added columns to this report to show relevant sales information such as the opportunity name, stage, and amount. End users running this report can leverage the buttons at the top right to modify and rerun the report, and if they wish, save their own version of the report for later use.

Figure 1-5. Current Quarter Sales report

Reports can be created by any user in your system by using a simple but powerful report editor. There are four report formats to choose from, allowing you to tailor the content of your report to your business needs. You'll learn about creating reports and the four types of report formats in Chapter 4.

Figure 1-6 shows another report using the Summary format. In this example, you can see all open cases in the system, grouped by owner. The report's groupings are collapsed, hiding the details to make it easier to see the subtotals and totals without seeing all the underlying records in the report.

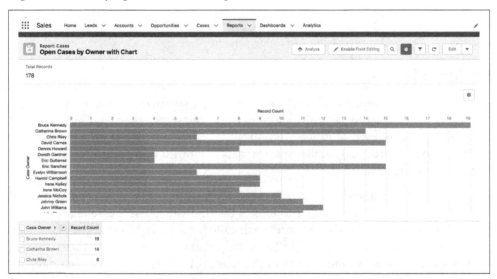

Figure 1-6. Open Cases by Owner with Chart report

There are a few interesting things you can do with reports that have been created and saved in your system. You can embed them into page layouts, as seen in Figure 1-7. You can also use saved reports to feed dashboard components, as you'll learn next.

Figure 1-7. Embedded report chart in a page layout

Dashboards

Dashboards are collections of charts and tables that summarize data in your system visually, often created for a particular department or type of analysis. They are made up of components, each of which are sourced by a single report in your system. It is common to have groups of similar types of data combined into a single dashboard for a user or team to view.

Figure 1-8 shows a support dashboard called My Support KPIs, which can be used by individual users or their managers to look at that individual user's case load and metrics. This is part of a free dashboard pack called the Preconfigured Service Cloud Dashboards (*https://oreil.ly/p82Uz*). There are controls on each dashboard component allowing you to expand the size of the chart, drill down to its underlying report, or download the component.

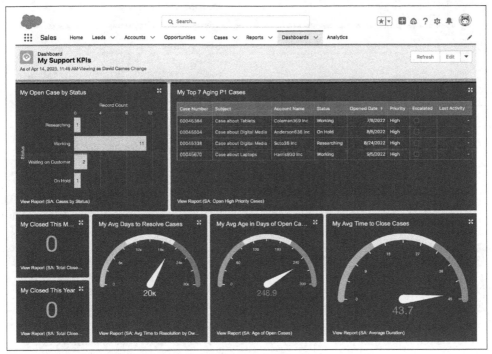

Figure 1-8. My Support KPIs dashboard

There are sets of free sample dashboards available on Salesforce's AppExchange (*https://appexchange.salesforce.com*). Your system administrator can download and install these samples, which can be modified to suit your organization's needs.

Dashboards are created using a simple drag-and-drop editor. When adding a component, you are asked to select a source report and then given the option to choose the component's type. Once a component is selected, you can adjust its many properties to tailor the resulting component to your needs. Dashboards are saved in folders that control who can see them.

Dashboards are commonly embedded into home pages for users to see when they first log in to the system. These might be thin panels with very specific information for individual users, or a full dashboard used to run a team. Figure 1-9 shows an example of an individual sales user's dashboard that appears at the top of their home page. This allows sales users to see a summary of their key metrics at least once each day. A system administrator or someone with dashboard creation permissions would create this dashboard, and then a system administrator would embed it within the sales users' home page.

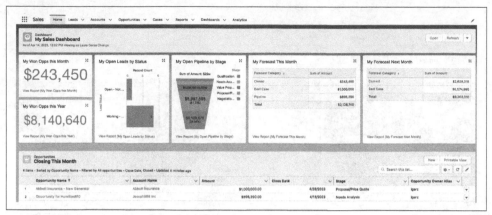

Figure 1-9. My Sales Dashboard in Home page

Use Cases for Reporting

Nearly all Salesforce users end up running reports and dashboards from time to time. A subset of users are power users, running their businesses, teams, and individual work on summary data and charts daily. Others may be more casual users, perhaps not even realizing that they are using reports and dashboards that are embedded into the screens they are viewing to do their jobs. The combination of business savvy and creativity goes a long way in Salesforce reporting. In this section, you'll read examples of use cases for reporting.

 There are 75 or so sample reports available to use in Salesforce Classic. You can switch to Classic, run a report, and use the Save As button to create a clone of any samples, which you can then use in Salesforce's Lightning user interface.

Leadership

It comes as no big surprise that reports and dashboards in Salesforce are often utilized by leadership in an organization. Their needs run across departments and may include specific types of reporting such as trending, ratios, and escalations. Leadership teams often rely heavily upon dashboards to track summary information about the business. This could include a set of dashboards offering key performance indicators (KPIs) or other types of analysis critical to running the business. Figure 1-10 shows the top row of a dashboard called Executive Sponsor: Key Metrics that comes included in the free Preconfigured Service Cloud Dashboards pack on the AppExchange. In it you can see a gauge showing the high number of open cases, a donut showing the ratio of priorities on open cases, and a zero for unassigned cases.

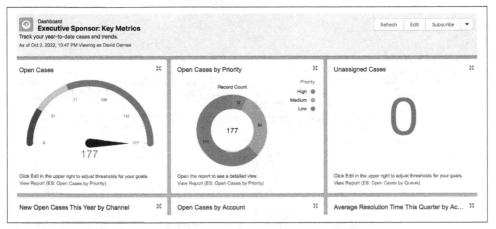

Figure 1-10. Leadership dashboard

Ideally, key metrics that the leadership team uses to run the business are also used by each department so that the organization is aligned in measuring and managing what is most important. For example, if the XYZ sales ratio is critical for management to run the business, you should have the same metric appear on the sales team's dashboard and where applicable on individual sales reps' dashboards so that everyone knows their contribution to that key metric.

Sales

Sales teams can make great use of reports and dashboards to manage their operations. Examples of individual reports might include a current quarter forecast, year-to-date sales, or sales pipeline by region. A VP of Sales might leverage a dashboard detailing sales KPIs, while their head of sales operations may want to conduct win/loss analysis or more closely monitor individual opportunities. Sales managers need reports and dashboards to run their teams, and individual sales reps to monitor their own performance.

Figure 1-11 is an example of a useful report for a head of sales wanting to understand what gaps their individual sales reps have in their opportunity pipelines. This is an example of a matrix report format, which is grouped by the report creator by key fields both vertically and horizontally. Matrix reports are great for seeing a bird's-eye view of data. Conditional formatting is used here to highlight specific data, in this case where there are gaps in each sales rep's pipelines.

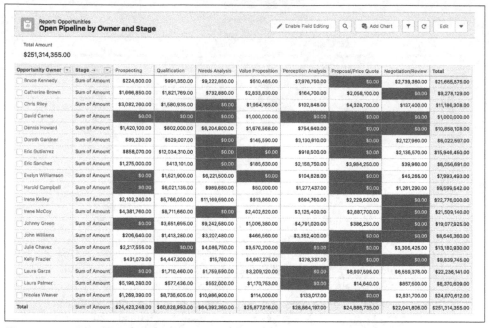

Figure 1-11. Open Pipeline by Owner and Stage report

Marketing

Marketing teams generally have many systems in their organization's go-to-market tech stack, so their reporting needs often extend outside of Salesforce. Within the system, it is common to track campaign effectiveness and the demand that is generated in the form of leads. You can create reports that show the lead-to-conversion ratio and campaign effectiveness, for example. Marketers also want to keep track of what their sales counterparts have done with the leads generated for them.

Figure 1-12 shows a list of sample campaign-related reports that are only available within Salesforce Classic. Notable in this list is the Campaign Call Down report, which combines lead and contact data with their associated campaign, allowing you to see everyone tied to a campaign.

Figure 1-12. Sample Marketing Campaign reports in Salesforce Classic

Marketers might also take advantage of the Leads with Converted Lead Information report type to create reports that show the progress that the sales team is making with leads that have been generated. Figure 1-13 shows such a report, with its unique combination of Lead, Contact, Account, and Opportunity fields.

Figure 1-13. Leads with Converted Lead Information report

Services

Teams using Salesforce Service Cloud functionality can also meet their reporting needs using reports and dashboards. When reporting on support cases, in particular, you'll note their many picklist fields make them very dashboardable! Service teams can create reports that show the agent case workload by status, case aging, and case origin trends, for example. It is common to see multiple dashboards in use for overall support KPIs, team performance, and individual agent workloads.

Figure 1-14 shows a chart added to the top of an Open Cases by Owner and Status report. This is a common way to track agent workload and their progress toward completing the cases they are assigned. Salesforce reports provide eight types of charts that can be added to your reports to fit your business needs.

Figure 1-14. Open Cases by Owner and Status report chart

Reports and Dashboards Versus BI Tools

Although this book is focused on Salesforce reports and dashboards, it is helpful to understand the limits of their capabilities, and where business intelligence (BI) tools take over. The reach of Salesforce reports and dashboards extends only to the data that is stored within that same Salesforce instance. This is a big limitation when leadership teams look to report across departments on data that is stored in other systems and databases. BI tools are often introduced to provide enterprise-level analysis for leadership teams needing to understand data across systems, regions, and departments.

As you'll learn in this book, reports and dashboards offer a set of tools that solve specific needs in reporting. Many organizations are able to run their businesses using Salesforce reports and dashboards. Individual users, whose main body of work is tracked within Salesforce, such as leads, opportunities, cases, and so on, can also be served by Salesforce's native reporting tools.

BI tools range much further than reports and dashboards in their support of querying and combining data sources, analyzing the data, providing predictive capabilities, and visually representing the data. Put another way, BI tools are far more sophisticated in what they can do than Salesforce reports and dashboards.

Salesforce currently offers two BI tools, Tableau and CRM Analytics. Tableau is a very powerful analytics tool that can be used independently of Salesforce. While its analytics can be surfaced in Salesforce, the vast majority of its use is outside of the system. CRM Analytics provides its users with the ability to explore and surface data from directly within Salesforce. CRM Analytics is a much lighter tool than Tableau, with fewer analysts that know how to use it, though it is more tightly embedded into Salesforce than Tableau.

There are many other excellent choices of BI tools on the market. Even with a BI tool in place, most companies still take advantage of Salesforce reports and dashboards. BI tool licenses can be costly, and so their licenses are often reserved for upper management, if used at all. This leaves reports and dashboards as the primary reporting tools for most Salesforce users. Given their ease of use and access, reports and dashboards serve most Salesforce users very well.

Conclusion

Reports and dashboards support the needs of all levels of users in your system across the various departments that use Salesforce. They can be accessed directly on their respective tabs, searched for and run on the Analytics tab, or embedded within page layouts. While there are no sample reports or dashboards in Salesforce's Lightning user interface, there are free examples that you can find and leverage as starting points in your system.

In the next chapter, you'll learn what additional permissions are needed to build dashboards and to take full advantage of reporting functionality in Salesforce.

CHAPTER 2

First Things First

Before you dive into reporting in Salesforce, it is important to understand which edition of Salesforce you are working on, and what reporting features come with it. You should then review the feature permissions that have been assigned to you, learn how data is organized and secured in your Salesforce system, and understand the out-of-the-box reporting foundations available to you. When reporting on currency fields, it is important to understand the capabilities and limitations of the Multiple Currencies module. Additionally, it is worth considering that each new Salesforce module enabled into your system, whether a free or paid add-on, may introduce its own reporting capabilities.

While many of the settings discussed in this chapter are controlled by your system administrator, your basic understanding of them is vital to ensuring that your reports and dashboards return the results you expect. The more you learn about how your data is organized and the security settings that apply, the stronger your report writing will be.

Salesforce Editions

While all editions of Salesforce offer customizable reports and dashboards, it is important to know which edition you are using to understand the full range of reporting features available to you. The current editions that Salesforce sells include Essentials, Professional, Enterprise, and Unlimited, with Enterprise being the most common and Unlimited including the maximum set of features. Figure 2-1 shows the current editions and indicates that advanced reporting features are only available in the Enterprise and Unlimited Editions of Salesforce.

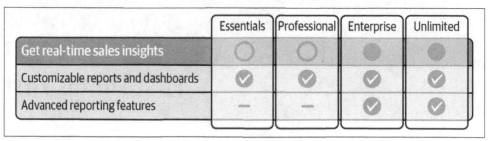

Figure 2-1. Sales Cloud Edition feature comparison

 If you are unsure which edition of Salesforce you are using, ask one of your system administrators, or you can go into Setup, look for the Company Information page, and see your Organization Edition listed.

Within Salesforce Help there is a page that lists out the many reporting features and which are available for each edition. You can find it at Reports and Dashboards Limits, Limitations, and Allocations (*https://oreil.ly/GIVCh*). The top of this long file is shown in Figure 2-2.

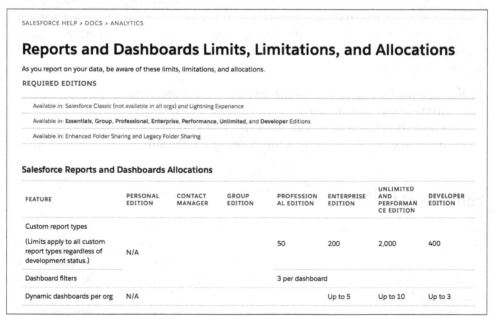

Figure 2-2. Report and dashboard limits

The limits on this page are updated during Salesforce's three release windows each year, as new features are introduced and limits are adjusted. This information makes this page very useful to you in understanding what is possible with Salesforce reporting in your instance. For the purpose of this book, we are focused on the Enterprise Edition's set of reporting features, and will note when the Unlimited Edition adds more.

Settings and Permissions

In order to get the most out of your work with reports and dashboards, you will want to ensure that you have the necessary profile permissions in your Salesforce instance. System administrators start with all report and dashboard permissions, so if you are one of them, you are good to go. Non-system administrators have to be more aware of what permissions they've been assigned, and may need to ask their system administrator for access to other features to be successful.

There are about 30 report and dashboard permissions that can be assigned to users in Salesforce using profile and permission sets. Only four of these permissions are assigned by default in the Standard User security profile, which is often copied as the basis for custom profiles. The four default permissions are: Create and Customize Reports, Run Reports, Export Reports, and Subscribe to Reports. This leaves more than 25 other reporting-related permissions that can be assigned to give users the reporting functionality they need to do their jobs. Figure 2-3 shows some of the report and dashboard subscription-related profile permissions. Note that what is enabled and not enabled by default is indicated by the corresponding checkboxes. Oddly, most users can subscribe to reports by default, but not to dashboards, unless a system administrator enables the permission.

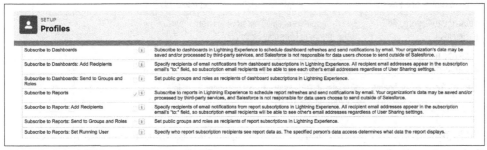

Figure 2-3. Profile permissions

One way to think about assigning these permissions is to think about how the key roles in your organization relate to reporting. In Tables 2-1 to 2-4, you'll see suggested permissions for end users, managers, report and dashboard super users, and report and dashboard admins working in Salesforce's Lightning user interface. Your system administrator can update individual profiles with these permissions, or create overlays called permission sets to use to assign these permissions to users in your system.

Table 2-1. Suggested reporting permissions for end users

Permission	Description	Notes
Create and Customize Reports	Create, edit, and delete reports in personal folders.	This is set by default.
Report Builder	Create, edit, and delete reports using the classic report builder interface.	Classic only. Likely deprecated.
Report Builder (Lightning Experience)	Create, edit, and delete reports using the enhanced report builder interface. Only available in Lightning Experience.	Lightning only.
Run Reports	Run reports and dashboards.	This is set by default.
Schedule Dashboards	Schedule when dashboards refresh, and send email notifications that include refreshed dashboards in HTML format.	Classic only.
Schedule Reports	Schedule report refreshes in Salesforce Classic, and send email notifications that include refreshed reports in HTML format.	Classic only.
Subscribe to Dashboards	Subscribe to dashboards in Lightning Experience to schedule dashboard refreshes and send notifications by email.	Lightning only.

Table 2-2. Suggested reporting permissions for managers

Permission	Description	Notes
Export Reports	Use Export Details and Printable View to export reports.	This permission allows for the quick download of large amounts of data, and thus should be only given out to those who need it.
Subscribe to Dashboards: Add Recipients	Specify recipients of email notifications from dashboard subscriptions in Lightning Experience.	
Subscribe to Dashboards: Send to Groups and Roles	Set public groups and roles as recipients of dashboard subscriptions in Lightning Experience.	
Subscribe to Reports: Add Recipients	Specify recipients of email notifications from report subscriptions in Lightning Experience.	
Subscribe to Reports: Send to Groups and Roles	Set public groups and roles as recipients of report subscriptions in Lightning Experience.	
View My Team's Dashboards	View dashboards owned by people under them in the role hierarchy.	

Table 2-3. Suggested reporting permissions for report and dashboard super users

Permission	Description	Notes
Change Dashboard Colors	Choose dashboard color theme and palette.	Lightning only.
Create and Customize Dashboards	Create, edit, and delete dashboards in personal folders.	
Create Dashboard Folders	Create dashboard folders and manage these folders if sharing rights allow.	
Create Report Folders	Create report folders and manage these folders if sharing rights allow.	

Permission	Description	Notes
Drag-and-Drop Dashboard Builder	Create, edit, and delete dashboards through the drag-and-drop dashboard builder interface.	Classic only.
Edit My Dashboards	Edit, move, save, and delete user's own dashboards in shared folders.	
Edit My Reports	Edit, move, save, and delete user's own reports in shared folders.	
Manage Dashboards in Public Folders	Create, edit, delete dashboards, and manage their sharing in all public folders.	
Manage Dynamic Dashboards	Create, edit, and delete dynamic dashboards.	Enterprise Edition instances can have up to 5 dynamic dashboards, and Unlimited Edition instances can have up to 10. More can be purchased.
Manage Reports in Public Folders	Create, edit, delete reports, and manage their sharing in all public folders.	
Subscribe to Reports: Set Running User	Specify which report subscription recipients see report data. The specified person's data access determines what data the report displays.	
View Dashboards in Public Folders	View and access dashboards in public folders, which does not include others' personal folders.	
View Reports in Public Folders	View and access reports in public folders, which does not include others' personal folders.	

Table 2-4. Suggested reporting permissions for report and dashboard admins

Permission	Description	Notes
Manage Custom Report Types	Create, edit, and delete custom report types.	
Manage Reporting Snapshots	Create, edit, and delete reporting snapshots.	

The suggested permissions by role in the tables are meant to help you think through your organization's needs. Separating out these last two permissions in Table 2-4 from what are assigned to super users may be too granular for your needs. Larger organizations are often more restricted in what permissions they grant users, whereas smaller organizations are more likely to grant additional permissions.

One other reporting permission currently exists on profiles, which is specific to myTrailhead functionality. MyTrailhead is an add-on feature to Salesforce and not covered in the scope of this book. The permission is called Manage Learning Reporting, and it allows users to create reports with associated objects for learning paths.

Salesforce Data Model

The data within your Salesforce instance is organized into objects. Leads, Accounts, Opportunities, Cases, and Campaigns are all examples of objects in your system. The objects that come with Salesforce are called standard objects, and ones that your system administrators build in your system are called custom objects. Custom objects allow you to store other information that is specific to your business. It is not uncommon for even small companies to have hundreds of custom objects! We can create reports on nearly all objects, standard and custom.

An example of a custom object for a software company might be Usage, which stores the software utilization data for that company's customers directly in Salesforce. This information might be brought into your Salesforce system via an integration or manually uploaded at some regular interval via data import. Along with the usage data, the integration would bring IDs that allow the utilization records to be associated with accounts and contacts. This linkage between objects provides the basis of reporting in a relational database like Salesforce.

In relational-database terms, Salesforce objects are tables, each of which contains a grouping of similar records, with individual pieces of information separated into fields. Contact is a table in Salesforce, with each record having fields for first name, last name, email address, and so on. Tables are connected using primary keys and foreign keys, which are also known as ID fields. Child tables have foreign keys that point to parent table primary keys, supporting the joining of the tables. This architecture allows you to associate contacts with accounts, for example, without requiring that you store all account information within the contact table. You only require that each contact specifies an account ID. This forms the basis for relational databases and their speedy queries.

One way to see a diagram of the objects in your Salesforce system and how they relate is to look at Schema Builder within Setup. Using this tool requires either that you are a system administrator or have been assigned the Customize Application profile permission. Figure 2-4 shows four objects: Campaign, Campaign Member, Contact, and Lead. It shows how they are related and a list of fields for each, in a diagram tool that you can manipulate. The Schema Builder is an older tool within Salesforce, with its own unique user interface, but it is one that can be helpful in learning your system's data model. This is especially valuable for getting up to speed on the data model of custom applications built upon custom objects in your system.

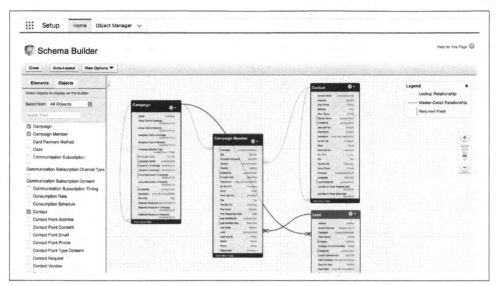

Figure 2-4. Schema Builder screen

Your ability to create reports successfully in Salesforce depends on your understanding how data in your system is organized into objects, and how those objects are related. There can be many hundreds of tables in your Salesforce system. When reporting on opportunities, as seen in Figure 2-5, you usually have access to all account fields along with the opportunity fields. This is true because of how the two objects, Opportunity and Account, are related to each other.

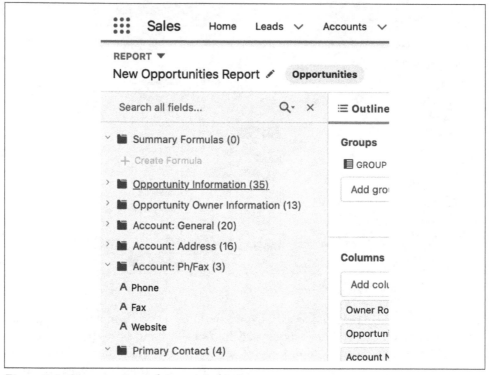

Figure 2-5. Opportunity and Account objects

Reporting Joins

Database tables are joined together in specific ways to support desired reporting results. The basis for these joins is the relationship defined between the tables. It either comes standard, such as with contacts and accounts, or is created by a system administrator as they are configuring your system. An example of a custom relationship between tables is a lookup between case and account called partner, which signifies that a partner company is involved in the case. This lookup provides a connection between the tables that can allow them to be reported on together.

When creating reports in Salesforce, it is important to know the tables (referred to as "objects" in Salesforce) involved and how they are connected to each other. Salesforce supports two types of joins in its reporting, equijoins and left joins. These joins determine the results you will see when you create a report.

Figure 2-6 shows an example of an equijoin. When two tables are joined via equijoin, in order to see an A record you have to have a related B record, and in order to see a B record you have to have a related A record. For example, you might look to create a report in Salesforce that pulls in records from the Case and Asset objects. There is a lookup field on Case that allows you to specify one asset that is associated with the Case. By creating an equijoin report on cases with assets, you will only ever see in the report results cases that have assets.

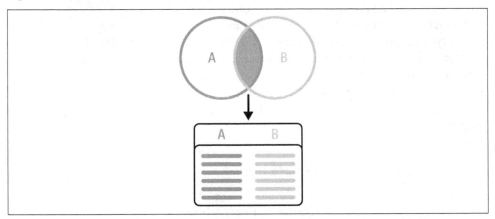

Figure 2-6. Equijoin

Figure 2-7 shows an example of a left join. When two tables are joined via left join, you will see all A records and related B records, whether or not there are any B records. In account-based marketing (ABM), you might create a report on accounts and their opportunities, whether or not there are any related opportunities. This would allow you to list all of your target accounts with any related opportunities.

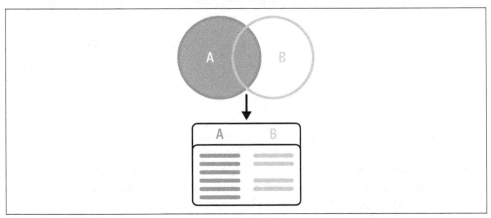

Figure 2-7. Left join

Standard Report Types

Each Salesforce instance starts off with about 75 standard report foundations called report types. As you'll learn in the next chapter, when creating a new report, you must first select a report type. Figure 2-8 shows this first step in creating a new report. The report types represent tables in your system that are joined as either an equijoin or left join to support reporting. If you choose the Accounts with Assets report type, you will only ever see accounts that have assets associated to them. In most cases, the word "with" is indicative of an equijoin between objects. Most of the standard report types are equijoins, which means that in your report results you will only get an A if there is at least one corresponding B.

Create Report

	Select a Report Type		
Recently Used			
All	Q Search Report Types...		▼ Filter (0)
Accounts & Contacts	**Report Type Name**	**Category**	
Opportunities	Accounts	Standard	▼
	Contacts & Accounts	Standard	▼
Customer Support Reports	Accounts with Partners	Standard	▼
Leads	Account with Account Teams	Standard	▼
	Accounts with Contact Roles	Standard	▼
Campaigns	Accounts with Assets	Standard	▼
Activities	Contacts with Assets	Standard	▼
Contracts and Orders	Accounts with Projects	Standard	▼

Figure 2-8. Standard report types

Your selection of a report type determines which objects and fields are available in the resulting report. Many of the standard report types have special fields available that do not exist on the underlying objects, but have been added to support reporting goals. Figure 2-9 shows the Opportunities report type and some special fields that are available when using it, such as Last Stage Change Date and Stage Duration. Close Date (2) is a special field that displays the close date, allowing you to use the Close Date Field in groupings and still see the actual close date value as a column.

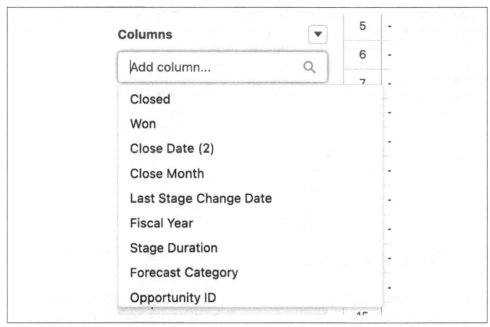

Figure 2-9. Special fields available on Opportunities report type

The best way to get to know the report types is to try them out and see what objects and fields are supported. When first using a new report type, scroll through the fields available to ensure you're using the best ones for your purpose.

Data and Data Access Considerations

Your organization decides whether its data is freely visible to all users or locked down based on each user's need-to-know. Understanding these data access policies around who sees what impacts your ability to create effective reports. Your data access permissions may differ from those that your report users have when looking at the same reports. This means that you might look at the same report as the person sitting next to you, and see different results!

Your system administrator defines visibility to records in your system using a combination of tools within Salesforce Setup. These include security controls like the Role Hierarchy, Org Wide Defaults, and Sharing Rules, and are rooted in the concept of record ownership. Figure 2-10 shows the Sharing Settings page within Setup where a system administrator controls the Org Wide Defaults and Sharing Rules for your org. In large organizations, this page can be very, very long, listing out hundreds of objects. You can see here that while Account is shared as Public Read/Write,

Opportunity's visibility is set to Private. These two settings mean that everyone can see and edit all accounts in the system, but only the record owner and users above them in the Role Hierarchy can see opportunities.

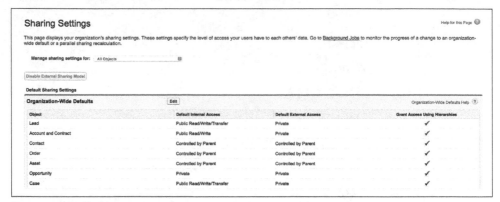

Figure 2-10. Sharing Settings page

While these security settings are controlled by your system administrator, it is important to know the basics about them. The Role Hierarchy resembles an org chart within your system, identifying who reports to whom. By default, users above you in the Role Hierarchy can see and edit the same records that you can. Org Wide Defaults define the baseline level of access for each object in your system, and Sharing Rules allow you to define exceptions to those rules. Who owns a record such as XYZ account is also important to how data is shared.

 A special reporting feature called the Account Owner report can be enabled by a system administrator in Salesforce systems where the organization-wide sharing access level is set to private for accounts. This allows a special report type of the same name to be used to create a report that lets users search for an account and who owns it, regardless of whether that user has permission to see that account.

Another security tool can play a role in what you see, or don't see, on reports and dashboards. It is called Field Level Security (FLS), and it allows your system administrator to choose which fields to hide completely or make read-only to certain profiles. When a field is hidden to you via FLS, you will not be able to see that field as a column on a report.

Using Multiple Currencies

One module used in many Salesforce instances around the world is Multiple Currencies. This feature is not enabled in a Salesforce instance by default. When turned on by a system administrator, it introduces new capabilities across Salesforce. Each user will then have a default currency and each record will have a currency, both of which impact reporting.

On reports, the Multiple Currencies module reveals a useful twin field for every field of data type Currency. The original field, such as Amount, will show amounts in the original currencies, while the twin field, which has "(converted)" in its name, will be displayed in the currency you choose on each report. Figure 2-11 shows two such "(converted)" fields next to the original Amount and Annual Revenue fields. The top arrows point to the Amount and Amount (converted) columns. Note that the Amount column contains two currencies, USD and CAD, and thus should no longer be used to sum values on reports. The bottom arrows show a pull-down menu where on a report you can select any of the active currencies in your Salesforce instance to see the current conversion using the rates updated by your system administrator.

Amount ▾	Amount (converted) ▾	Annual Revenue ▾	Annual Revenue (converted) ▾
USD 10,000.00	USD 10,000.00	USD 42,011,000.00	USD 42,011,000.00
CAD 5,000.00	USD 3,881.69	CAD 300,000,000.00	USD 232,901,172.27
USD 20,000.00	USD 20,000.00	CAD 64,877,585.00	USD 50,366,885.33
CAD 0.00	USD 0.00	USD 54,902,000.00	USD 54,902,000.00
USD 15,000.00	USD 15,000.00	USD 6,000,000.00	USD 6,000,000.00
USD 343,360.00	USD 343,360.00	USD 116,793,000.00	CAD - Canadian Dollar
USD 2,500.00	USD 2,500.00	USD 80,741,000.00	✓ USD - U.S. Dollar
USD 25,000.00	USD 25,000.00	USD 28,119,000.00	Currency: USD ▾

Update Preview Automatically

Figure 2-11. Multiple Currencies impact on report builder

When you enable the Multiple Currencies module, currency fields such as Amount will display the various currencies in use in your system and its twin, the Amount (converted) column, will show the converted amounts. The totals for both columns, however, will sum up the converted amounts, making both columns useful on reports and dashboards.

One other impact of Multiple Currencies comes in how we can use currencies within report filters. Specifically, you can prepend currency amounts with a currency code, for example, "Amount less than USD 1000000" when filtering the data in your report. If you do not specify a currency code, amounts are assumed to be in the personal currency of the user running the report.

 When reporting on currency fields in Salesforce, keep in mind that currency conversions, even on very old records, will use the current exchange rate. This will alter your report values as currency rates change over time. Salesforce provides Advanced Currency Management to introduce dated exchange rates, but only on opportunity-related data.

Add-On Modules Introduce Additional Reporting Features

While not covered in depth in this book, it is worth noting that many of Salesforce's free add-on modules and paid add-on products introduce additional reporting-related features. Some of these features are more obvious than others, and some are tucked away to be found only by those who go looking for them. When readying to take advantage of a new module, you should review relevant Salesforce Help documentation and explore your system for related reporting features.

Salesforce provides optional Teams modules on three objects—Accounts, Cases, and Opportunities—to help track team member involvement on and grant record-sharing access to these records. While each is slightly different, these Teams features, when enabled by your system administrator, provide additional fields, report filters, and report types. Figure 2-12 shows three "team-selling" filters that are available to use on opportunity reports when Opportunity Teams is enabled.

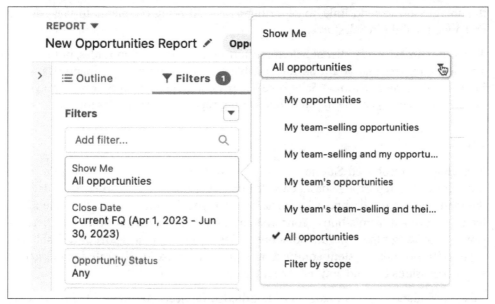

Figure 2-12. Opportunity Team-Selling filters

If you have a Salesforce CRM Analytics Plus license (and an additional profile permission assigned), you have access to a powerful feature called Einstein Discovery for Reports. It appears in the top right corner toolbar of reports in the form of the Analyze button, as shown in Figure 2-13. Clicking the button on a report scans the report data using Einstein Discovery's artificial intelligence and statistical analysis. A sidebar panel will open on the report with analysis of the report's data across a number of categories that you can drill down further into.

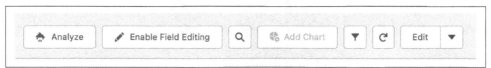

Figure 2-13. Analyze button

While Salesforce's Configure Price Quote (CPQ) product comes with no reports or dashboards, it does provide a set of standard and custom report types you can use to build reports. Other modules, such as Collaborative Forecasting and Enterprise Territory Management, introduce objects that can be referenced in custom report types and special filter options to support your report and dashboard goals. You will learn more about the power of custom report types in Chapter 10.

If your organization uses Slack, there is a free add-on called CRM Analytics for Slack that can be enabled by your system administrator. This feature allows you to subscribe to up to seven reports or dashboards directly from within Slack. You can use this integration to send links to reporting assets, allowing recipients to view details and open the links in Salesforce.

This is not an exhaustive list of Salesforce add-on products and modules, but rather a sample to suggest that you look for possible additional reporting capabilities when implementing new features. Salesforce Help documentation and some good old-fashioned tinkering can be useful in uncovering reporting capabilities for each.

Conclusion

This chapter introduced Salesforce's editions and described where in Help you can learn about the report and dashboard features that are standard in each. It detailed the many report and dashboard permissions that you'll need to take advantage of the features outlined in this book. Your system administrator uses profiles and permission sets to assign these permissions out to users. If you are a report and dashboard super user, but not a system administrator, you may need to advocate for the necessary permissions to build and manage them effectively.

Salesforce's data model is made up of hundreds of objects, and forms the basis upon which all of reporting is built. These objects are joined together to form reporting foundations called report types, which are the first step in building a new report. Each new module you implement may offer unique reporting features worth exploring. Beyond this, there are security controls that govern who sees what data in the system. There is clearly a lot to think about before you get started with reporting.

In the next chapter, you'll learn all about the Reports tab and how you can use it to control which reports users see in your system.

CHAPTER 3

Reports

Reports provide a quick way to query the data in your Salesforce system. They also serve as a tool to run your business, manage a team, or track your individual workload. There are many use cases for reports in an organization. Marketing managers create reports to track the impact of their campaigns. Customer service directors use reports to monitor the performance of their teams in resolving cases. Vice presidents of sales run their pipeline review meetings with reports. The list goes on and on.

Most users have the ability to create reports on the data that they can see within their systems. They can create a report to see the data, and they can save it to reuse and share with others. When a user does not have the ability to create reports, a report can be made on their behalf by a super user or administrator.

Whether you are creating or accessing a report, all the action will happen on the Reports or Analytics tabs. There, they are organized into folders that control sharing access to their contents. In this chapter, you will step through the basics of reports and walk through their primary home on the Reports tab.

What Is a Report?

Reports in Salesforce are built upon the data that is within your system. They are intended to give users an easy way to see their data in detail or aggregate, monitor trends, and identify issues for follow up. You run existing reports by clicking on their name. At their core, reports are made up of source data that is filtered and then displayed in rows and columns on the screen. The information shown might also group records, leverage formulas, include summary columns, and display charts.

In Figure 3-1, you see the top of a report on open activities by account. The report is grouped by account name, with the individual activities exposed as rows within. The count of the open activities is listed at the top, and there are controls provided to users to adjust and manipulate the report while looking at it.

Report: Activities with Accounts
Open Activities by Account
This report shows a list of all open activities in the system grouped by account.

Total Records
223

Account Name ↑	Subject	Date	Assigned	Type	Priority	Status
Abbott358 Inc (1)	Email exec mas [5858]	9/6/2022	Eric Sanchez	Email exec	Normal	Not Started
Subtotal						
Adkins907 Inc (1)	Put a proposal tum [7633]	9/13/2022	Eric Gutierrez	Put a proposal	High	Not Started
Subtotal						
Aguilar870 Inc (2)	Setting up demo rogzifvib [3234]	8/12/2022	Nicolas Weaver	Setting up demo	Normal	In Progress
	Task exec fezi [2163]	8/28/2022	Nicolas Weaver	Task exec	Normal	In Progress
Subtotal						

Figure 3-1. Simple report on Open Activities by Account

Overview of the Reports Tab

The Reports tab is one of three places in Salesforce where you can see a list of all reports you have access to in your system. (The other two places are the Analytics tab and the Mobile app, which you'll learn about later.) The Reports tab offers a simple set of categories on the left, a category-specific search across the top, and additional controls over on the right. The list of reports and folders displays a set of relevant columns that you can customize.

If you've selected one of the report categories on the left side, such as the default view Recent in Figure 3-2, you will see a list of reports and their relevant details organized into columns. Let's go over the default columns. The Report Name column tells you exactly that, the report name. The name is a link that will run the report and show it to you. Some organizations devise a naming scheme to facilitate understanding of what each report will yield. While not required, the Description column can be helpful by offering a few sentences on the purpose, data, or structure of the report. The Folder column tells you where the report is housed and provides a link to view all items in that folder. The Created By and Created On columns are self-explanatory and don't ever change. The Subscribed column shows a checkmark if Salesforce will email the report to users on a regular basis or if it meets certain criteria. In the top left corner, there are 157 items in this user's Recent category.

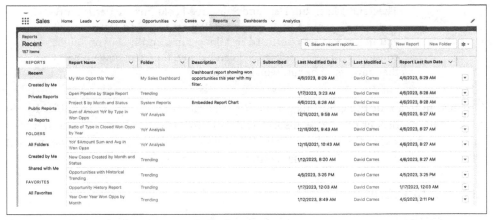

Figure 3-2. Reports tab categories and columns

Your first-ever glance at the Reports tab will likely show you no reports at all. This is because the default view on the tab is Recent, showing you your own recently viewed reports. Clicking All Reports on the lefthand side will show you the full list of reports in folders you have access to.

There are a few other columns that are not visible by default. These include Last Modified By, Last Modified Date, and Report Last Run Date. You can add them to your Reports tab view, or remove others, by clicking on the gear at the top right of the tab and choosing Select Fields to Display, as in Figure 3-3. One of these columns, the Report Last Run Date column, shows the last time a report was run by a user or called by a dashboard to populate a dashboard component. This is useful information for determining reports not regularly used. Another option when clicking this gear is to Reset Column Widths, which can be helpful if the columns in the list on the Reports tab appear incorrectly sized.

Figure 3-3. Customize which columns are visible to you

The Report Last Run Date and Subscribed columns are particularly useful to display on the Reports tab. Report Last Run Date can tell you if a report was not used in a long time, and if so, you might consider retiring it. Subscribed can help each user manage reports they have set to be auto-emailed to them.

One last note about the columns on the Reports tab is that they are sortable. If you click a column header once, it will sort the list of reports or folders by the contents of that column in ascending order. If you click the same column a second time, the list will be sorted by the contents of that column in descending order.

Reports Tab Categories

The categories on the left side of the Reports tab, shown in Figure 3-4, allow you to choose the kinds of reports, folders, and favorite items that you can view in the main part of the screen. The categories are broken into three sections: Reports, Folders, and Favorites. The categories within them are fairly self-explanatory, but let's go through them.

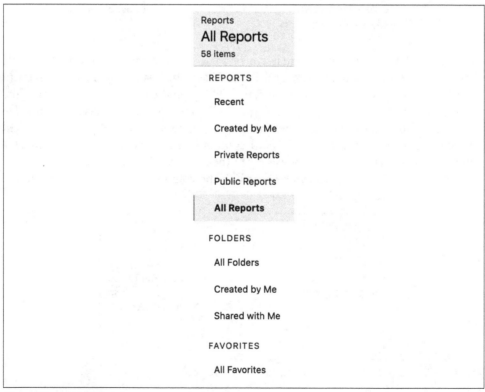

Figure 3-4. Reports tab categories

Under Reports, you will see the categories shown in Table 3-1.

Table 3-1. Report categories

Category	Description
Recent	Shows you reports that you've accessed the most recently.
Created by Me	Shows you reports that you've created.
Private Reports	Shows you reports that are only visible to you.
Public Reports	Shows you reports that are visible to everyone.
All Reports	Shows you all reports that you have access to, regardless of owner.

Next, under Folders, you will see the categories shown in Table 3-2.

Table 3-2. Folder categories

Category	Description
All Folders	Shows you all folders that you have access to in your system.
Created by Me	Shows you the folders created by you.
Shared with Me	Shows you folders created by others that have been shared with you.

Finally, under Favorites, you will see one category, All Favorites, which shows you all the reports you've marked as a favorite for quick access.

Depending on whether you select the Reports, Folders, or Favorites category, the columns displayed will be adjusted to match the category. You'll learn about folders and favorites a little later in this chapter.

Reports Tab Search

There are a few ways you can search for reports in Salesforce. There is the global search at the top center of all screens, which searches across all data in your system and supports partial word searches. With regard to reports, the global search tool searches the title of the report and any text in the description field. Another is the search feature built into the Reports tab, which works differently than Salesforce's global search capability in a couple of important ways.

First, the category selected on the left dictates the scope of the search feature built into the Reports tab. For example, if you select the category Created by Me, the search context will include all reports created by you, as shown by the arrows in Figure 3-5. Note too that the placeholder text in the Reports search box now reads, "Search reports created by me."

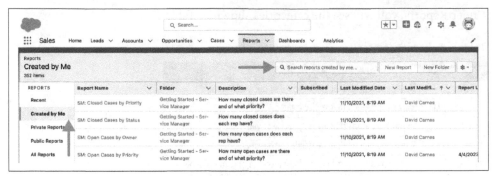

Figure 3-5. Search context driven by category

Second, as you type in the Reports search box, it will immediately refresh to compare your search term to the start of each word in the report names listed for that category. The search mechanism highlights your search term within the start of any matching report name words below. You can search for a report with as few as two characters. Figure 3-6 shows the search for "op" within the Recent category yielding report name words that begin with those same letters, highlighting them in the results.

Figure 3-6. Reports tab search highlights first letters of matching words

 Every time you go to the Reports tab, the initial category will be Recent, which means that the initial search context will also be "Search recent reports." If you want to search through all of your reports or all of your folders, you will need to select one of those categories first.

Reports Tab Folders

Report access is controlled by the folders in which they reside. So, someone who has access to a certain folder also has access to all of the reports within. Folders can be nested up to four levels deep. Figure 3-7 shows the list of all of the top-level folders that you have access to. Note that for each there is no indicator of how many reports or nested folders are in each. Click on a folder name to see the contents of that folder.

Figure 3-7. Top-level folders

Chapter 8 is dedicated to using and managing folders. You'll learn that your ability to see folders and access their contents is controlled by a sharing mechanism on each folder.

Reports Tab Actions

There is a list of actions available to the right of each report or folder name. Your system's list may differ slightly, depending on which features are enabled in your system and what permissions you have. In Figure 3-8, you can see that we can Run, Edit, Subscribe, Export, Delete, Add to Dashboard, Favorite, and Move each report using its action menu. The options are described in Table 3-3.

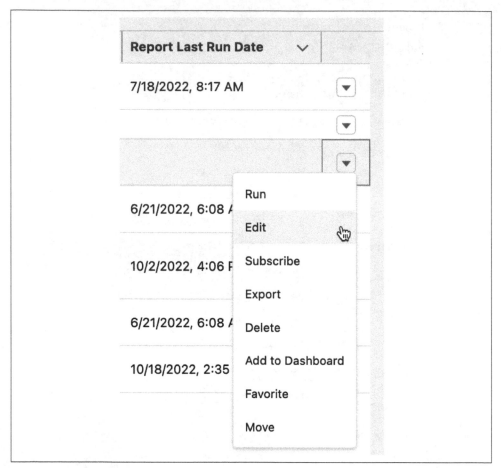

Figure 3-8. Report actions

Table 3-3. Report tab actions

Action	Description
Run	Runs the report.
Edit	Edits the report.
Subscribe	Allows you to receive a copy of the report via email at a set time or when it meets defined criteria.
Export	Allows you to save a copy of the report results to Excel or a .csv file.
Delete	Deletes the report and moves it to the recycle bin.
Add to Dashboard	Allows you to add this report to a new or existing dashboard.
Favorite	Marks this report as one of your personal favorites.
Move	Lets you change the folder where the report is stored.
Open in Quip	If you have a Quip license assigned to you, this action appears, allowing you to open the report directly within Quip.

Reports Tab Menu

When clicking on the Reports tab, if you happen to click on the down arrow embedded in the tab, you will see a list of up to five of your favorited reports above a list of up to five recent reports. As you'll learn later in this chapter, favorites allows each user to create shortcuts to up to two hundred items, including reports. Figure 3-9 shows five favorited reports and a list of recent reports, any of which you can click on to open that report. Each user's list of favorites and recents is unique to them, making this a handy menu for anyone to find and run their own frequently used reports quickly.

Figure 3-9. Reports tab menu

Running Reports

In Salesforce, the act of selecting a report and clicking on its name to view it is known as "running" a report. When running a report, there are many features available on the report to help you navigate and get more from that report. Some examples include filters, charts, toggles, subscriptions, exporting, and favoriting. It is important to understand these features to get the most out of running your reports.

Filters

When running a report you are not familiar with, it is a good idea to take a look at what filters are applied to that report. This will help you understand what data you should expect to see in the report. There is a funnel icon button at the top right of each report that allows you to show or hide the report's filters, shown in Figure 3-10. The figure shows the filters on a report on cases, with three standard filters and a fourth filter Open Equals True applied that has a lock icon. The lock indicates that that filter can't be changed by users when running the report. The other three filters in the filter panel can be changed to adjust the report in the run environment. While you can't add or remove filters using this feature, you can still adjust a report's existing filters. Click on the funnel icon again or the arrow to the right to close the filter panel.

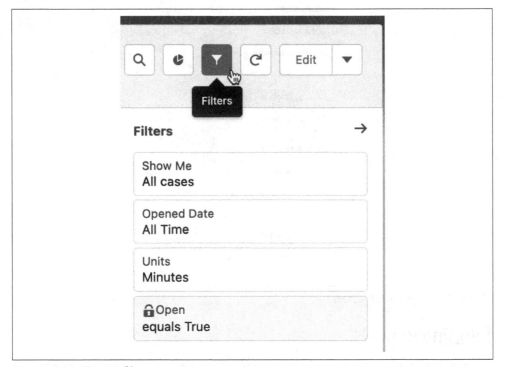

Figure 3-10. Report filters

 Filters are meant to be played with on reports! If there isn't a lock on a filter, you are free to adjust it to see how the report results change.

Charts

Salesforce allows us to organize the data in each report by using columns to group the information, such as showing a list of leads grouped by the lead owner. When running a report that is grouped, the Add Chart button will be active, allowing you to add a chart to the report. For example, let's say you have an Opportunity report that is grouped by owner and stage, shown in Figure 3-11. Clicking the button will add a horizontal bar chart to the report and give you options to change the chart type and its properties.

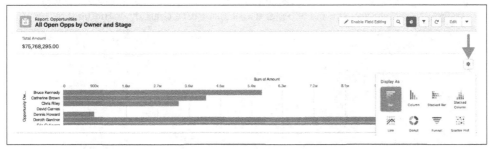

Figure 3-11. Add Chart button

> If the Add Chart button is disabled, you probably need to add a grouping to the report. Charts can only be created for reports that have groupings.

When you've added a chart to the report, look for the gear icon on the right, as indicated by the arrow in Figure 3-12. You can keep the chart as a horizontal bar or change it to one of the other seven kinds of charts that you can see listed. If any of the chart options are grayed out, it is because the report requires a second grouping to use them.

Figure 3-12. Report chart settings

The eight report charts available each have strengths and best uses, as shown in Table 3-4.

Table 3-4. Report chart types

Chart Type	Notes
Bar	Beyond being the default chart, bars are great for displaying many groupings and also for having up to four measures per group.
Column	Columns are excellent for showing progression across time.
Stacked Bar	Stacked bars show off a second grouping's values, but can get busy quickly.
Stacked Column	Stacked columns show off a second grouping's values.
Line	For a few groups' values changing over time, line charts are a great choice. They get busy quickly.
Donut	Donuts show the proportion of values in each slice. Having more than 8 or 10 slices makes them unreadable.
Funnel	Funnels are made for displaying open sales pipeline data grouped by stage but can also be used for any other data going through a process.
Scatter Plot	Scatters show correlations in data.

Each type of chart has its own properties that you can adjust by clicking on the gear icon. Figure 3-13 shows the properties for a stacked bar chart. Here you can see that we can enter a title, adjust the x and y axes, add a reference line, and choose where the legend appears. Stacked bars and columns, for example, also offer the ability to stack to 100%, revealing the proportions of each grouping to one another. Donut and funnel charts have the option Combine Small Groups into Others set by default, which can cause confusion, but can also be used to reduce complexity. To remove the chart from the report, click the Remove Chart button.

 Reporting in any system is all about managing the real estate on the screen. The default legend position on a report chart is "Right," but often you can make better use of space on a chart by changing it to "Bottom."

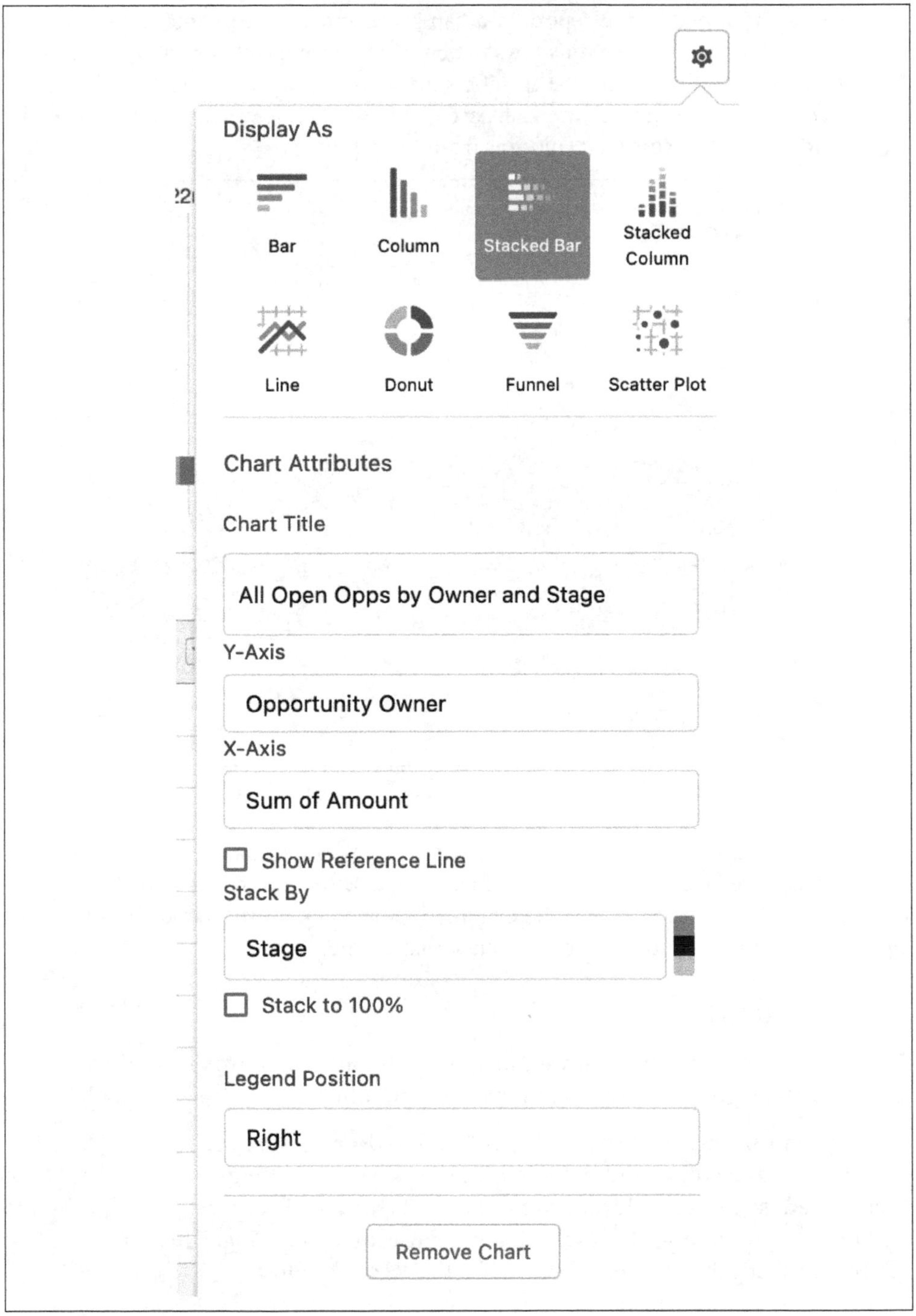

Figure 3-13. Report chart properties

Once a chart is added to the report, you can hover over its segments to see the data behind the segment. Figure 3-14 shows the cursor hovering over Eric Gutierrez's horizontal bar data and revealing the specific sum driving that chart segment. Hovering over a chart segment also shows the percentage of that segment compared to the whole and lists out all summed columns from the report.

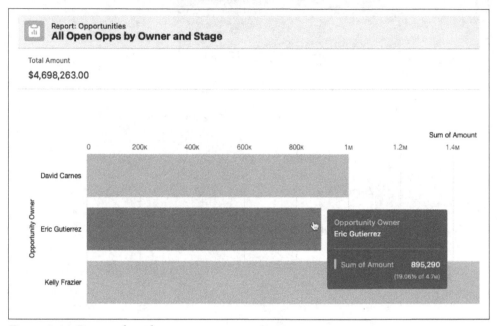

Figure 3-14. Report chart hover

If you click on any chart segment, the report is filtered by that segment. The rest of the chart is grayed out, and the records for just that segment are listed below. To undo that segment filter and return to the original report, click on the same chart segment again. Or, to filter by another segment, click that segment.

Column Actions

There a number of actions that we can apply to reports when we've run them. These include sorting, grouping, and even removing the column.

Each column header on the report can be clicked on to sort the report data. Click once to sort ascending, and a second time to sort descending. Columns that have been sorted, such as the Industry column in Figure 3-15, can be identified by the small arrow pointing up for ascending or down for descending. This report will be sorted alphabetically in ascending order by the account industry.

Account Name ▼	Industry ↑ ▼	Opportunity Name
Owens441 Inc	Agriculture	Opportunity for McLaughlin130
Gordon630 Inc	Agriculture	Opportunity for Dennis260
Bass271 Inc	Agriculture	Opportunity for Lee1827
Obrien994 Inc	Agriculture	Opportunity for Hughes845
Robertson5 Inc	Agriculture	Opportunity for Medina1844
Robertson5 Inc	Agriculture	Opportunity for Gordon852

Figure 3-15. Column sort

Clicking on the dropdown icon next to any column's heading reveals that column's action menu. Figure 3-16 shows the actions that we can take on the Stage column: you can sort the column in ascending or descending order, group the rows or columns by this field, or we can remove the column. In this example, the option to group columns by this field is grayed out because reports have to be grouped by a row first before they can be grouped by a column.

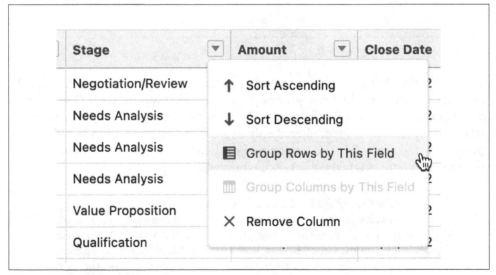

Figure 3-16. Report actions menu

Drill Down

An old and lesser used feature in reporting is our ability to drill down into grouped data, selecting one or more groups, and then changing the grouping. Your ability to drill down appears after you add your first grouping on a report. Figure 3-17 shows one user's open opportunity pipeline grouped by stage where two of the groups have been selected for a closer look. When you click one or more of the boxes next to a grouping (as shown by the left arrow), the Drill Down button (as shown in the right arrow), appears in the buttons at the top of the report.

Stage ↑	Opportunity Owner	Account Name	Opportunity Name	Fiscal Period	Amount	Expected Revenue	Proba
✓ Prospecting (2)	Eric Gutierrez	Rodgers956 Inc	Opportunity for Santiago1975	Q4-2022	$122,200.00	$12,220.00	
	Eric Gutierrez	Ingram644 Inc	Opportunity for Grant1452	Q4-2022	$735,870.00	$73,587.00	
Subtotal							
Qualification (5)	Eric Gutierrez	Rowe333 Inc	Opportunity for Harrington1112	Q4-2022	$905,000.00	$90,500.00	
	Eric Gutierrez	Keller1 Inc	Opportunity for Shaw336	Q4-2022	$389,120.00	$38,912.00	
	Eric Gutierrez	Wright507 Inc	Opportunity for Allison281	Q1-2023	$9,250,000.00	$925,000.00	
	Eric Gutierrez	Rodriquez412 Inc	Opportunity for Holmes1012	Q1-2023	$1,348,890.00	$134,889.00	
	Eric Gutierrez	Reynolds298 Inc	Opportunity for Jennings981	Q1-2023	$141,300.00	$14,130.00	
Subtotal							
✓ Needs Analysis (1)	Eric Gutierrez	Joseph988 Inc	Opportunity for Hamilton810	Q2-2023	$895,290.00	$179,058.00	
Subtotal							
Perception Analysis (1)	Eric Gutierrez	Dean95 Inc	Opportunity for Rhodes1746	Q3-2022	$918,500.00	$642,950.00	

Figure 3-17. Drill Down button

Clicking on the Drill Down button reveals a simple screen where you can change the grouping for the data in those groups. Figure 3-18 shows the Drill Down screen where you can select another group, in this case the account industry, to view this data. The report reruns itself, filtered only to show the values in the selected groups, grouped by the new field. The resulting report looks like any other, grouped by that new value, with the original groups selected added as filters on the report.

When using the Drill Down feature, choosing to not add a Group By value is a quick way to apply a filter on the groups you selected. After you've chosen certain groups and clicked Drill Down, click the X in the Group By box, then click the Apply button. In essence, you can use this to filter your report without visiting the Edit screen.

Drill Down

Filter by Stage
Prospecting, Needs Analysis

Group By

Industry ✕

Cancel   Apply

Figure 3-18. Drill Down selection

Search Report Table

While looking at a report that you've run, you can search within the results and see matches to your search term highlighted. Figure 3-19 shows arrows where you click a magnifying glass to begin a search, and enter a search term such as the word "media." Here the search yields two matches in the Industry column, the first of which is indicated by the bottom arrow. The search box shows the number of matches and allows you to toggle through each of the matching results one by one using the up and down arrow controls, with the current match highlighted brightly and all others in a lighter shade of highlight.

Figure 3-19. Search report table

You can search on numbers, such as those in the amount column, but be mindful of the locale setting, which may include commas. To match 1249 within $1,249,000.00 in the amount column, your search would require a comma in the millionths place, as in "1,249."

Toggles

If the report you are looking at is grouped by at least one item, a set of toggle switches will appear on a fixed bar at the bottom of the report. Figure 3-20 shows a report on opportunities, grouped by stage, with the toggles all switched on at the bottom. Table 3-5 lists the toggle switches.

Stage ↑ ▼	Account Name ▼	Opportunity Name ▼	Fisca
Prospecting (19)	Duncan433 Inc	Opportunity for Hawkins22	Q3-2
	Maldonado464 Inc	Opportunity for Todd162	Q4-2
	Thornton799 Inc	Opportunity for Nunez399	Q4-2
	Gray676 Inc	Opportunity for Wilkerson900	Q1-2(
	Maxwell670 Inc	Opportunity for Barton1670	Q4-2
	Lawrence491 Inc	Opportunity for Franklin560	Q4-2

Row Counts ✓ ⬤   Detail Rows ✓ ⬤   Subtotals ✓ ⬤   Grand Total ✓ ⬤

Figure 3-20. Grouped report toggles

Table 3-5. Toggle switches

Toggle	Description
Row Counts	Shows or hides the number of records per grouping and total number of records on the report.
Detail Rows	Expands or collapses the report.
Subtotals	Shows or hides the subtotals by grouping on the report.
Grand Total	Shows or hides the grand totals of summary columns appearing at the top of the report, above the chart, if any.
Stacked Summaries	This toggle appears only on Matrix reports. Puts all summarized column values one on top of the other. When toggled off, the summary values appear side by side, which can widen the report considerably.

Save and Save As

Report actions include Save and Save As, which do what they do in most systems. Clicking Save allows you to save the current report with your changes applied. If it is a new report that hasn't been saved yet, you will be asked to give it a name, optionally include a description, and specify which folder to save it to. Clicking Save As allows you to save a copy of a report that you are looking at. Figure 3-21 shows the words "Copy of" prepended to "All Open Pipeline Report" when selecting Save As. You can change the name as desired, provide a report description, and change the folder the report is stored in.

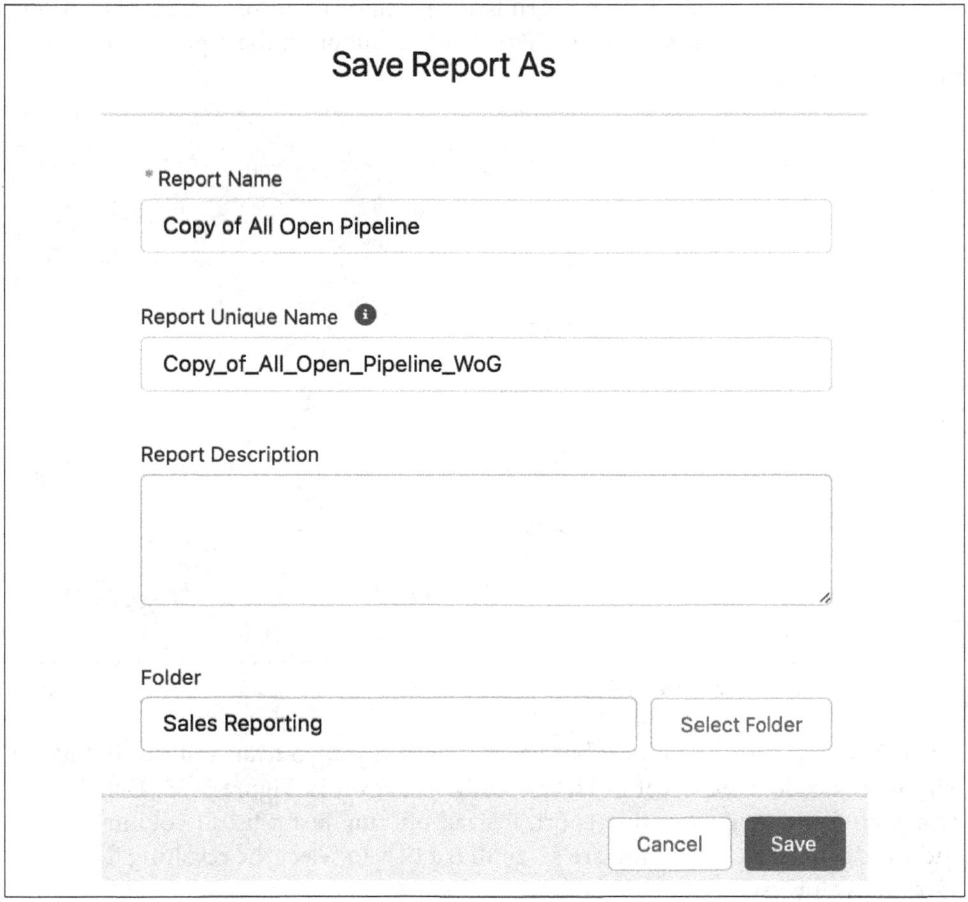

Save Report As

* Report Name

> Copy of All Open Pipeline

Report Unique Name ⓘ

> Copy_of_All_Open_Pipeline_WoG

Report Description

Folder

> Sales Reporting

> Select Folder

> Cancel   Save

Figure 3-21. Save Report As

You may have run a report in a folder that allows you to see, but not modify the reports in that folder. In that case, Save As is your only option for saving the report. This allows you to create your own copy of the report.

Export

By default, all Salesforce users can run a report and export its data. Some organizations choose to restrict who can export report results, to make it harder for users to walk away with sensitive company data. They restrict this by having a system administrator remove the Export Reports permission on these users' profiles. If your profile allows exporting reports, you will see Export as an option in the report action menu, as in Figure 3-22.

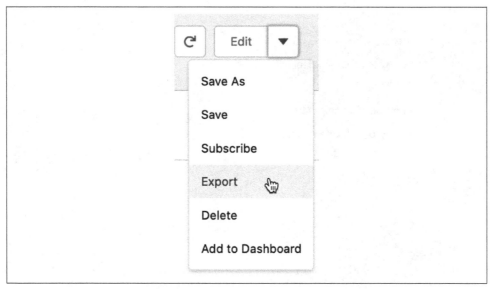

Figure 3-22. Export a report

If you have just created a report but haven't saved it yet, you can still run it, but you will only be able to export it as Details Only, as shown in Figure 3-23. Details Only brings no formatting from the report, instead offering just a list of column headers and rows of records below. You are given the option to select the resulting file format as .xls, .xlsx, or .csv.

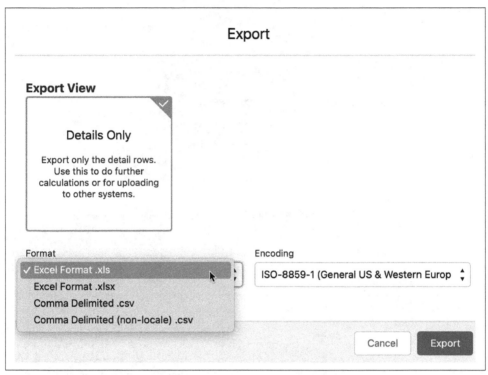

Figure 3-23. Export Details Only

When exporting a previously saved report, you have the additional option to export as a formatted report. This will include the report header, all report groupings, and the filter settings in the resulting Excel file. Figure 3-24 shows Formatted Report and Details Only as export options on a saved report. Charts are never included in exported reports.

 In the Reports and Dashboards Settings in Setup, a system administrator can check a box that "Hides the option to export a report in XLS format in Lightning Experience." They can also tick a box to "Exclude Disclaimer from Formatted Report Exports in Lightning Experience."

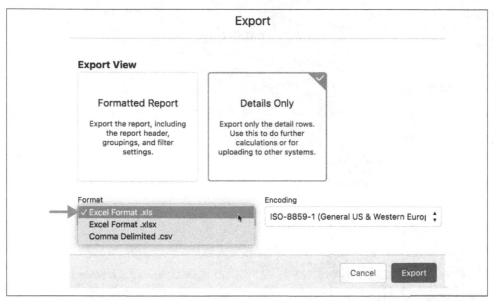

Figure 3-24. Export formatting options

Activating the "Hides the option to export a report in XLS format in Lightning Experience" checkbox is strongly recommended. A Salesforce report downloaded in XLS format is actually formatted as HTML but designated as an Excel spreadsheet. This makes the document unusually large and may set off virus-detection alerts that notice the XLS is incorrectly formatted.

Subscriptions

Report subscriptions allow users to set a schedule or define conditions upon which to receive an emailed copy of a specific report. Each user can subscribe themselves to up to 7 reports in Salesforce Lightning (up to 15 in Salesforce's Unlimited Edition). The number of subscriptions that a user receives can be more than that limit if other users add them to their own report subscriptions. Figure 3-25 shows the Subscribe action in a report's action menu. When selecting this, a drop-down menu appears, allowing the user to add or modify a subscription. If the user has an existing subscription on this report, a button is shown in the lower lefthand corner allowing the user to Unsubscribe from (i.e., delete) the existing subscription.

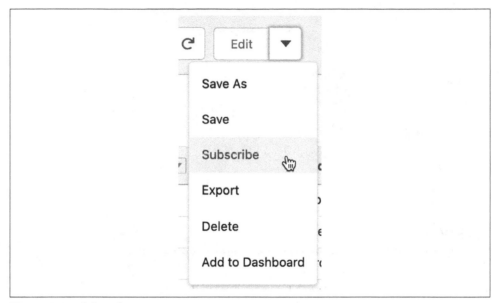

Figure 3-25. Subscribe action

 You can add the Subscribed column to your view on the Reports tab and then sort by that column descending to quickly see what reports you have already subscribed yourself to.

Figure 3-26 shows the Edit Subscription screen where you specify the frequency by which you want to receive the emailed report: daily, weekly, or monthly. You can specify the day or days of the week and the hour of the day you want to receive the report subscription. You have the option to include an attachment of the export of the report, if your profile permissions include the Export Reports permission. You can also specify the recipients of the report if you have the Subscribe to Reports: Add Recipients profile permission. When teeing up a subscription, you can also choose to Run Report As another user, based on their data permissions.

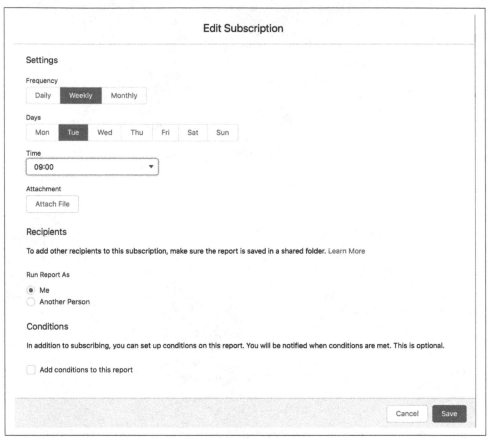

Figure 3-26. Report subscriptions

In order to add other recipients to a report subscription, the folder the report is stored in must already be shared with those users.

Salesforce can alert you when something important happens to data within a report. By adding conditions to a subscription, Salesforce will only email you when a threshold is met. An example of this would be to send the subscription on a case report only when there are more than 10 high-priority cases for your top-tier customers. To add a condition, as shown in Figure 3-27, click the "Add conditions to this report" checkbox and then use the filter tool that is revealed to add one or more conditions. The Conditions feature also allows you to send a "Summary + report," or just the "Summary only" to be alerted via email that the specified condition has been met.

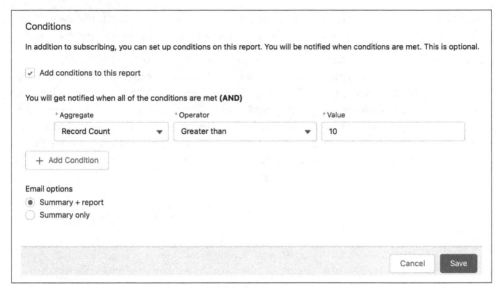

Figure 3-27. Report subscription conditions

 Use report subscriptions with conditions to monitor your data for exceptions. For example, you can set a condition based on "Record Count Greater than 0" on a report showing anomalies to alert you on a regular schedule if such records exist.

Inline Editing

After many years of the Salesforce community asking for it, we now have the ability to edit reports inline. Inline editing allows you to make changes to the data in multiple fields and multiple records in the report, directly on the report. When running a report, if you see values that need to be changed, you can click the Enable Field Editing button, shown in Figure 3-28.

Figure 3-28. Enable Field Editing button

Clicking the Enable Field Editing button reveals a pencil icon to the right of editable fields that appears when you hover over each field. If the pencil appears, then you can click that field from within the report and save it to the database. There are quite a few data types supported, and even the ability to update fields on other objects displayed in the report. This feature is active in Salesforce by default, but can be disabled for everyone by a system administrator in the report and dashboard settings.

Figure 3-29 shows the editing of multiple fields on an Opportunity report. You can tell from the figure that you are in edit mode as the color of the button changes and its text now reads "Field Editing Enabled." These fields are of type text, picklist, and date and include key ones from the opportunities. Ones that are edited appear highlighted, awaiting your clicking the Save button at the bottom of the report. On the left of the image, you can see the pencil that appears when hovering over a field that is editable, and when that is clicked, a small window appears to update its value. If a field is not editable, the image of a lock appears.

| Report: Opportunities All Open Pipeline | | | | | | Analyze | Field Editing Enabled | Add Chart | Edit |

	Total Records 193	Total Amount $245,513,755.00	Average Amount $1,272,091.99					
	Opportunity Name	Fiscal Period	Close D...	Stage	Amount	Next Step		Lead Source
1	Opportunity for Daniel1888	Q1-2023	1/17/2023	Id. Decision Makers	$1,384,600.00	work with key stakeholder to identify decision makers		Seminar - Internal
2	Opportunity for Phillips1889	Q1-2023	2/2/2023	Value Proposition	$50,000.00	-		Phone Inquiry
3	Opportunity for Hall1897	Q1-2023	3/3/2023	Needs Analysis	$2,551,000.00	determine pain points and goals for this project		Employee Referral
4	Opportunity for Drake Corp	Q4-2022	10/17/2023	Proposal/Price Quote	$70,368.00	get them a quote, fast!		Partner
5	Opportunity for Robbins1143	*Opportunity Name			$365,072.00	-		Advertisement
6	Opportunity for Jennings981	Opportunity for Drake Corporation			$141,300.00	-		Partner
7	Opportunity for Lloyd988	Q3-2022	8/18/2022	Proposal/Price Quote	$2,243,150.00	-		Public Relations

Figure 3-29. Inline editing a report

Inline editing will smartly save all the changes that you make that are valid, while letting you fix any that aren't. If a change you make violates a validation rule in your system, the other changes you made are saved, and that one is highlighted in red to be fixed before saving. When your changes are accepted, a green box appears saying that "Your changes are saved."

 Inline editing is a great way for sales reps to keep their open pipeline opportunities up-to-date. It is also excellent for quickly fixing data when you notice mistakes in report results.

After making inline edits, click the Refresh button, the one with the circular arrow, in the upper righthand corner of the report. Dependent values (like formula fields, row and column summaries, and grand totals) may not show updated values until the report is refreshed.

Favorites

A helpful feature that all users should take advantage of in reporting is favorites. This gives you the ability to create up to two hundred of your own private shortcuts to individual records, lists, folders, reports, dashboards, and more. No one else can see your favorites. Figure 3-30 shows the All Favorites category selected, and the resulting list of favorited reports and report folders.

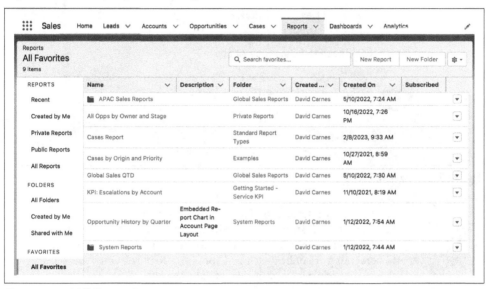

Figure 3-30. All Favorites

Favoriting a report can be done by clicking on the star while looking at the report or folder you want to favorite. Clicking on the star again will unfavorite the item. You can also use the Favorite/Unfavorite actions in the action menu to the right of each report or folder.

Your list of favorited reports and folders can also be seen when viewing your favorites list, as in Figure 3-31, when clicking on the tiny down arrow next to the star. Here you can click on the name of any favorite to quickly open that favorited item. Note the Edit Favorites link, which allows you to manage your list of favorited items.

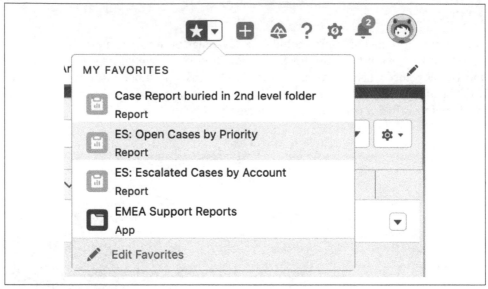

Figure 3-31. Favorites list

 A little-known feature of favorites is that you can relabel any favorited item. Instead of seeing the report name "Global Pipeline Analysis," you can use favorites to relabel the favorite for yourself to something friendlier, such as "Tom's Big Report." Only you see this change while looking at a list of your favorites.

Conclusion

The Reports tab offers an easy way to explore and find the reports in your system. It organizes all reports into categories that you can filter and search to discover which reports exist in your system. It offers folders and favorites to help you organize and prioritize the reports you create. From the Reports tab, you can quickly take action on any report or folder that you can see.

In this chapter, you saw that there are many actions you can take on a report when running it. Some of these include exporting, subscribing, and favoriting your reports. The exact list of actions you can take depends on your profile permissions.

In the next chapter, we will step through creating reports. You will learn about grouping, filtering, adding charts, and using conditional formatting. Let's go create some reports!

CHAPTER 4

Creating Reports

Reports are remarkably useful for gathering and presenting information, and you can create them to show information stored within Salesforce. For example, you could create a quick report to check on the current numbers in your system. You could also create a more complex report with an analysis of a particular area of your business to be used by management. There are many possibilities for you to explore. In this chapter, you'll walk through how to build a report and go through the various options.

In a nutshell, when you create a new report, you will be asked to select a data foundation for the report, called a report type, which locks you into reporting on a specific set of objects and fields. From there you are brought into the report builder, where the magic happens in a simple interface where you can click and drag and drop to create a report. In this chapter, you'll learn each of the steps to create reports in your system.

Create a New Report

There are two ways to start creating a new report in Salesforce. Your first option is to click the New Report button at the top right corner of the Reports tab, shown in Figure 4-1.

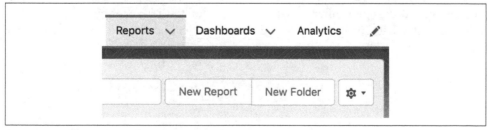

Figure 4-1. New Report button

If your company uses the Analytics tab, discussed in Chapter 9, you could start a new report by clicking the Create button at the top right of the tab. Figure 4-2 shows the Create button clicked to reveal three options, including to create a report.

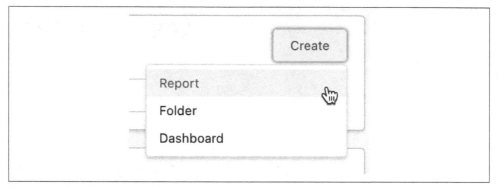

Figure 4-2. Analytics tab Create Report

 By default all users have the ability to create reports in Salesforce. If the buttons to create reports are not visible, these permissions have been disabled on your profile. Your system administrator controls what permissions are assigned to users through profiles and permission sets.

Regardless of which route you take to create a report, the next step involves selecting a report type.

Selecting a Report Type

After you start a new report, you will be brought to the Select a Report Type screen, shown in Figure 4-3, and asked to select which data foundation, or report type, to use as the basis for your report. The report type defines the underlying objects that will be available in your new report's dataset and how the objects are connected. There are about 75 standard report types, in addition to any custom report types that your system administrator has created for the users in your system. Selecting your report type is the most important decision you will need to make in this process because you will not be able to change it after this point. Consider the reporting goal you have in mind, and the data, such as objects and fields, that will be required to achieve it. So, choose wisely.

If you are unable to see a custom report type that someone mentioned has been created for you, it may mean that the custom report type is not "Deployed." It may still be set to the default status "In Development," which limits its visibility to system administrators and those with the Manage Custom Report Types profile permission.

To the left of the Select a Report Type screen, you'll see a list of report type categories. By default, the Recently Used category will be selected. This is especially useful if you've created many reports before or you use the same ones each time. However, if you are new to reporting, you won't see any report types to select. You might instead select the category All or one of the specific categories of report types below it. The context of the search feature on this screen is driven by the category you select.

Create Report

Category	Select a Report Type	
Recently Used	🔍 Search Report Types...	
All	**Recently Used Report Types**	
Accounts & Contacts		
Opportunities	**Report Type Name**	**Category**
Customer Support Reports	Opportunities	Standard ▼
Leads	Leads	Standard ▼
Campaigns	Cases (CRT)	Custom ▼
Activities	Reports	Standard ▼
Contracts and Orders	Opportunity History	Standard ▼
Price Books, Products and Assets	Leads with converted lead information	Standard ▼
Administrative Reports	Cases	Standard ▼
File and Content Reports	Opportunities (CRT)	Custom ▼
Other Reports	Opportunity Trends	Standard ▼
Hidden Report Types	Opportunities with Products	Standard ▼
	Activities with Accounts	Standard ▼
	Opportunities with Historical Trending	Custom ▼
	Case Lifecycle	Standard ▼
	Lead History	Standard ▼
	Accounts	Standard ▼

Figure 4-3. Select a Report Type screen

If you need to search for a particular report type, to give you the widest range of the search, select the category All or one of the other specific categories before you start your search.

In Salesforce's Unlimited Edition, at the top right of the Select a Report Type screen, is a special filter that can be used to refine your search by indicating up to 20 objects or fields you are interested in building your report on. In Figure 4-4, you can see that the Filter button has been clicked and two Opportunity object fields have been added to filter on report types that include those fields. This filter capability is useful for those unfamiliar with the custom report types in your system. On this screen, you can choose to search by objects or fields, and then click the Apply button.

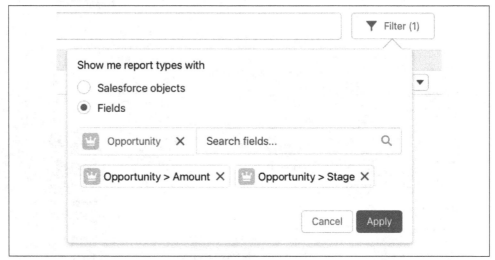

Figure 4-4. Select a Report Type filter in Unlimited Edition

 Your knowledge of report types goes a long way in your ability to be an effective report writer in Salesforce. Learn as much as you can about the standard report types and make use of custom report types, which are discussed later in this book.

To learn more about any report type in the list, you can click on its name or on the action menu pulldown to the right and select Details. Figure 4-5 shows a report type selected and its details appearing over on the right. The left arrow shows you how you can click on a report type name to open up the details. The two arrows on the right show how you can use the action menu to view the same details.

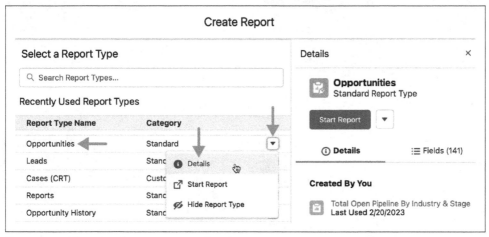

Figure 4-5. Showing the report type details

The Report Type Details panel offers a convenient way to learn about each report type. Figure 4-6 shows that you can see reports created by you and created by others using this report type. You can also see a list of objects that are involved in the report type.

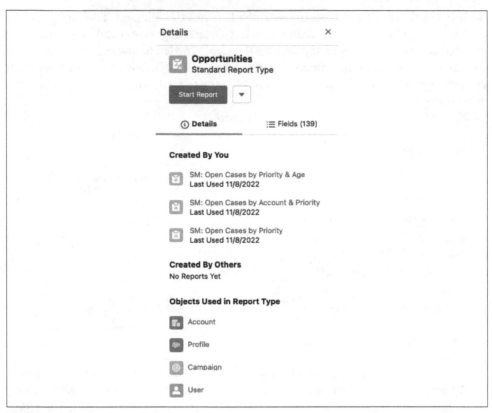

Figure 4-6. Report Type Details panel

There is a separate subtab available on the same Details panel where you can see a list of all fields available on the report type. Figure 4-7 shows this tab, with a simple search mechanism above the list of all fields. This provides a great way to learn about potentially useful report types before you commit to creating a report with them.

Figure 4-7. Report Type Details Fields tab

One final useful indicator on the Report Type Details screen appears for custom report types. In the Objects Used in Report Type section of the Details panel, for custom report types you can see the type of join between the objects. Figure 4-8 shows the details for a custom report type called Accounts with or without Opportunities. It shows a Venn diagram of the intersection between these two objects, and by hovering over the circle with the "i", you can see that this report type is built on a "Left Join" along with a quick description of what that means.

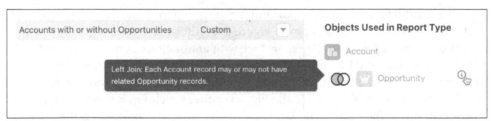

Figure 4-8. Objects used in Report Type

 There are two kinds of joins supported in custom report types in Salesforce: Inner Joins and Left Joins. You will learn more about using these joins when creating report types in Chapter 10.

Once you've selected a report type to use, the next step is to click the Start Report button. There are two ways to access this button, as shown in Figure 4-9. You can click on the action menu to the right of the report type in the list and select Start Report, as shown by the left two arrows. You can also click on the Start Report button from the Details panel, as shown by the right arrow. From here you will be brought into the report editor to start designing your report. Once a report is started, it is no longer possible to change its report type.

Figure 4-9. Start Report button

Report Builder

The report builder is where you will do the majority of the work to build a report.

It can be helpful to think of the report builder as having four main regions of controls that you use when building reports. Figure 4-10 shows the four regions on a new report built on the Opportunity report type with annotations to mark each region. In the first region, in the top left of the report builder, you can see Outline and Filter tabs, along with a small control in the top left called Fields. The center of the report builder, shown by number two, is the Preview pane, which has a toggle to allow you to turn on or off the preview-updating as you build your reports. The third section has useful controls for editing and saving your report. Along the bottom is the fourth region, where toggles and a conditional formatting tool may appear while you build your report.

Figure 4-10. Report builder regions

Outline Tab

When creating a report, you'll often want to get to work adding and removing columns. Each report type has a number of columns as default, including ones you aren't interested in seeing. Beyond this, horizontal real estate is precious in reporting, and you'll want to display only columns that relate to the purpose on the report. Adding and removing them can be done in a few ways, and is mainly done using the Outline tab. The Outline tab, as shown in Figure 4-11, gives us the ability to add and remove groups to our report in the Groups section at the top, and below that, the ability to add, move, and rearrange columns in the Columns section at the bottom. Note the last two fields shown are a slightly different color, with a # symbol before each name. These are summary columns, which if clicked, allow you to add subtotals for those columns in the form of sum, average, max, min, and median.

Figure 4-11. Outline tab

To add a grouping, start typing in the name of the field you want to group the report's rows by in the Add Group search box. Alternatively, you can drag a field from the Columns section up and drop it just below the Group Rows Add Group search box. Figure 4-12 shows the Opportunity Owner column that has been dragged up to group the report's rows.

Figure 4-12. Drag to add a grouping

You have the ability to add up to three groupings on report rows. Grouping a report by rows makes the report into what is called a *Summary Report* format. After adding your first grouping on rows, you also have the ability to group by up to two columns, making the report into a *Matrix Report* format. Later in the chapter, you'll learn about each of the four report formats.

Below the Outline tab, there is the list of columns that currently appear on the report. You can add a column by starting to type in the name of a column you know you want to add to the report. Clicking in the Add Column field will also show you a list of all fields available in the report type, which you can scroll through to add your desired field. Figure 4-13 shows adding the Fiscal Year column to the report by selecting it from the Add Column list. Once selected from this list, the field will be added to the bottom of the list of columns, making it the right-most column appearing on the report.

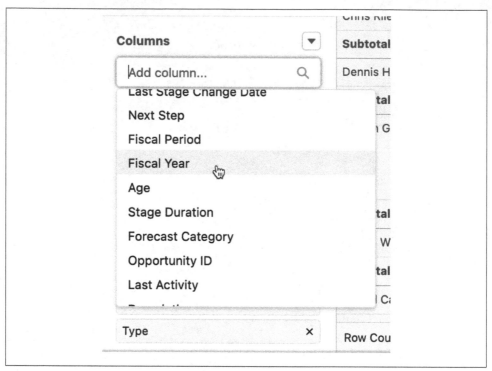

Figure 4-13. Adding a column

To remove columns from the report, you can click on the X to the right of the desired column. Figure 4-14 shows the X next to the Owner Role column, which will take it off the report. If you make a mistake removing a column, you can add it back using the procedure previously described.

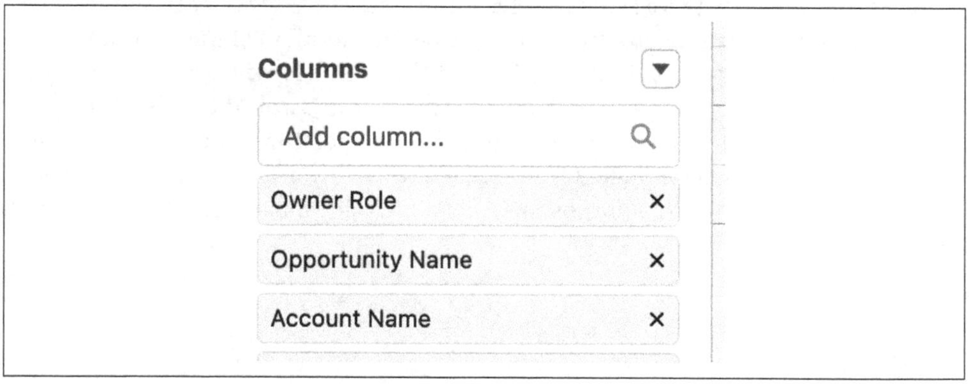

Figure 4-14. Removing a column

To the right of the word "Columns" is an action menu offering up to four actions. Figure 4-15 shows that we can currently add a bucket column, a summary formula, a row-level formula, or we can remove all columns. You'll see what bucket columns can do in a moment, and learn all about formulas in the next chapter. In the meantime, the Remove All Columns action can be handy for quickly wiping the slate clean of all columns, allowing you to add others you may want.

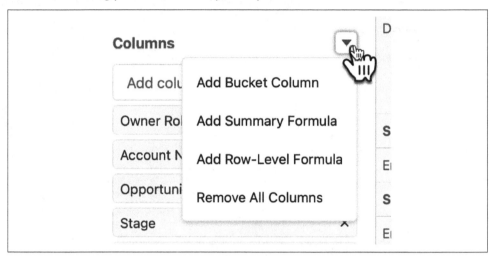

Figure 4-15. Columns action menu

Bucket columns

Bucket columns allow you to create ad hoc groupings in your reports, based on numeric, picklist, and text columns. They allow you to categorize report records based on criteria that you come up with, and then sort, filter, and group by the new bucket columns as needed. You can create up to five bucket columns per report. Each bucket column can group records into up to 20 buckets.

A nice example of a bucket column uses the Industry field on the Account object as its source. There are 32 values that come standard in this column in Salesforce. What if you wanted to group them into just three groupings, such as Core, Emerging, and Other in a new column called Market Category? Figure 4-16 shows the screen that appears when you select Add Bucket Column in the columns action menu. Notice that a default column is set, which we will want to change to Industry for our example.

Figure 4-16. Edit Bucket Column

With the Industry field selected, and a name given to the bucket column, we can assign the picklist field values to buckets that we create. Figure 4-17 shows that one bucket has been created, out of a possible 20, called Core. Additional picklist values have been ticked, and the Move To button at the bottom of the Edit Bucket Column screen has been clicked, allowing you to add the newly checked items to Core, to the pile of Unbucketed Values, or to a New Bucket, which you will label in the subsequent screen as Emerging.

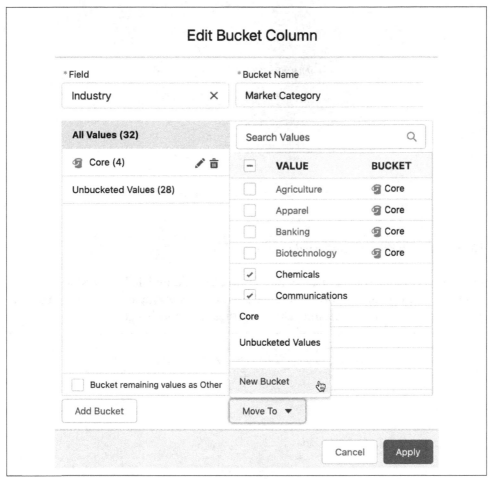

Figure 4-17. Editing a bucket column

When working with text and picklists, there is a handy checkbox that allows you to "Bucket remaining values as Other." Figure 4-18 shows the box checked.

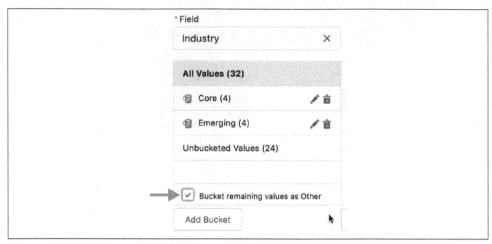

Figure 4-18. "Bucket remaining values as Other" screen

Once you click the Apply button, your new bucket column will be added as the right-most column on your report. Figure 4-19 shows this example added to a report to collapse our 32 Industry column values into these 3 simple buckets.

Industry	Market Category
Technology	Other
Apparel	Core
Communications	Emerging
Banking	Core
Biotechnology	Core

Figure 4-19. Bucket column output

 There is nothing preventing you from being creative with your bucket names. You could even use emojis. Doing this adds instant color to your reports. You can then sort, filter, and group on the bucketed emojis just like you would any other text.

With numeric fields that feed a bucket column, you are asked to set less-than-or-equal-to and greater-than ranges. You can also add up to 20 total thresholds to assign those records into up to 20 buckets by clicking the Add button in between each existing threshold. Figure 4-20 shows a bucket column created on the Amount field on an

Opportunity report, with buckets created for "Tiny," "Just Right," and "Huge" opportunities.

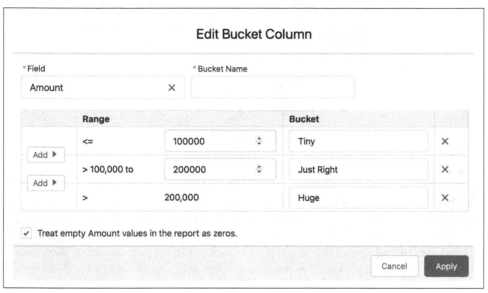

Figure 4-20. Numeric bucket columns

 You'll never see a bucket on a report with zero records in it because there is no option to show buckets that have no records matching their criteria.

Show Fields Pane

Just to the left of the Outline Tab is the control to open the Show Fields pane. It is a useful tool that is easy to miss within the busy report builder. This tool is optional when building reports, but it can be valuable especially if you are not familiar with what columns are available to the report type you selected. It is also helpful in that it indicates each field's data type. To use the Show Fields pane, click on the > symbol next to the word "Fields" marked by the arrow in Figure 4-21.

Figure 4-21. Show Fields carrot

The Show Fields pane, as seen in Figure 4-22, gives us a searchable, scrollable, and collapsible list of all fields available in the selected report type. It indicates each field's data type as text, numeric, checkbox, date, or picklist with an icon to the left of each field name. To add one of the fields as a column on the report from the Show Fields pane, you have two options. You can double-click on it to add it as the left-most column on your report. You can also drag and drop the column to your desired location in between two columns in the Preview pane to the right.

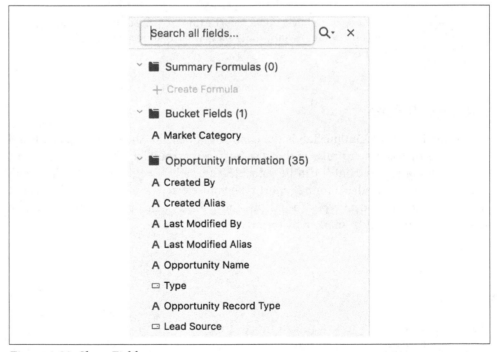

Figure 4-22. Show Fields pane

There could be thousands of fields available in the report type you've chosen to create a report on. If you are unfamiliar with the report type you are using, it can be helpful to scroll through the list of fields in the Show Fields pane to get to know what is available. The fields are organized into folders that typically correspond to their objects and whether they are standard or custom. Collapsing folders can be helpful to hide fields that aren't relevant to you at that moment.

By clicking on the magnifying glass and starting to type the name of a desired field, you will see a list of matching fields appear below. In Figure 4-23, you can see a search started by typing in the first few letters of the word "name." Those same letters are highlighted in the resulting fields below. If you click the magnifying glass icon, the search feature also lets you navigate fields by selecting their data type, which filters that list to show only matching data types below. This can be helpful because you may not know a field's name but know that the field you are looking for is a checkbox.

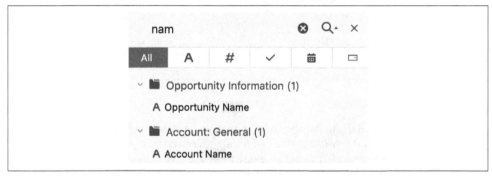

Figure 4-23. Show Fields pane search

When you double-click on a field using the Show Fields pane, it is added as the left-most column on the report. This is the opposite of using the Add Columns box on the Outline tab, which deposits new fields on the far-right of the report.

Filters Tab

The Filters tab is where you can add, remove, or adjust filters in your reports. Immediately to the right of the tab, you might see a blue circle with a number in it. That number indicates how many filters are currently restricting records in the report. If there are no filters restricting records, the blue circle doesn't appear. Figure 4-24 shows a circle with the number one in it, and below that the Filter tab, where you can add additional filters or adjust the existing ones. The list of standard filters differs for each report type.

Figure 4-24. Filters tab

When starting new reports, keep an eye out for the blue circle and the number within. Many of the standard report types have one or more unwanted filters set every time you start a new report. These filters are easy to adjust, but may prevent you from seeing the data you are interested in until changed.

To modify a standard filter, click on it. Figure 4-25 shows changing this Opportunity report's standard filter on the Close Date field from its default of the current fiscal quarter to the range of All Time. This essentially removes the filter on Close Date by showing opportunities with any date in that field. By clicking on the Close Date filter, a window appears to the right, allowing us to select a predefined date range or to customize by hard-coding the dates we want.

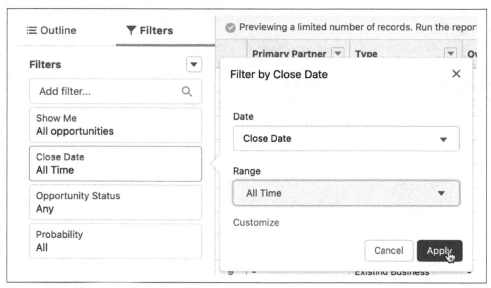

Figure 4-25. Editing a standard filter

A rookie mistake when working with filters is to forget to click the Apply button when adding or editing a filter. If you forget and click somewhere else, the Filter Edit window goes away, but your changes are not saved.

Depending on the report type used to create a report, you may see two, three, or four standard filters available to use. It is worth exploring each report type's standard filters to see which have special features you can take advantage of in reporting. In Figure 4-26, you can see the Show Me filter selected on a report based on the Opportunities report type. By default, it allows you to filter by My Opportunities, My Team's Opportunities, and All Opportunities. When the Opportunity Teams or Enterprise Territory Management features are enabled in your system, the list of filter options grows even longer. When the All Opportunities filter is applied, you can further filter opportunities shown in the report by an opportunity owner role and even further by a specific opportunity owner in the Narrow by Person field as needed.

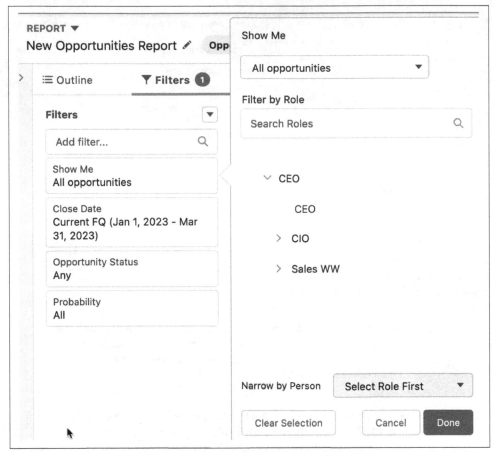

Figure 4-26. Special standard filters

The standard filters on each new report are useful up until a point, and after that you will need to make use of advanced filters. Add new filters to your report by typing in a field name within the "Add filter" window, selecting the appropriate field, and then specifying the operator and value you want to filter on. Figure 4-27 shows adding a filter on the Opportunity field Type, which is a picklist. To the right of the new filter appears a window that allows us to adjust the operator and select one or more values for it.

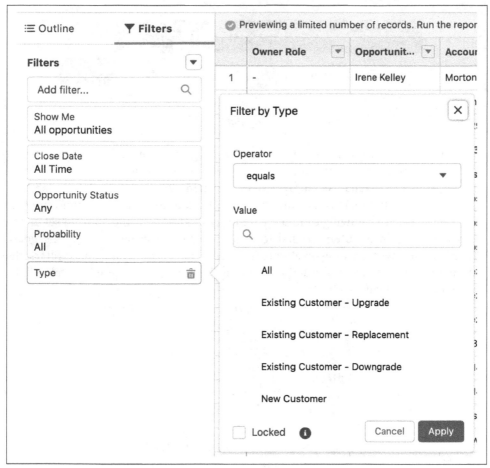

Figure 4-27. Adding an advanced filter

Be sure to scroll down on the list of available operators. Many new report writers miss out on using the Contains, Does Not Contain, and Starts With operators because they don't scroll down to see all the operator choices.

The Locked checkbox at the bottom of each advanced filter will, when checked, prevent users from adjusting the filter when running the saved report. Figure 4-28 shows the box checked on a filter and also the help text that appears when hovering over the "i" in the circle next to it.

Figure 4-28. Locked checkbox on advanced filters

You can add up to 20 advanced filters to any report. When you add them, assume that they are all connected by an "and." This means that they will all be enforced when filtering your report data. As report writers, we often need more flexibility than that, which is where filter logic comes in. This powerful filtering feature is found in other places in Salesforce, allowing us to use parentheses, "and," "or," and "not" to set up the exact combination of filters needed to achieve a particular report's filtering goals. When you first start working on a report's filters, prior to adding advanced filters, the Add Filter Logic option in the action menu to the top right of the Filters tab will be grayed out, as in Figure 4-29.

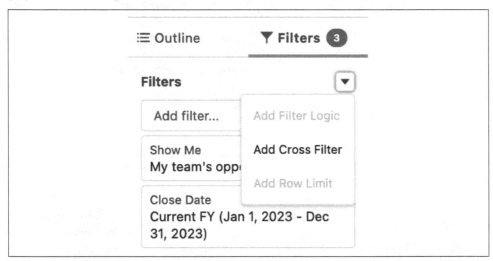

Figure 4-29. Add Filter Logic grayed out

As soon as you add your second advanced filter, the Add Filter Logic option will no longer be grayed out and will be usable in the action menu at the top right of the Filters tab. Once you select it, the Edit Filter Logic pane will appear. Salesforce has added reference numbers to the left of each filter and written the word "AND" in an editable box between the numbers representing each filter. In Figure 4-30, you can see a simple example where the Industry field filter has been assigned "1" and the Billing State field filter has been assigned "2." By using the Edit Filter Logic pane, the "AND" has been changed to an "OR" in between the numbers 1 and 2. This means that data matching either of the underlying advanced filters will be returned by the report. When you work on a report with many filters, filter logic helps you meet your complex filtering needs.

Figure 4-30. Edit Filter Logic pane

 It is easiest to first add all the advanced filters you want to a report and then circle back to add the filter logic that fine-tunes them.

Cross filters

Another type of powerful filter that is available in reports, cross filters, is often avoided because it seems complicated. Cross filters allow you to filter a parent object, such as accounts, whether or not there are any child objects, such as contracts, cases, or opportunities. With a little understanding of your Salesforce instance's data model, you can make great use of cross filters in your reporting as each report can support up to three cross filters. Figure 4-31 shows that you can add a cross filter by using the pull-down action menu to the right of Filters.

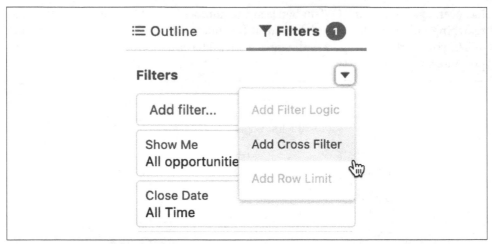

Figure 4-31. Add a cross filter

Once you've selected the Add Cross Filter action, the Edit Filter pane will appear. Figure 4-32 shows that you can specify the object from your report type, such as Opportunity, decide whether you want the report to pull records with or without the child object, and choose the child object. The list of available child objects for the selected object in the Show Me picklist will depend on the data model in your Salesforce instance. In this example, the filter will only show opportunities that do not have associated products.

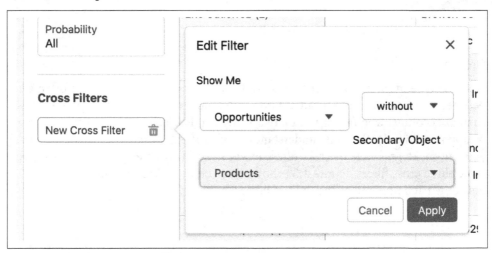

Figure 4-32. Editing a cross filter

Not only can you have up to three cross filters per report, but you can also filter each of the cross filters. Once you have added a cross filter, you can further refine it by adding a field subfilter to it. Figure 4-33 shows adjusting a cross filter so that it shows accounts without cases where the Escalated field is set to True.

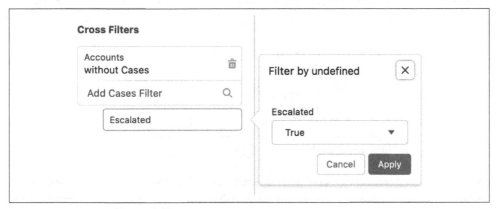

Figure 4-33. Cross filter subfilter

 Cross filters and their subfilters can be used effectively to isolate anomalies in your database. You might use them to look for customers who have no won opportunities, or target accounts that have no emailable contacts.

Row limit filters

Row limit filters are not new to Salesforce reports, though they were more recently added to reports in the Lightning user interface. They allow you to restrict the report output to a specific number of records, between 1 and 99, while ignoring the rest in the dataset. They are perfect for displaying a top 10 list of largest deals ever, or a list of the top 5 most expensive campaigns, for example. To use them, you need to have an ungrouped report that has at least one column sorted; otherwise, the option in the filter menu is grayed out. Figure 4-34 shows the Add Row Limit filter option grayed out.

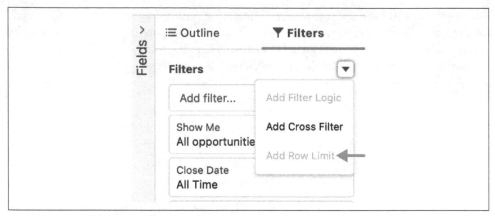

Figure 4-34. Add Row Limit grayed out

With an ungrouped report, and with at least one column sorted, the row limit filter option becomes available. Figure 4-35 shows what this looks like in the report builder.

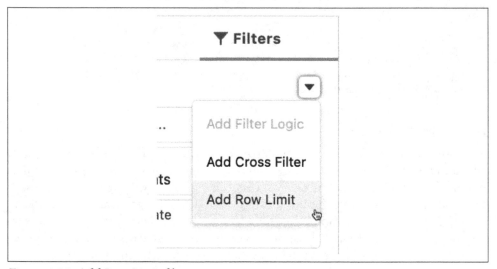

Figure 4-35. Add Row Limit filter

Once added, the default number of rows in a row limit filter is 10 as seen in Figure 4-36. You can adjust this by entering any number between 1 and 99 here and clicking the Apply button.

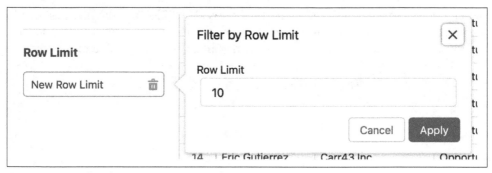

Figure 4-36. Filter by Row Limit

It is helpful to users to indicate that records have been limited by a row filter in the name of the report, such as "Top Five Performing Campaigns This Year" or "Ten Oldest Open Cases."

Personalized filters

Salesforce offers another special type of filter that only applies to fields that "look up" to the user object. Examples of standard fields include ones such as Created By and Last Modified By. You likely have custom fields in your system where this filter becomes especially valuable, such as Executive Sponsor. These filters are called personalized filters because they provide a dynamic way to run a report filtered by the user who is running the report. The arrow in Figure 4-37 shows that when filtering on a field that looks up to the user object, the "Use relative value" link appears.

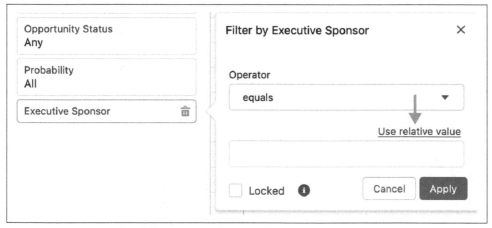

Figure 4-37. Personalized filter: Use Relative Value

When clicked, the "Use relative value" link inserts "$USER" into the filter, as seen in Figure 4-38. Once applied, this will create a "my filter" on this field, showing the person running the report only records where they are the user populated in the field.

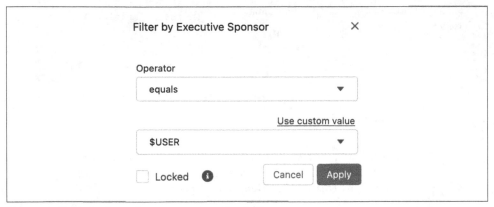

Figure 4-38. Relative value in a personalized filter

Relative date filters

A powerful way to zero in on your desired report data becomes available when filtering your reports on fields of Date and Date/Time data types. Relative date filters allow you to dynamically include or exclude records based on dynamic date ranges indicated by phrases such as "THIS QUARTER," "YESTERDAY," or "7 WEEKS AGO." Any variation of capitalization when using relative date filters is acceptable. The arrow in Figure 4-39 shows the link "Use relative date," which appears when filtering on a Date field.

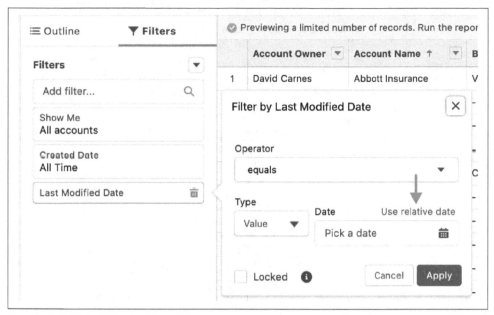

Figure 4-39. Use Relative Date filter

There is a document entitled "Relative Date Filter Reference" in Salesforce Help (*https://oreil.ly/Y3UtS*) that lists out all of the relative date values you can use in filters. These are very useful across Salesforce, be it in report filters, dashboard filters, list views, and so on.

Clicking on the "Use relative date" link reveals a Relative Date box where you can type in the relative date value you want to use to filter the report. Figure 4-40 shows that the operator is set to "equals" and the Relative Date is "THIS WEEK."

Figure 4-40. Relative Date filter example

When first using relative date values, it is best to stick with "equals" or "not equal to" as the operator. Unexpected results can occur with these dynamic date ranges when trying out the variations of "less than" or "greater than" as operators.

Preview Pane

The second big region in the report builder is the Preview pane. By default, the Preview pane does not refresh itself to update the report preview unless you toggle on the Update Preview Automatically switch. Figure 4-41 shows the toggle turned on, meaning that the preview will update itself as you make each change to the report in the report builder.

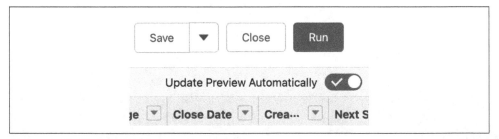

Figure 4-41. Update Preview Automatically screen

Please do not make business decisions based solely on the data in the Preview pane. In most cases, the pane shows just a small subset of the data that will appear when the report is run. It is intended to serve as a way to give you a sense of what the report will look like.

Within the Preview pane, you will see the columns that have been selected to appear in your report. To the right of each column is an action menu pulldown that gives you a set of controls related to that column. Figure 4-42 shows the action menu for the Account Name column. You can sort ascending or descending. You can group rows or columns by this field. You can create a bucket column with Bucket This Column. You can show the count of unique items appearing in this column by selecting Show Unique Count. Finally, you can move the column left or right in the column order, or remove the column entirely, using this menu.

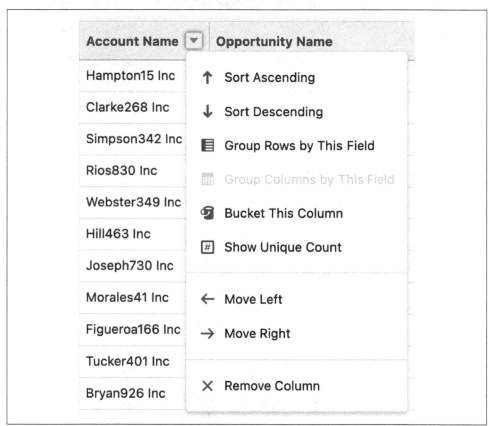

Figure 4-42. Column header action menu

For columns that can be summed, such as the Amount column on an Opportunity report, there is an option to summarize that column using sum, average, max, min, or median. For grouped columns, there are additional options to control how the grouping is handled. For example, when you group a report by dates, such as by the Close Date on an Opportunity report, the default grouping is by day. Unless your business is very transactional, this is almost never what you want. Figure 4-43 shows how to use the action menu to change Group Date By to Calendar Quarter. The top left arrow shows engaging the action menu. The center arrow selecting Group Date By reveals a list of options, and the bottom arrow shows the current selection of Calendar Quarter.

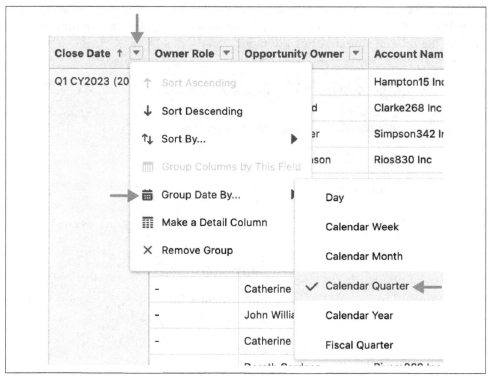

Figure 4-43. Group Date By

Clicking on any of the column headers once will sort the report by that column ascending. Clicking it a second time will sort the report by that column descending. Figure 4-44 shows the up arrow that appears next to the column name once it has been sorted ascending.

Figure 4-44. Column sort order

Report Controls

Across the top of the report builder is a set of controls related to the report you are working on. All new reports are given a default name based on the report type you have chosen. Figure 4-45 shows the top left corner of the report builder, where you can see the default label given to your new report, with a pencil to the right. Clicking on the pencil allows you to rename the report. To the right of the pencil, you can see the word "Opportunities" in a gray oval. This is the report type that the report is based on. Up above the report label is the word "Report" with a black triangle next to it. We will use that triangle a bit later in this chapter to change the report format to a joined report.

Figure 4-45. Relabel report

Across the top, to the right corner of the report builder, there is an additional set of controls. There are Undo and Redo buttons, which work in your current editing session, tracking more than 25 recent changes that you can go back or forward to. Figure 4-46 shows these two buttons and the text that appears when you hover over the Undo button. The Redo button to the right is grayed out because no changes have been undone in this editing session.

Figure 4-46. Undo and Redo buttons

To the right of the Undo and Redo buttons is the Add Chart button, as seen in Figure 4-47. This button is grayed out until at least one grouping is added to the report. Next to it is the Save & Run button, which does exactly those two steps. The Save button has either one or two choices, depending on whether you've already saved the report. Clicking it shows the choices Save As and Properties. Save As will let you create a clone of the report by just giving it a new name. Properties will allow you to update the report's name, description, and assigned folder. If you've made changes to the report and click the Close button, you will be asked if you want to save the changes or discard them. The Run button will run your report as is. It is not necessary to save a report before running it.

Figure 4-47. Report buttons

 The Save As feature is useful when you are creating, editing, or running a report and want to create another version of it. All settings from the original will be brought over to the new copy, and you just need to give it a new name and folder location to save it in.

When first using the Save & Run or Save buttons, you will be given the chance to change the report name, add a description, and specify the folder you want to save the report in. Figure 4-48 shows the Save Report screen. When first saving a new report and adjusting the Report Name field, click anywhere else on the screen and the Report Unique Name field will be autopopulated. All reports have to have a unique name in your Salesforce instance. The Report Description is an optional field, but a useful one to help orient your report users to the purpose and structure of the report. Note that the default folder for every new report is the report creator's Private Reports folder. Items in the Private Reports folder can only be seen by the person who saved the report. To change the folder, or create a new one, click on the Select Folder button before you click Save.

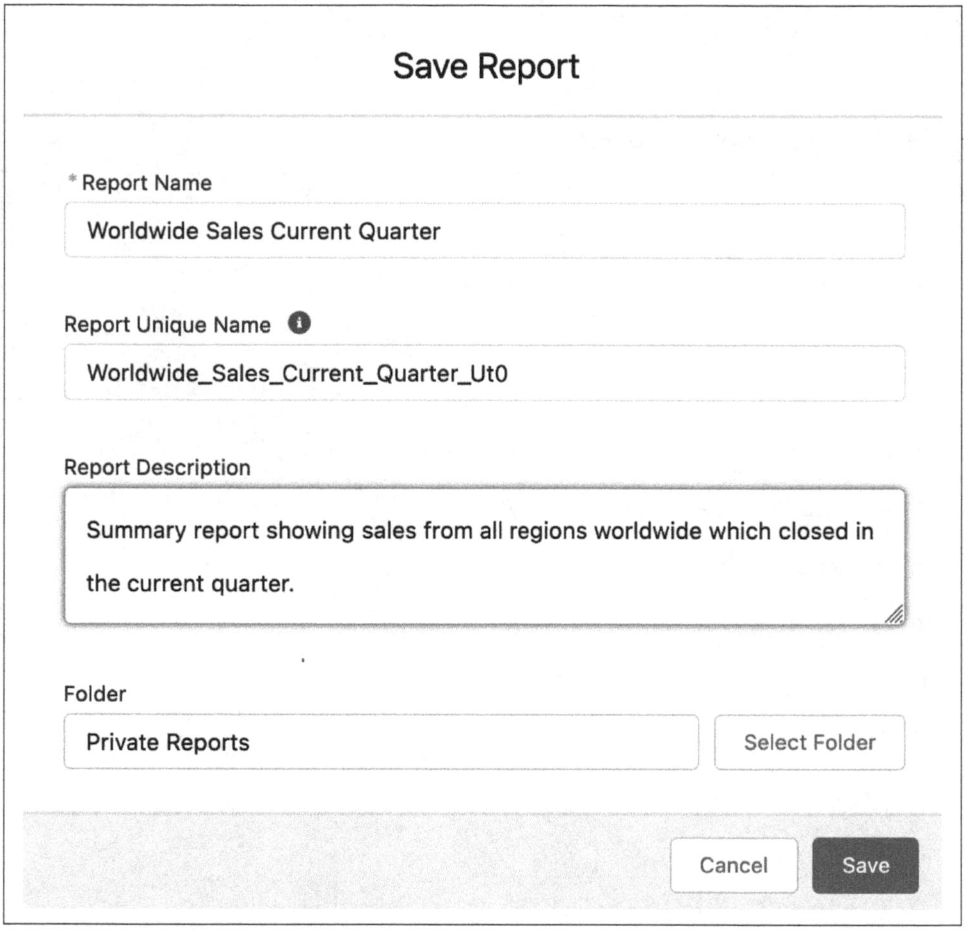

Figure 4-48. Save Report screen

On the Select Folder screen, you can navigate into a folder and, if desired, into its subfolders to select the best folder in which to store your saved report. Figure 4-49 shows this screen and the Sales Reports folder as selected. Also available in the bottom left of this screen is the New Folder button, allowing you to create a new folder as part of the save process for the new report. Once you have selected the folder you want, click the Select Folder button to finish the save.

Select

All Folders > **Sales Reports**

| 🔍 Search folders... |

📁 Customer Success Reports	▶	📁 EMEA Sales Reports	▶
📁 Customer Support Reports	▶		
📁 Einstein Bot Reports	▶		
📁 Einstein Bot Reports Summer '22	▶		
📁 Einstein Bot Reports Winter '23	▶		
📁 EMTrailheadReport	▶		
📁 Getting Started – Service Agent	▶		
📁 Getting Started – Service Exec Overview	▶		
📁 Getting Started – Service KPI	▶		
📁 Getting Started – Service Manager	▶		
📁 Marketing Reports	▶		
📁 Sales Reports	▶		

📁 New Folder   Cancel   **Select Folder**

Figure 4-49. Select Folder screen

 If you create a new folder in this way, remember to go into that folder to review and, if needed, adjust the report sharing to allow others to view, edit, or manage reports in the folder. The worst thing is creating an incredible new report, storing it in a new folder, and no one being able to see the report.

Charts

As you saw in the last chapter, you can add a chart when you run a report. You can also add charts when editing a report in the report builder. Figure 4-50 shows an arrow pointing to the icon for the Add Chart button once it has been clicked on a report that has been grouped. The default chart shown is a horizontal bar, which can be changed by clicking on the small gear, as shown by the right arrow, and selecting one of the other seven chart types. Below the Display As choices, there are chart properties, such as the chart title, the axes, and others, which you can update.

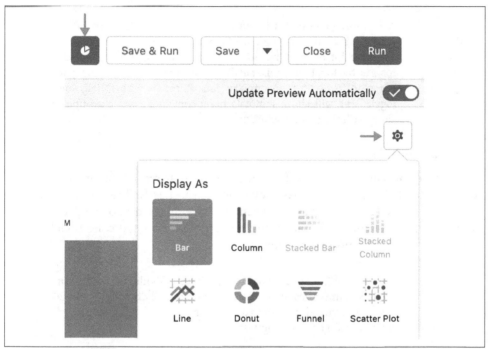

Figure 4-50. Add Chart button and Display As screen

Toggles

The fourth region of the report builder is the set of toggles that appear across the bottom once a report has been grouped. Figure 4-51 shows the default position of these toggles, all set to display row counts, detail rows, subtotals, and the grand total. (Another toggle, Stacked Summaries, is shown on matrix reports. See the Matrix section later in this chapter to learn more.) Row Counts reveals or hides the number of records in each grouping. Detail Rows will collapse or expand the entire report, showing only subtotals and the grand total. Subtotals will hide or reveal the subtotals on the report based on its groupings. Grand Total will hide or reveal the report's grand total. Also shown is the Conditional Formatting button, which appears with the first grouping and first summarized column.

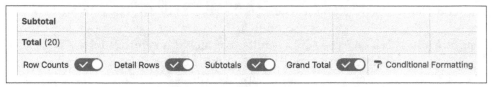

| Subtotal | | | | | |
| Total (20) | | | | | |

Row Counts ✔️ Detail Rows ✔️ Subtotals ✔️ Grand Total ✔️ ⌄ Conditional Formatting

Figure 4-51. Toggles and Conditional Formatting

 A Salesforce report that is run will show up to the first two thousand rows in the browser. Looking at that many records would involve a lot of scrolling. In many cases, it is helpful to collapse reports by toggling off Detail Rows to allow anyone using your report to focus on the summary data. A report with Detail Rows toggled off will show subtotals based on your report groupings along with the report's grand total.

Conditional formatting

Conditional formatting allows you to add color to your report's summed numerical columns, highlighting numbers based on criteria you specify. These can be standard columns on which you have chosen to sum, average, max, min, or median, or summary formulas that you have written on the report. You can add conditional formatting on up to five columns in each report.

 Conditional formatting does not apply to individual records, only grouped summaries. If you need to conditionally highlight anomalies in individual records, you can use a row-level formula and show colorful emojis as output.

Clicking the Conditional Formatting button will open the Conditional Formatting Rules screen. This shows the list of formatting rules already created on this report. Figure 4-52 shows this screen without any rules added yet. Clicking the Add Conditional Formatting Rule button will allow you to add a new rule.

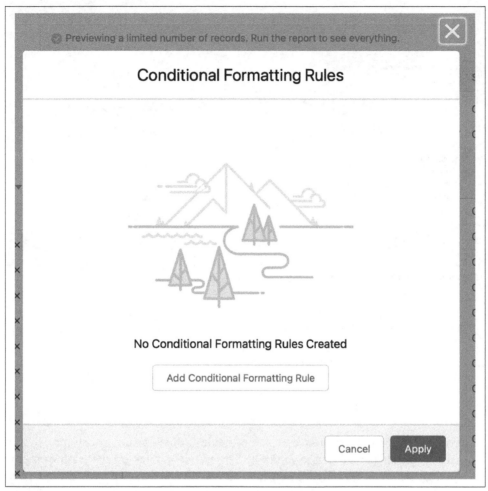

Conditional Formatting Rules

No Conditional Formatting Rules Created

Add Conditional Formatting Rule

Cancel   Apply

Figure 4-52. Conditional Formatting Rules

Clicking Add Conditional Formatting Rule will take you to a window that lets you set thresholds that correspond to the background colors to the right. Figure 4-53 shows a new rule based on the Sum of the Amount column, with thresholds set for less than or equal to 250,000, greater than 250,000 up to 500,000, and greater than 500,000. The default colors are red, yellow (orange), and green, though they each can easily be changed to one of millions of colors by clicking on the corresponding color box.

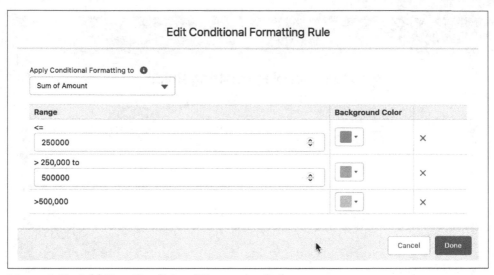

Figure 4-53. Add New Conditional Formatting Rule

 A powerful technique when using conditional formatting is to drop the number of colors shown from three to two, and then set one of those two remaining to display no color. Sometimes three or even two colors in the background of a column's results is just too much color on the report. This technique allows you to highlight just one threshold that you want on the summary column, and show just one color.

Figure 4-54 shows the newly saved rule on the Sum of the Amount column. To edit this rule, click the pencil icon to the right. To remove it, click on the trash can icon. By clicking the Apply button, this new formatting rule will be displayed on the report.

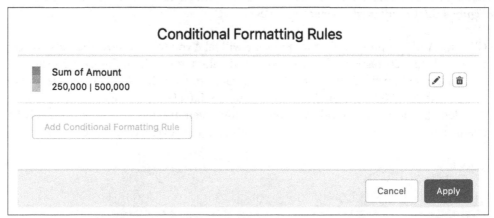

Figure 4-54. Saved Conditional Formatting Rule

Once saved, the conditional highlighting is applied to the summary column. The font changes from black to white, and the entire background of the cell becomes the formatting color specified. Figure 4-55 shows an Opportunity report grouped by calendar quarter and owner with the Sum of Amount formatted.

Report: Opportunities
Won Opps by Calendar Quarter

	Total Records	Total Amount
	400	**$689,065,761.00**

Close Date ↑ ▼	Opportunity Owner ↑ ▼	Sum of Amount	Record Count
Q1 CY2021	David Carnes	$101,000,000.00	3
	Subtotal	**$101,000,000.00**	**3**
Q2 CY2021	David Carnes	$69,000,000.00	2
	Eric Gutierrez	$1,981,936.00	2
	Irene Kelley	$2,250,950.00	1
	Irene McCoy	$27,800.00	1
	Johnny Green	$2,451,210.00	1
	Julie Chavez	$206,587.00	1
	Subtotal	**$75,918,483.00**	**8**
Q3 CY2021	Bruce Kennedy	$1,436,125.00	2
	Catherine Brown	$259,500.00	1
	Chris Riley	$9,602,013.00	5
	Dennis Howard	$240,747.00	1

Figure 4-55. Conditional formatting in action

If you disable the summary column that is used in a conditional formatting rule or remove the groupings in the report, all conditional formatting rules on the report will be lost.

Report Formats

One final thing to know when creating reports in Salesforce is the set of four report formats that are available. These formats provide the structure of the report and are largely driven by the presence or lack of groupings in your data.

Tabular

A tabular report is an ungrouped report. These are excellent for lists of information, such as a call list or an address list you might want to give a fulfillment vendor to send out holiday gifts to clients. Figure 4-56 shows a report-created listing of all reports in the system. This is an excellent example of a tabular report you might want to create to help manage the cleanup of the Reports tab. Once run, you might immediately export it to Excel to review and make notes.

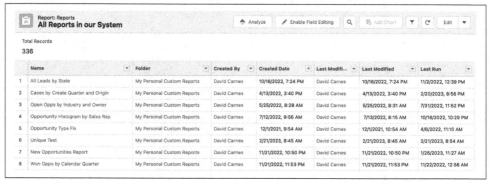

Figure 4-56. Tabular report example

Summary

Summary reports are reports in which rows are grouped. In a summary report, you can group rows up to three times. As mentioned earlier in this chapter, once a report is first made into a summary report by adding the report's first grouping, a number of options become available. Figure 4-57 shows the list of all accounts in a system grouped by the Account Owner and Type fields. This report also has Detail Rows toggled off to collapse the results to just show the groupings and the record counts.

If you are not sure which report format to select in a given situation, it generally doesn't hurt to start with a summary report. In many reporting situations, you want to see information grouped along with subtotals for those groupings.

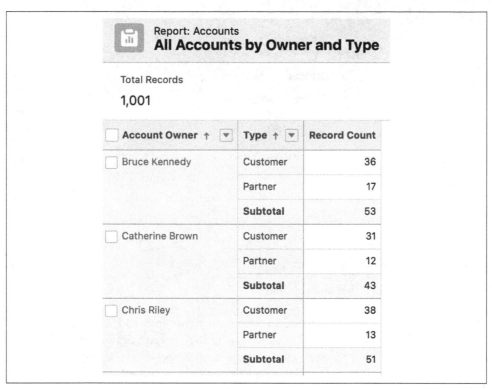

Figure 4-57. Summary report example

Matrix

Matrix reports allow you to group vertically (rows) up to two times and horizontally (columns) up to two times. A nice example of a use case for a matrix report is when you create a bird's-eye view of your open opportunity pipeline, grouped by owner vertically and by stage horizontally. Figure 4-58 shows the start of this example. As soon as your first row grouping is added, the Group Columns section appears. Once you've added row and column groupings, a new control appears to the left of the trash can that allows you to flip the row and column orientation. The trash can quickly deletes all groupings.

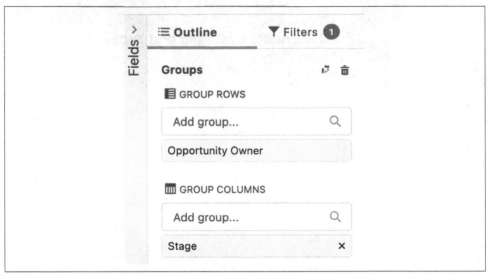

Figure 4-58. Grouping rows and columns

With Row Counts toggled off, and the Amount fields summed, this matrix report shows a compact set of information about the health of each sales owner's open pipeline. Figure 4-59 shows the sum of the amount each owner has in each sales stage. When a matrix report is run, clicking on any one of the cells will filter the record set below the matrix to just that cell.

Report: Opportunities
Open Opps by Owner and Stage

Total Amount
$245,877,355.00

Opportunity Owner ▾	Stage →	Prospecting	Qualification	Needs Analysis	Value Proposition	Perception Analysis	Proposal/Price Quote	Negotiation/Review	Total
Bruce Kennedy	Sum of Amount	$224,800.00	$991,350.00	$9,222,850.00	$510,465.00	$7,976,750.00	$0.00	$2,739,360.00	$21,665,575.00
Catherine Brown	Sum of Amount	$1,666,850.00	$1,821,769.00	$732,680.00	$2,633,830.00	$164,700.00	$2,058,100.00	$0.00	$9,278,129.00
Chris Riley	Sum of Amount	$3,082,260.00	$1,580,935.00	$0.00	$1,954,165.00	$102,848.00	$4,328,700.00	$137,400.00	$11,186,308.00
David Carnes	Sum of Amount	$0.00	$0.00	$0.00	$1,000,000.00	$0.00	$0.00	$0.00	$1,000,000.00
Dennis Howard	Sum of Amount	$1,420,100.00	$602,000.00	$6,204,800.00	$1,676,568.00	$764,640.00	$0.00	$0.00	$10,868,108.00
Doroth Gardner	Sum of Amount	$89,230.00	$529,007.00	$0.00	$3,609,705.00	$11,708,105.00	$0.00	$2,127,960.00	$18,064,007.00
Eric Gutierrez	Sum of Amount	$858,070.00	$4,357,660.00	$895,290.00	$0.00	$918,500.00	$0.00	$2,135,570.00	$9,165,090.00
Eric Sanchez	Sum of Amount	$1,312,950.00	$413,101.00	$0.00	$185,630.00	$2,158,750.00	$3,984,250.00	$39,960.00	$8,094,641.00
Evelyn Williamson	Sum of Amount	$0.00	$1,621,900.00	$6,221,500.00	$0.00	$104,828.00	$0.00	$45,265.00	$7,993,493.00
Harold Campbell	Sum of Amount	$0.00	$6,021,135.00	$989,680.00	$39,600.00	$1,277,437.00	$0.00	$1,261,290.00	$9,589,142.00
Irene Kelley	Sum of Amount	$2,102,240.00	$5,766,050.00	$11,169,590.00	$913,860.00	$594,760.00	$2,229,500.00	$0.00	$22,776,000.00

Details (191 Rows) ⓘ Click an intersection in the table above to filter details.

	Owner Role ▾	Account Name ▾	Opportunity Name	Fiscal Period ▾	Amount ▾	Expected Revenue ▾	Probability (%) ▾	Age ▾	Close D... ▾	Created Date ▾
1	-	Webster349 Inc	Opportunity for Butler582	Q1-2023	$224,800.00	$22,480.00	10%	137	1/11/2023	7/8/2022
2	-	Pittman435 Inc	Opportunity for Watson1794	Q4-2022	$991,350.00	$99,135.00	10%	118	12/12/2022	7/27/2022

Figure 4-59. Matrix report example

Matrix reports are generally unreadable if the detail rows are shown. There is just too much data to look at. Most often these reports are displayed with Detail Rows toggled off, which collapses the report to the grouping level.

When creating a matrix report, an additional toggle switch appears at the bottom of the report. This toggle is called Stacked Summaries, and can be seen in Figure 4-60. This feature comes into play once your report has multiple summed columns.

Figure 4-60. Stacked Summaries toggle

Stacked summaries, by default, appear one on top of the other. You can adjust them to appear side by side by turning off the toggle. Figure 4-61 shows the report becoming taller with three summary columns stacked for each grouping.

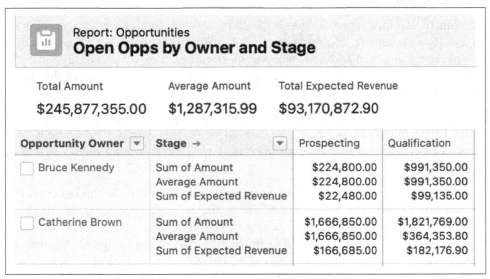

Figure 4-61. Matrix report with stacked summaries

The same matrix report will look quite different with Stacked Summaries turned off. It will be shorter and much wider because the summary columns will be displayed side by side for each column grouping. Figure 4-62 shows the very different orientation and look of the same report as shown in Figure 4-61 with Stacked Summaries turned off.

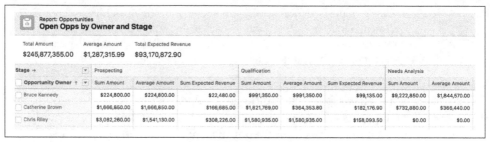

Figure 4-62. Matrix report without stacked summaries

Where possible, try to avoid creating reports where users will have to scroll left and right to read the report output. This can happen when you turn off Stacked Summaries. Scrolling up and down through report results is acceptable to most users, but the user experience when scrolling horizontally is less appealing.

Joined Reports

The fourth and final report format is joined reports, which allow you to combine up to five separate reports into one report. This is done by changing the report to be a joined report, and then adding new report blocks for each report you want to include. The key to making this work is to have a common element across each of the report blocks that group the joined report.

A classic example of a joined report is to combine a report showing all won opportunities by account, with another showing all open opportunities by account with another block showing all open high-priority cases. In the following steps, you'll learn how to create this joined report.

Change a report into a joined report by using the dropdown in the top left corner of the report. As shown in Figure 4-63, click the black triangle next to the word "Report" in the top left corner of the report builder. Once clicked, select the option for Joined Report and click Apply. The initial report is created using the Opportunity report type.

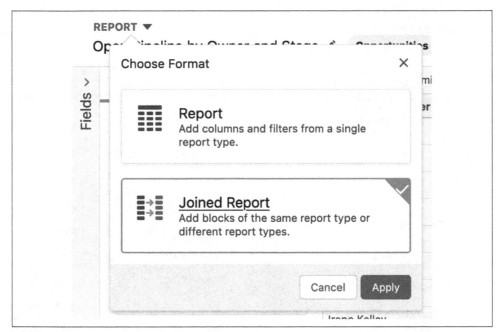

Figure 4-63. Creating a joined report

As seen in Figure 4-64, a new button appears immediately to the right entitled "Add Block," which is how you will add additional report blocks to the joined report. Report blocks are self-contained reports, with columns, filters, and formulas. Before adding a second report block, it helps to relabel the current block by clicking on the pencil to the right of the label in the Preview pane and changing its name. In this case, you might relabel it to "Won Opps," and sum and average the Amount column. Note in this example that the columns for this block have been relabeled "Won Opps" as well. The same is true for the filters for this block on the Filters tab.

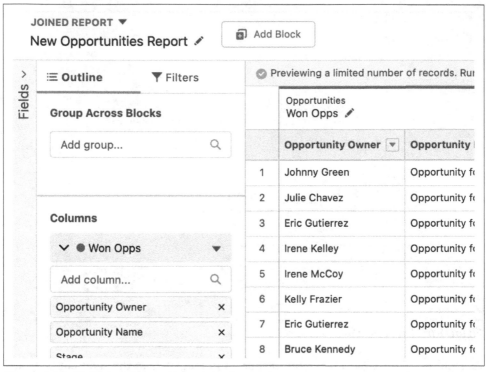

Figure 4-64. First steps in creating a joined report

There are some limitations to what report types can be added as a block on a joined report. In Salesforce Help there is a list of standard report types that can't be added to joined reports. There are also some report types that are not compatible with each other based on their objects and joins. When you try to add an offending report type, a red error message will warn you that it isn't compatible to be added as a block.

Let's take this example a bit further by adding a second report block. Click the Add Block button at the top of the report. This button will ask you to select another report type to add to this same report, just like you do when you create new reports. This is shown in Figure 4-65, where you can see the "Include default columns" checkbox and the Add Block button. When adding each new block, you can reuse the same report type or select another one. In this case, you will select the same Opportunities report type and make adjustments to its columns and filters to show all open opportunities.

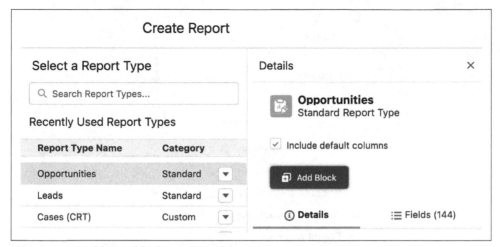

Figure 4-65. Adding a block to a joined report

 Joined reports become very busy quickly. When adding additional blocks, consider unchecking the checkbox "Include default columns." This allows you to start the new block without the clutter of the default columns from the report type you selected, and add only the ones you want.

For each block, as needed, you will want to repeat the steps of relabeling the block, adjusting the filters, adjusting the columns, and adding any summary columns. Then you will want to add a grouping that spans across all the blocks in your joined report, as shown in Figure 4-66. When the grouping on Account Name is added, you will want to toggle off the detail rows to simplify the final appearance of the report and make the report run faster.

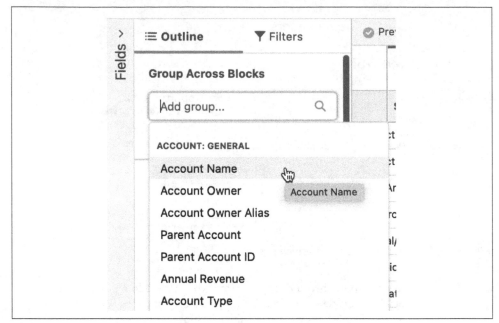

Figure 4-66. Grouping a joined report across blocks

Joined reports include records expansively. In a joined report, the groups with records across all blocks ("the intersection") are shown, and also the groups with records in any block ("the union").

Joined reports support a number of innovative ways to view data in your system. While this example, as seen in Figure 4-67, shows data from Opportunities, Accounts, and Cases in the same report, much like a scorecard, you could also be creative and show the same report type block over and over. As you'll see in the next chapter, joined reports have their own special type of formula available, the cross block formula.

	Opportunities Won Opps			Opportunities Open Opps		Cases Open High Priority Cases
Account Name ↑ ▼	**Sum of Amount**	**Average Amount**	**Record Count**	**Sum of Amount**	**Record Count**	**Record Count**
Abbott358 Inc	$98,850.00	$98,850.00	1	-	-	-
Adkins42 Inc	$773,640.00	$773,640.00	1	-	-	-
Adkins907 Inc	-	-	-	$1,741,100.00	1	-
Aguilar870 Inc	-	-	-	$1,072,200.00	2	1
Allen182 Inc	-	-	-	$4,067,300.00	1	-
Allison992 Inc	-	-	-	$2,592,000.00	1	-
Alvarez45 Inc	$200,400.00	$200,400.00	1	-	-	-
Alvarez72 Inc	$52,440.00	$52,440.00	1	-	-	-
Anderson269 Inc	$249,600.00	$249,600.00	1	-	-	-
Anderson638 Inc	$93,714.00	$46,857.00	2	$578,880.00	1	1
Armstrong345 Inc	$316,726.00	$316,726.00	1	-	-	-

Figure 4-67. Joined report example

Joined reports are excellent sources of data to populate scatter plot charts. This type of chart allows you to show correlations in data, which can often be generated by putting two report blocks side by side in a joined report.

Conclusion

This chapter stepped through the ways to start creating a new report and the significance of selecting the right report type for the task at hand. It introduced the report builder and its many controls that help streamline report creation, and it described the options for filtering your report to get at the data you want. By understanding the common use cases for the four report formats, you will expand your reporting repertoire considerably.

The next chapter is focused on incorporating formulas into your reports. Formula writing is a skill set that, much like in Microsoft Excel, will extend your range as a report writer.

CHAPTER 5

Formulas

Formulas solve problems in reporting, much like they do in spreadsheets. They can be used to change the data type of a field, adjust its value by leveraging functions, or combine it with other field values. Formulas can calculate ratios and do math across summary columns. They can even perform calculations across blocks in joined reports. When reporting, if you are stuck trying to figure out how to present data a certain way, a formula may be part of the solution. Keep formulas in the back of your mind for these situations.

You'll learn in this chapter that formulas are written with a combination of field references, operators, literal values, functions, and comments. The report builder offers three kinds of formulas you can add to reports: row-level formulas, summary formulas, and cross-block summary formulas, each with its own special uses. Custom formula fields can also be created on objects and then included in your reports.

What Are Formulas and Why Do They Help?

Formulas are made up of field references, operators, literal values, functions, and comments. They help you automatically calculate a value based on the inputs you specify. Although this definition tells you what a formula does, it is often easiest to explain it by demonstrating their power in an example. To calculate a win ratio, for example, you'll need to add a formula to an Opportunity report that is filtered to only show closed (won or lost) deals. The win ratio formula itself is pretty simple, as pointed out by the arrow in Figure 5-1. It divides the count of won deals by the count of closed deals.

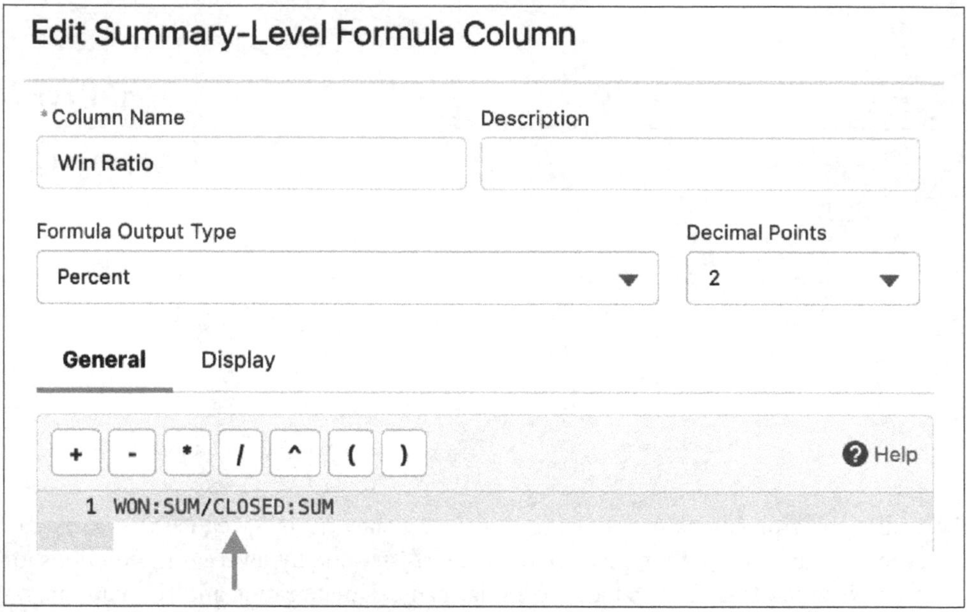

Figure 5-1. Win ratio formula in editor

When the formula is added to the report, it displays as a column. In this case, as it is a summary formula (which you'll learn about shortly), the formula results are shown at the subtotal and grand total levels. In Figure 5-2, you can see arrows pointing to the historic win ratio for the company and for each individual sales rep. This formula divides the sum of two other columns, not displayed on the report in this case, to achieve the desired results.

Figure 5-2. Win ratio formula on report

Another, somewhat whimsical, example of a formula in a report is when you use emojis to highlight sales opportunities of certain sizes. You can display a whale when the amount is over 1,000,000, a target with an arrow in it for amounts above 250,000, and a potato for opportunities whose amount falls below that lower threshold. Get it, "small potatoes"?[1] To achieve this, you can add a formula that evaluates every individual record using simple logic to assign emojis based on the corresponding record amounts. Using a row-level formula, we can take advantage of two IF() functions to set the thresholds, as seen in Figure 5-3. The IF() function allows you to test a condition and return some output if true, and other output if false. In this example, you can see two IF() functions, one nested in the other, to achieve the desired results.

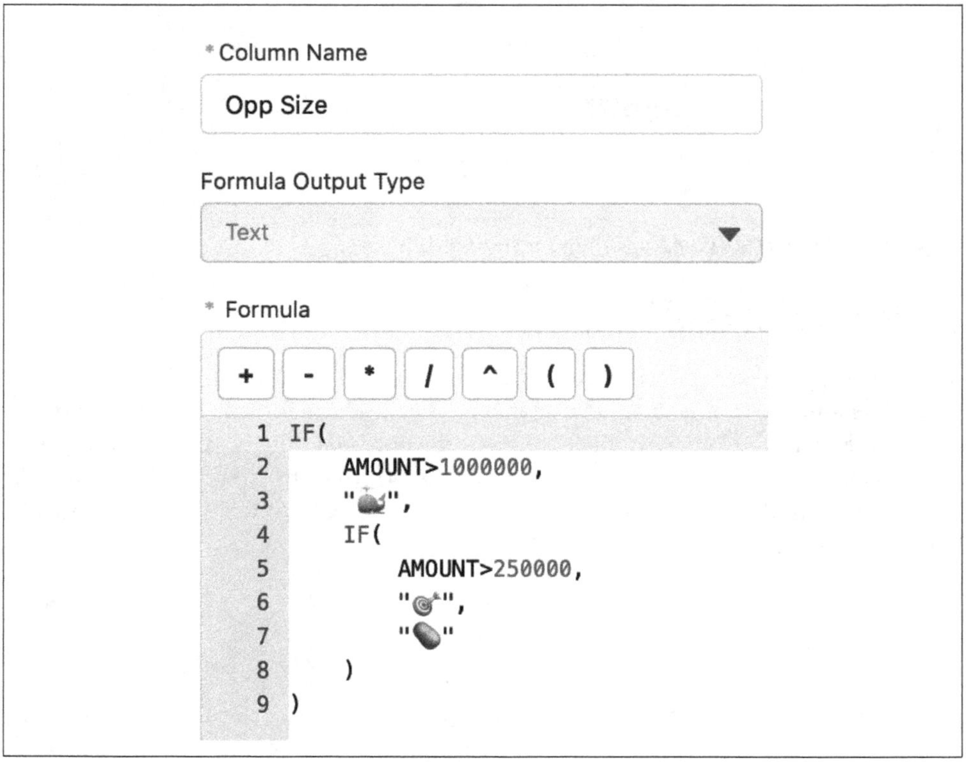

Figure 5-3. Opportunity-sizing emoji formula

1 "Small potatoes" is an informal American-English expression meaning something insignificant or unimpressive.

When added to the report, this formula's output, as seen in Figure 5-4, adds color, making opportunities easily identifiable by their size. Emojis are just another form of text in Salesforce, and as such, can be used in sorting, filtering, and grouping.

Figure 5-4. Opportunity-sizing emoji formula output

Building Blocks of Formulas

When writing or editing formulas in a Salesforce report, you will use the formula editor. It has a number of features that make it easier to write formulas quickly and correctly. While in the report builder, to open the formula editor, you can add a new formula or click on an existing formula in the list of columns. To add a formula while in the report builder, click on the action menu to the right of Columns, as shown by the arrows in Figure 5-5.

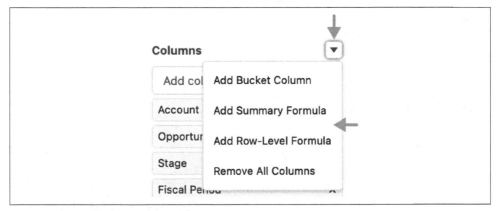

Figure 5-5. Adding a new formula

To edit an existing formula while in the report builder, click on the formula name in the list of columns. Alternatively, for row-level formulas, you can use the action menu to the right of an existing formula column in the Preview pane and select Edit Formula, as shown with the arrows in Figure 5-6.

Figure 5-6. Edit an existing row-level formula

 Salesforce won't let you add a formula to a report until the report has been given a name. Save your new report before adding a formula, or you will see the "The report name cannot be null." error above the Validate button in the formula editor when you validate or save the formula.

Formula Editor

The formula editor is largely consistent across the three types of formulas you can add to reports. It asks you to specify a column name, choose the output type of the formula, and write a valid formula. The output type can be either number, date, date/time, and text for row-level formulas or number, percent, or currency for summary formulas. It provides a description field to allow you to optionally share what the formula is for, and a Validate button to check the syntax to ensure the formula is written in a way that the editor can understand. Figure 5-7 shows the editor for the emoji formula from earlier in this chapter. The formula editor has syntax highlighting to make the formulas easier to read. Formula text is black, numbers are brown, and functions are blue. Note that the rows of text in the formula are numbered as well. Just above the box with the formula itself are a set of buttons for some, but not all, of the operators you can use. Similarly, to the left there is a list of all the fields you can insert and a list of many of the functions you can take advantage of in the editor.

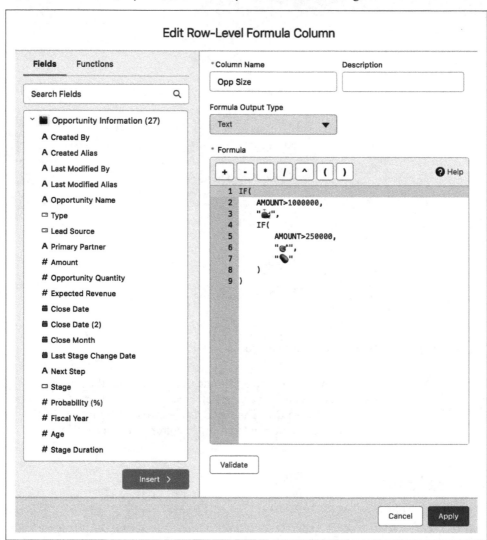

Figure 5-7. Formula editor

The Validate button tests that your formula has valid syntax. It cannot, however, determine if your formula achieves what you set out for it to do. To confirm that, you will have to test your formula.

When typing in the editor, you'll notice the handy typeahead functionality appear, offering to complete your words. You can ignore this, or use its suggestions to write your formula. Simple icons to the left of each suggestion indicate its purpose. In Figure 5-8, you can see the cube to the left of the word "casc" indicating that there is a function available. By clicking on the suggested word, Salesforce will insert sample syntax for that function.

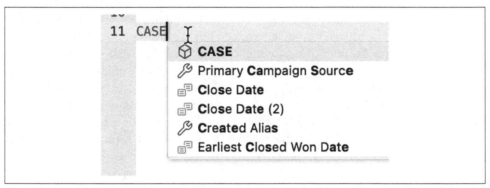

Figure 5-8. Formula editor typeahead

There are about one hundred functions in Salesforce that can be used to create formulas, but the formula editor only shows a subset of them. If there is a function that you know of that isn't visible in the report builder's formula editor, it is still worth trying to add it to a formula. Oftentimes, the hidden function works fine.

Depending on the type of formula you are writing on your report, the editor may have a second tab. The Display tab, as shown in Figure 5-9, appears on summary and cross-block summary formulas, allowing you to specify at which grouping level you want the formula to appear. The default is All Summary Levels, though this will not make sense to use for all of your formulas and isn't a valid choice when certain functions are used. The Display tab also gives you the option to display your formula at the Grand Total Only, or to select Specific Groups and indicate for which report grouping the formula should be calculated.

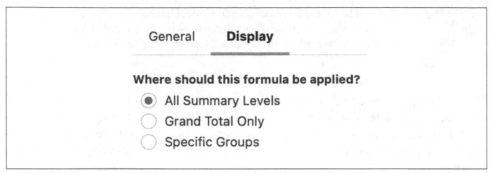

General   **Display**

Where should this formula be applied?

- ● All Summary Levels
- ○ Grand Total Only
- ○ Specific Groups

Figure 5-9. Formula editor display tab

Something to keep in mind when writing formulas is that there is an outer limit to the complexity of formulas that are supported. You can have up to 3,900 typed characters in each formula, and formula complexity is limited to 15,000 bytes, based on the fields referenced and functions used in the formula. As is true when writing formulas in Excel, you can only nest so many IF() functions before the complexity of the formula exceeds the limits. The 15,000 byte complexity limit is generous, especially for formulas you will typically write on reports, so most of the time you will not bump up against it. The Validate button can help keep your formula complexity in check by telling you if your formula goes past the limits.

Rather than nesting a bunch of IF() functions and increasing your formula complexity dramatically, you might be able to use the CASE() function. It checks a given expression, such as a field value, against a series of values, and then allows you to designate appropriate output for each.

Field References

Nearly all of the formulas you will write will have one or more field references in them. These tell the formula which fields you want included in your formula, to evaluate, perform a calculation on, concatenate, and so on. The emoji formula you saw earlier references the Amount field twice, as seen in Figure 5-10.

```
1  IF(
2      AMOUNT>1000000,
3      "🐋",
4      IF(
5          AMOUNT>250000,
6          "🐢",
7          "🐁"
8      )
9  )
```

Figure 5-10. Formula field reference

The formula editor provides a searchable and scrollable list of fields to choose from to add to your formula. As you saw on the Report tab search, the search mechanism will react to each letter you type, highlighting matching results in yellow. Figure 5-11 shows a search on the letters "opp" typed into the search box and a partial set of matching fields appearing in the field list below.

Fields　　Functions

opp|　　🔍

⌄ 📁 **Opportunity Information (2)**

A Opportunity Name

\# Opportunity Quantity

⌄ 📁 **Opportunity Owner Informatio...**

A Opportunity Owner

A Opportunity Owner Alias

Figure 5-11. Formula editor search

While not required, indenting lines within your formulas to correspond with functions makes them much more readable and easier to find mistakes. The formula editor makes consistent indenting easy by setting the starting cursor position the same as the last line each time you click the Return key.

To the left of each field label is an icon that indicates which data type category the field is in, such as text, number, picklist, or date. You can see these icons in Figure 5-12 along with the Insert button. To use this, click the field you want to insert, and then select the Insert button. The field name will be added to the formula writing space to the right, based on where your cursor position in the formula was before you inserted the field.

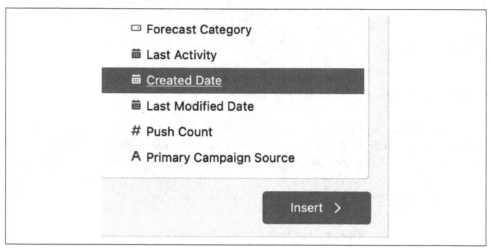

Figure 5-12. Formula editor field insert

 While you can manually type in field references when writing formulas, it is always worth using the field insert mechanism in the formula editor. This is because formulas use the underlying database name for each field, and not the field label you're used to seeing. There are many standard fields, and occasional custom fields, where the label and the name used in formulas don't line up. This occasional mismatch will cause errors in your formulas, and makes the field insert mechanism a must-use, even for formula pros.

Operators

Operators play an important role within formulas. They specify the type of calcula-tion, evaluation, or concatenation that you want to perform on the elements within a formula. Figure 5-13 shows the seven mathematical operators that have buttons directly in the report formula editor. The full list of operators available to use in your formulas is longer, including logical and text operators. Logical operators help you evaluate and compare items in the formula, such as equals, not equals, or greater than. Text operators support concatenation of field references and text.

Figure 5-13. Formula editor operators

Literal Values

Sometimes it is useful to use literal values in your formulas. A literal value is exactly what is written. It is a value that will be used as it is included in a formula every time the formula is evaluated. When concatenating two text values, it is often helpful to include punctuation and spaces in between for readability. Figure 5-14 includes two examples of this, inserting ": " in between the first two fields and " - " between the second set of fields.

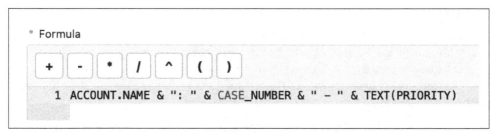

Figure 5-14. Concatenate with literal values

Another example of literal values can be seen in a row-level formula that you might add to an Opportunity report to further discount the expected value of deals in your pipeline. In Figure 5-15, you can see the value 0.9 being used to discount the expected revenue value of each opportunity.

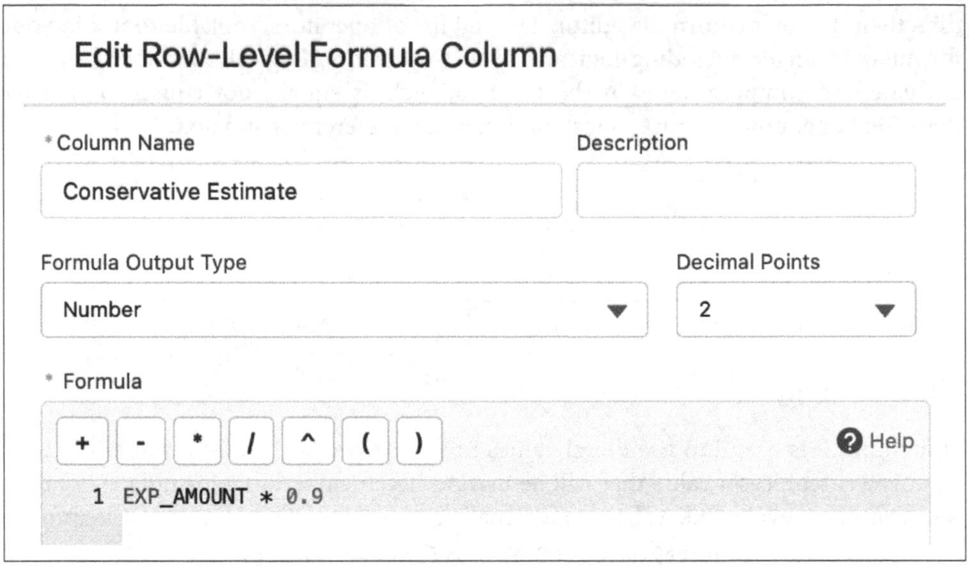

Edit Row-Level Formula Column

* Column Name

Conservative Estimate

Description

Formula Output Type

Number ▼

Decimal Points

2 ▼

* Formula

| + | - | * | / | ^ | (|) |

❓ Help

1 EXP_AMOUNT * 0.9

Figure 5-15. Adjust expectations with literal value

Functions

Functions do the heavy lifting within formulas. They are predefined formula snippets that solve different formula needs, performing simple or complex calculations. At present there are about one hundred functions available to you when writing formulas. Occasionally Salesforce will add new functions to help solve specific challenges with formulas in reporting.

Functions are thoughtfully grouped in the editor and in documentation into categories for Date and Time, Logical, Math, Text, Summary, and Advanced Functions. Having a sense of what type of function you might need in a situation will help you narrow down which category might have functions most useful to you. A short list of some helpful functions, their syntax, and a brief explanation can be seen in Table 5-1.

Table 5-1. A short list of useful functions

Function	Syntax	Uses
DATE	DATE(year,month,day) Accepts a four-digit year, a two-digit month, and a two-digit day.	Manufactures a valid date by assembling the parts.
TODAY	TODAY()	Returns today's date.
AND	AND(,)	Returns TRUE if all values or logical tests, each separated by a comma, are true, and FALSE if any value is false.
ISBLANK	ISBLANK()	Determines if an expression has a value and returns TRUE if it doesn't. If it contains a value, this function returns FALSE.
IF	IF(logical_test, value_if_true, value_if_false)	Evaluates a logical test and returns one value if it is true and another if it is false. Can be nested.
CASE	CASE(expression,value1, result1, value2, result2, ..., else_result) where you replace expression with the field you want to test, value1 with your comparison, and result1 with what you want returned. Continue through value and result pairs, separated by commas, and then finally a result if there are no matching values.	Compares an expression against a set of values. If the expression matches a value, it returns the corresponding result. Otherwise it returns the else_result.
TEXT	TEXT(value)	Converts the value of a picklist, number, currency, date, date/time, or percent field into text. Very helpful when working with picklists.

This is nowhere near an exhaustive list of the functions available to you when writing formulas in your system. It is worth exploring and getting to know the functions that can help you achieve your formula goals.

Within Salesforce Help, there is the useful documentation page All Formula Operators and Functions (*https://oreil.ly/fB02a*). It lists out the complete set of each, providing definitions, the expected syntax, and useful examples.

Comments

A little known and even less used feature in formulas is the ability to add comments. Comments are visible within the formula syntax, but are ignored when the formula is evaluated. They are a great way to remind yourself of the purpose of a formula you've written or to highlight something within a section of the code. To start a comment within a formula, type in *, after which you can write your comment. To close your comment, follow it with */. Figure 5-16 shows a formula example filled with comments.

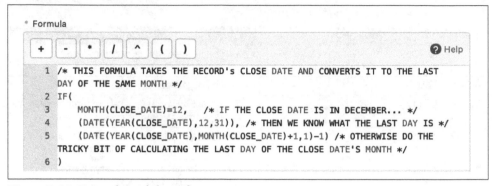

Figure 5-16. Formula with lots of comments

Another use case for taking advantage of comments within formulas comes when you are troubleshooting why one isn't working the way you expect. You might comment out a section of the formula to essentially test around it. If a formula doesn't work, but works when a section of it is commented out, that can give you a clue where the problem is.

Row-Level Formulas

Tabular, summary, and matrix reports that you create in Salesforce each support one row-level formula. These are created in the report builder by using the action menu to the right of the word "Columns" and selecting Add Row-Level Formula, as seen in Figure 5-17. Row-level formulas make their calculations on every report row, based on formula elements such as field references from that row. Joined reports don't give the option to create row-level formulas.

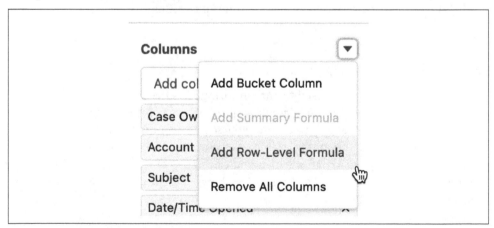

Figure 5-17. Add Row-Level Formula

Row-level formulas can be used in many ways to solve problems in your reports. You might create one to highlight data anomalies that you then fix using inline editing in your report. You might create another to concatenate the values of a few fields, or one that calculates the age of a record by subtracting the created date from the TODAY() function. Another simple example can be seen in Figure 5-18, where the formula evaluates each lead in the report's Lead Source and assigns each possible value a numerical score.

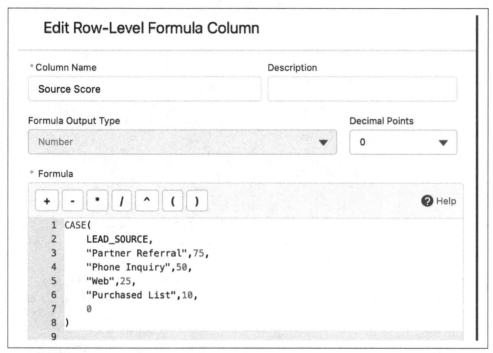

Edit Row-Level Formula Column

* Column Name

Source Score

Description

Formula Output Type

Number

Decimal Points

0

* Formula

| + | - | * | / | ^ | (|) | ? Help

```
1  CASE(
2      LEAD_SOURCE,
3      "Partner Referral",75,
4      "Phone Inquiry",50,
5      "Web",25,
6      "Purchased List",10,
7      0
8  )
9
```

Figure 5-18. Lead source score row-level formula

Different functions behave differently. If the previous example used IF() functions instead of CASE(), Salesforce would have required you to wrap each mention of LEAD_SOURCE in a TEXT() function to be able to extract the value. The CASE() function doesn't require use of the TEXT() function to perform its work.

The resulting score is listed as a column on the report with the telltale "fx" to the left of the column name, as shown in Figure 5-19. This example could be beefed up as an overall lead score calculation by expanding the formula to include multiple field references with each adding specific amounts to the calculation.

Lead Sou... ▼	*fx* Source Score ▼
Web	25
Web	25
Phone Inquiry	50
Purchased List	10
Partner Referral	75

Figure 5-19. Lead source score output

You might look to use a row-level formula to evaluate whether each record on a report is acceptable or if it violates some condition that you want to test. This type of formula can be useful if the purpose of the formula is to help you use inline editing in the report to fix the incorrect source values.

In Figure 5-20, you can see a row-level formula on a case report that evaluates each case's origin and priority. In this example, if the case priority is "High," then the case's origin should be "Phone," and is thus in violation if the origin is "Email" or "Web." To achieve this, the formula starts with an IF function that allows us to perform a logical test, which if true yields the word "Violation" and if false returns "OK." The logical test uses the OR function to set up the condition of a case having either "Web" or "Email" as its origin, and embeds that within an AND function to determine if the corresponding case also has a case priority that is "High."

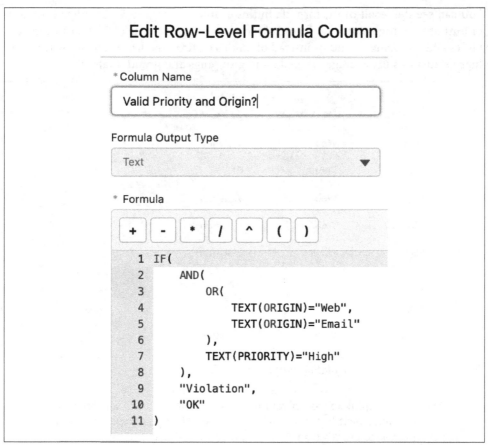

Edit Row-Level Formula Column

* Column Name

Valid Priority and Origin?|

Formula Output Type

Text ▼

* Formula

```
+   -   *   /   ^   (   )
```

```
 1  IF(
 2      AND(
 3          OR(
 4              TEXT(ORIGIN)="Web",
 5              TEXT(ORIGIN)="Email"
 6          ),
 7          TEXT(PRIORITY)="High"
 8      ),
 9      "Violation",
10      "OK"
11  )
```

Figure 5-20. Case origin violation row-level formula

A clear way to name a formula that returns good or bad values is to phrase its name as a question, such as "Valid Priority and Origin?"

You can see the result of the formula in this example in Figure 5-21. Other variations of output you might consider for this kind of formula are True or False, or even simple 1s and 0s. Using 1s and 0s instead of emojis or text enables you to show the summary statistics sum, average, or median in groupings and grand totals.

Priority ↑ ▾	Case Origin ▾	ƒₓ Valid Priority and Origin? ▾
High	Web	Violation
High	Phone	OK
High	Web	Violation
High	Web	Violation
High	Email	Violation
High	Chat	OK
High	Chat	OK
High	Web	Violation

Figure 5-21. Case origin violation output

A helpful way to test your formulas is to display all of the input columns next to the formula you've created in your report to allow you to quickly scan the expected outputs for any inaccuracies.

Summary Formulas

Summary formulas become available in your reports once you've added at least one grouping. If you try to add one before you've grouped a report, the option will appear grayed out in the Columns action menu, as in Figure 5-22. This option will also appear as grayed out once you've hit the limit of adding 5 summary formulas to a standard report and 10 summary formulas to a single block in a joined report.

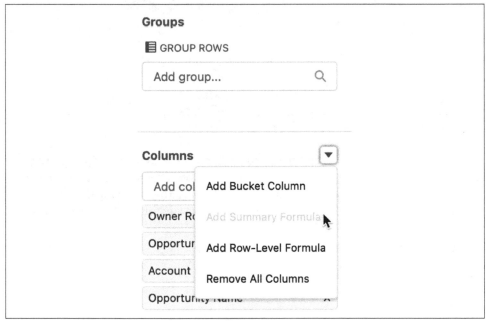

Figure 5-22. Add Summary Formula grayed out

Summary formulas allow us to return number, percent, or currency output values. They are great for doing math, such as calculating averages or differences. Summary formulas can also return the max (high) or min (low) values in a set or even the median value or count of unique values. When adding a field reference to a summary formula, scroll down next to the word "Sum" to see the other options, as shown in Figure 5-23. If you are about to insert a non-numeric field into your formula, your only insert option will be to use Unique, which returns the count of unique values in that set. Unique is a very useful tool in reporting.

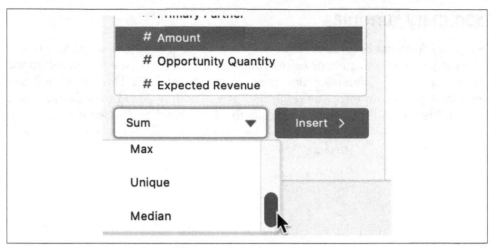

Figure 5-23. Summary formula insert options

Summary formulas are excellent for calculating ratios, such as the win ratio example from earlier in the chapter, lead conversion ratios, or case escalation ratios. In Figure 5-24, we see a summary formula that calculates the case escalation percentage by case owner. It divides the number of escalated cases by the total number of cases.

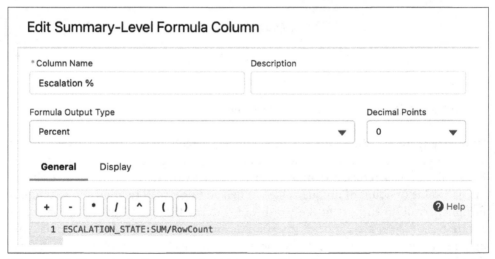

Figure 5-24. Case escalation percentage summary formula

The output you can see in Figure 5-25 appears as all other report formulas, with the "fx" to the left of the column name. This summary formula uses the default display setting, meaning it will appear at each subtotal level and at the grand total level. The formula output was set to percent without decimal places.

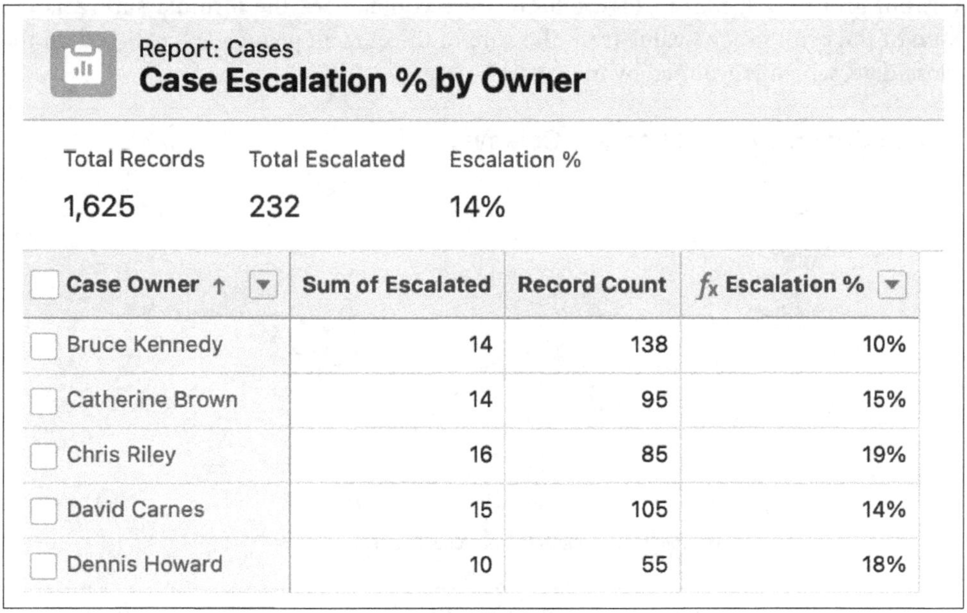

Report: Cases **Case Escalation % by Owner**			
Total Records 1,625	**Total Escalated** 232	**Escalation %** 14%	
Case Owner ↑ ▼	**Sum of Escalated**	**Record Count**	*fx* **Escalation %** ▼
Bruce Kennedy	14	138	10%
Catherine Brown	14	95	15%
Chris Riley	16	85	19%
David Carnes	15	105	14%
Dennis Howard	10	55	18%

Figure 5-25. Case escalation percentage output

Another excellent use of summary formulas is to calculate the change in value from one group to the next, especially when grouping on dates. This can be done using a special function that is available on summary and matrix reports called PREV GROUPVAL(). It pulls in the prior group's value, allowing you to compare it with the current group's value, as in Figure 5-26. Here you can see the formula subtracts the sum of the prior group's value from the sum of the current group's value, based on the close date, which is grouped by month.

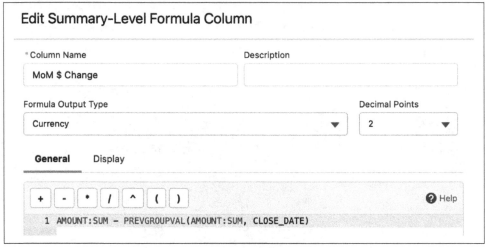

Edit Summary-Level Formula Column

*Column Name	Description
MoM $ Change	

Formula Output Type	Decimal Points
Currency ▼	2 ▼

General   Display

```
+  -  *  /  ^  (  )                              ❓ Help
1  AMOUNT:SUM - PREVGROUPVAL(AMOUNT:SUM, CLOSE_DATE)
```

Figure 5-26. Month over month change using PREVGROUPVAL()

The default syntax for the PREVGROUPVAL() function requires no specified offset. It is implied that the offset is 1 to look at the immediate prior group's value. By adding ,3 or ,12 within the parentheses at the end of the function, you can offset to the prior quarter's first month (3 months prior) or the prior year's corresponding month (12 months prior).

In Figure 5-27, the output of this example shows us month over month (MoM) the change in sales bookings as a dollar amount with two decimal places. The first month's grouping has no value in the formula's column because there is no previous value to compare it to. This powerful function can also be used for more complex math, such as displaying the percentage of the change from one group to the next.

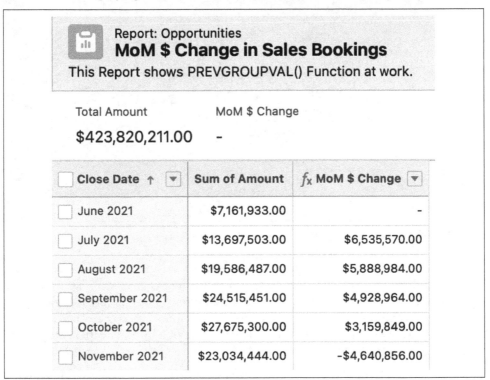

Figure 5-27. Month over month change output

When adding your first summary formula using a PREVGROUPVAL() function, a common mistake is to not set the display grouping. Even if you only have one grouping, you still have to go to the Display tab to set the specific group, or you will see an error when you try to save the formula. Figure 5-28 shows Specific Groups selected and then below that the specific row grouping Close Date identified.

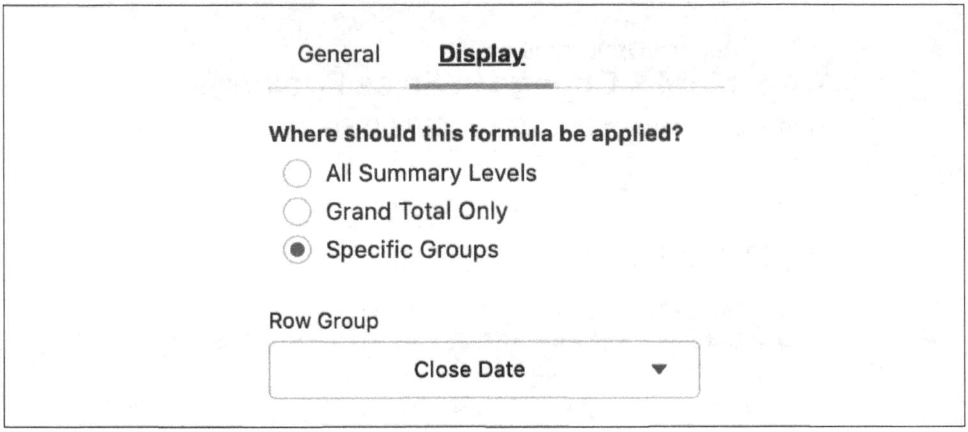

General **Display**

Where should this formula be applied?

○ All Summary Levels

○ Grand Total Only

● Specific Groups

Row Group

| Close Date ▼ |

Figure 5-28. PREVGROUPVAL() display requirement

Summary and matrix reports can each have up to 5 summary formulas per report, while joined reports can have up to 10 summary formulas per block. That means that by using a joined report we can have up to 50 summary formulas on a single report. One key thing to note is that summary formulas cannot reference other summary formulas, and so you may need to re-create portions of a formula you already added to a report to extend it slightly in a separate formula.

One final example of a summary formula in action involves taking advantage of another special "advanced" function called PARENTGROUPVAL(). Like PREVGROUPVAL(), PARENTGROUPVAL() allows you to compare one report grouping to another. However, instead of comparing against the same group, it allows you to cross group levels. You learned earlier that each summary report can have up to three groups, and each matrix report up to four groups. The ability in each case to do math across groups is very useful.

In Figure 5-29, you can see that the formula is dividing the current group's sum of the amount by the parent's sum of the amount. Since the report is grouped twice by close date, to get the quarter grouping and annual grouping, we have to be specific about which grouping we want to apply the function to. In this case, CLOSE_DATE2 refers to the outer grouping on the year. As before with PREVGROUPVAL(), we also need to be very specific about the display grouping, which in this case is applied to the grouping on CLOSE_DATE, referring to the inner grouping on the quarter.

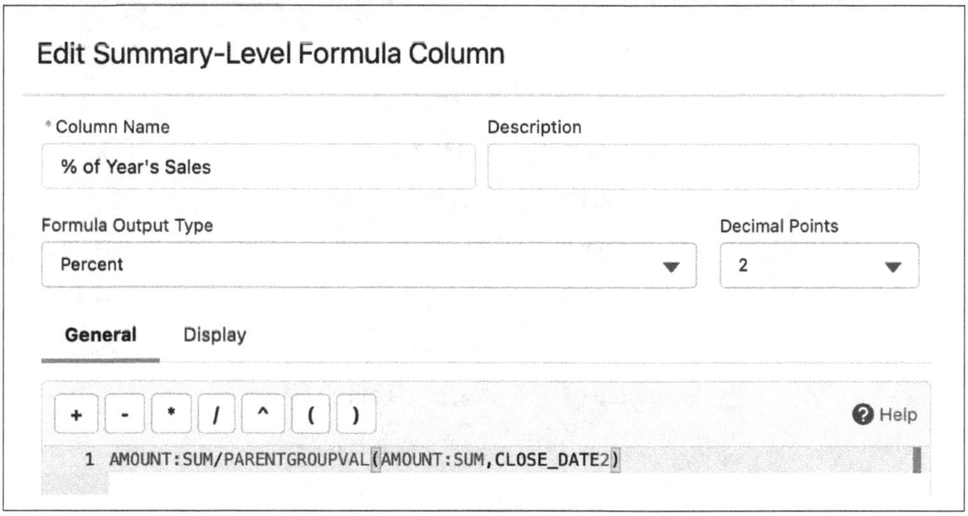

Edit Summary-Level Formula Column

* Column Name

% of Year's Sales

Description

Formula Output Type

Percent

Decimal Points

2

General   Display

| + | - | * | / | ^ | (|) |

? Help

```
1  AMOUNT:SUM/PARENTGROUPVAL(AMOUNT:SUM,CLOSE_DATE2)
```

Figure 5-29. Percentage of Year's Sales using PARENTGROUPVAL ( )

The output of the formula using the PARENTGROUPVAL() function, as seen in Figure 5-30, is a handy percentage, which we can't display any other way on a report. It tells us that the $7.1 million in Q2 CY2021 is 5.70% of that year's $125.7 million total.

Report: Opportunities			
Quarterly Sales as Percentage of Year			

Total Amount	% of Year's Sales
$423,820,211.00	-

☐ Close Date (2) ↑ ▼	Close Date ↑ ▼	Sum of Amount	*fx* % of Year's Sales ▼
☐ CY2021	Q2 CY2021	$7,161,933.00	5.70%
	Q3 CY2021	$57,799,441.00	45.98%
	Q4 CY2021	$60,744,023.00	48.32%
	Subtotal	**$125,705,397.00**	
☐ CY2022	Q1 CY2022	$107,698,798.00	36.13%
	Q2 CY2022	$115,689,242.00	38.81%
	Q3 CY2022	$74,726,774.00	25.07%
	Subtotal	**$298,114,814.00**	
Total		**$423,820,211.00**	

Figure 5-30. PARENTGROUPVAL output

Cross-Block Summary Formulas

When working with joined reports, a special kind of formula is available supporting math across the blocks. In the formula editor, when adding fields from each block, array notation is included to ensure that the blocks are referenced in addition to the field references. The first block is referred to as "B0," the second as "B1," and so on until "B4" if your joined report has five blocks. Each joined report will support up to 10 of these formulas, in addition to up to 50 summary formulas.

To create a cross-block summary formula, create a joined report, and then use the Outline Tab action menu to Add Cross-Block Summary Formula using the action pull-down menu for the appropriate block. Figure 5-31 shows this for the block labeled Open Pipeline.

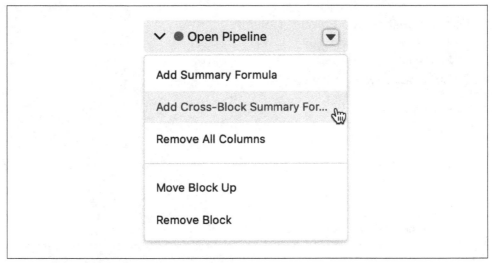

Figure 5-31. Add Cross-Block Summary Formula

 When working on a joined report, the option to Add Cross-Block Summary Formula will appear as grayed out until you add your first group to the report in the Group Across Blocks box.

A nice example of a cross-block summary formula can be seen in Figure 5-32, where field references from the first block are used to calculate the win rate by industry in the second block, and then those percentages are multiplied by the sum of the amount of open opportunities. This yields a projection of won deal amounts based on past performance.

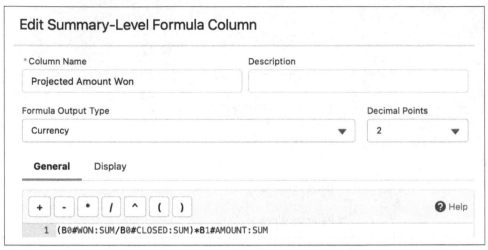

Figure 5-32. Projected Amount Won cross-block summary formula

You can see from Figure 5-33 that the cross-block summary formula called Projected Amount Won is applied at each subtotal and also at the grand total of the report.

Joined Report
Cross Block - Win Rate with Projection

Industry ↑	Opportunities Won Opps		Opportunities Open Pipeline	
	Sum of Amount	f_x Win Rate	Sum of Amount	f_x Projected Amount Won
Retail	$23,982,794.00	72.73%	$4,033,235.00	$2,933,261.82
Technology	$52,983,019.00	66.67%	$10,124,568.00	$6,749,712.00
Telecommunications	$13,773,149.00	70.59%	$9,584,467.00	$6,765,506.12
Transportation	$21,294,127.00	85.71%	$6,197,000.00	$5,311,714.29
Utilities	$16,457,625.00	63.16%	$9,747,149.00	$6,156,094.11
Total	$572,944,761.00	74.81%	$245,877,355.00	$183,931,509.75

Figure 5-33. Projected Amount Won output

Custom Formula Fields

One thing to keep in the back of your mind is that if the three types of formulas you can create directly on a report don't meet your needs, you can always ask a system administrator to create a custom formula field on a object, which you can then include on a report. Custom formula fields give you the ability to create cross-object formulas, which allow you to reach across up to 10 objects to pull a field reference back into your formula. They can also be reused over and over on various reports you and your team create, centralizing updates and reducing the possibility of mistakes across what could be many reports.

Here's a useful example that involves adding a custom formula field on the case object. This formula would look up the associated account's owner's first name and mobile phone, and format them nicely to appear on a case report to share back with the customer if they call to complain about having been sold the wrong product. Figure 5-34 shows two cross-object field references pulling in the values from the user object, via the associated account object and the account owner field. The values are formatted so that the account owner's first name appears, then a colon and a space, followed by the account owner's mobile phone number.

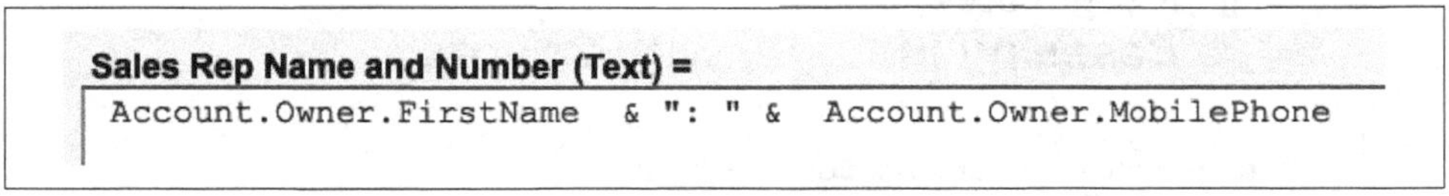

Sales Rep Name and Number (Text) =

```
Account.Owner.FirstName  &  ": "  &  Account.Owner.MobilePhone
```

Figure 5-34. Custom formula field with cross-object formula

The Power of One

Before Salesforce introduced the ability to leverage the Unique summary option within formulas or column actions, a clever way of counting things on reports involved creating Power of One formulas. This technique requires having your system administrator add a custom formula field to each key object you report on, using the name of the object such as Account as the field name. The formula field is set up to return a number without decimal places, and the formula you write is literally just the number 1, as shown in Figure 5-35.

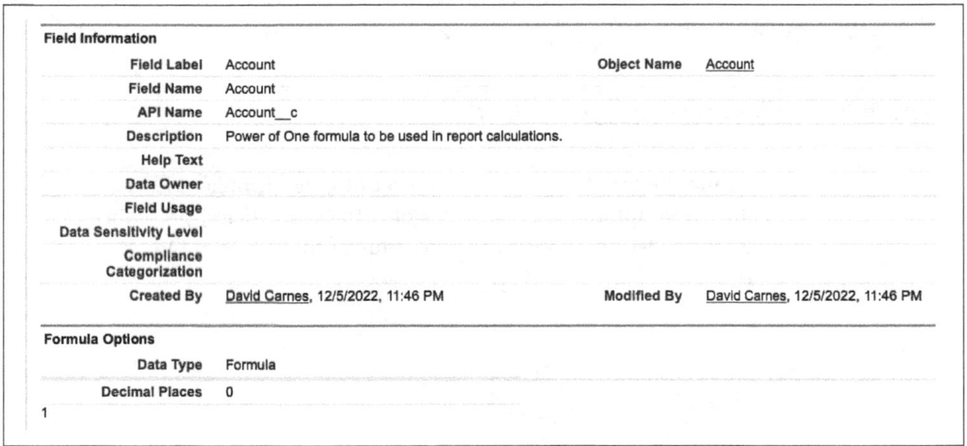

Field Information

Field Label	Account	**Object Name**	Account
Field Name	Account		
API Name	Account__c		
Description	Power of One formula to be used in report calculations.		
Help Text			
Data Owner			
Field Usage			
Data Sensitivity Level			
Compliance Categorization			
Created By	David Carnes, 12/5/2022, 11:46 PM	**Modified By**	David Carnes, 12/5/2022, 11:46 PM

Formula Options

Data Type	Formula
Decimal Places	0

1

Figure 5-35. The Power of One formula

When reporting on a single object, the Power of One column will match the record count shown by the report. When reporting on multiple objects, however, the single record count column on the report shows only the count of the child object's records and the count of the higher level object records is essentially lost. This is one situation where the Power of One is very valuable. In Figure 5-36, you can see a case report that includes Power of One formula fields for accounts and cases. As expected, the Power of One column for cases matches the record count column on the report. This example would be even more interesting if a third object, such as Assets, and a fourth object, such as Activities, were included, as we would suddenly be able to see counts of records for each of those objects.

Report: Cases
Cases by Industry with Counts

Total Records	Total Account	Total Case
1,625	799	1,625

Industry ↑	Sum of Account	Sum of Case	Record Count
Agriculture	35	67	67
Apparel	58	118	118
Banking	52	118	118
Biotechnology	46	107	107
Communications	21	49	49

Figure 5-36. The Power of One report output

 Searching the web for "Salesforce Power of One formula" will yield exalting descriptions and examples of it in blog articles, presentations, and videos demonstrating the value of the Power of One formula in Salesforce reporting.

Testing Formulas

The best time to start testing your formulas is even before you write them. This means that you should take the time to think through your formulas before creating them, identifying the inputs needed, the calculations you want to perform, and the expected results. It is important that you get in the habit of considering the full range of possible permutations and the impact each will have on the expected output of your formulas. Once you have written your formula, be sure to test out the formula using the data values in your report. Sometimes you will need to manufacture some realistic test records to ensure you are covering the range of possible inputs in your formula.

 When testing your formulas, consider the impact of negative values, zeroes, null values, misspelled data, and other anomalies that may be present in your data.

Conclusion

Formulas solve problems across the Salesforce platform, and in particular when reporting. They are written using a helpful formula editor that makes it easier to construct your formulas correctly. Formulas are made up of a number of components, such as field references, functions, and operators, which require syntax to be written a specific way, or errors will result. One of the most important steps in formula writing is testing, which should begin even before writing each new formula, by thinking through its expected inputs, calculations, and outputs.

You saw in this chapter that there are three kinds of formulas you can create directly on reports within the report builder: row-level formulas, summary formulas, and cross-block summary formulas. A fourth kind of formula, the custom formula field, remains available as an option for your system administrator to add to an object on your behalf in your system. Once created, custom formula fields can be used over and over on your reports.

Now that you've learned all the great things you can do with reports, the next thing is to shift gears and start learning about dashboards.

CHAPTER 6

Dashboards

Dashboards in Salesforce provide a powerful way to visualize data stored within your system. Whether you're an entry-level salesperson, a midlevel support manager with a team of direct reports, or a senior executive at a nonprofit organization, you can leverage dashboards to better understand your data and make decisions. It is common for system administrators or other users with the appropriate permissions to create custom dashboards showing charts, tables, and metrics in support of the various roles within an organization.

For example, your company's VP of Sales might log in to Salesforce and immediately see a dashboard embedded into their homepage showing key sales figures. They can use this information to gauge whether their team is on track to hit their goals. Their sales managers might each have a dashboard with charts and tables showing their team's performance. Those managers might also use another dashboard to meet with their individual sales team members to coach them on their deals. Figure 6-1 shows an example of a dashboard for an individual sales rep to see their leads and sales pipeline. They can use this to quickly determine their performance and what information they are communicating to their superiors.

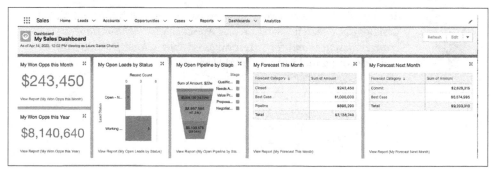

Figure 6-1. Sales rep dashboard

In this chapter, you'll step through dashboard features and explore the Dashboards tab. You'll learn how to access and interact with dashboards in your system and see tips on their use.

What Is a Dashboard?

Dashboards are built on top of reports that exist in your system, and they can show a wide array of data in one place to help drive decision making. Dashboards are made up of components, such as charts, gauges, metrics, and tables, which are organized on a grid. Components are the cards that appear on a dashboard. Each component type has its own properties, and they all offer the ability to display a title, subtitle, and footer text.

Unlimited Edition now uses "Widgets" in place of the word "Components" on Dashboards. For the purpose of this book, we will refer to both as "Components."

The different component types allow you a variety of ways to represent the underlying data in your system. Each component is fed by a source report within the system, with the exception of the two new widget types available in Unlimited Edition allowing you to insert image or text. There is an art to organizing components in compelling ways that tell powerful stories to drive actionable decision making, which you'll see in the next chapter.

New Salesforce instances often do not come with any sample dashboards. Notable exceptions include industry-specific templates, such as Salesforce Health Cloud or Nonprofit Success Pack (NPSP). To get started, you'll have to build one or download a dashboard pack from Salesforce's AppExchange (*https://appexchange.sales force.com*). There are several free packs available that can be used as-is or modified to suit your needs.

To find and download two dashboard packs, each with four sample dashboards, search Salesforce's AppExchange (*https://appex change.salesforce.com*) for "Preconfigured Sales Cloud Dashboards" and "Preconfigured Service Cloud Dashboards."

In Figure 6-2, you can see an example of a Sales dashboard made up of a variety of types of components, such as a horizontal bar chart, a gauge, a funnel chart, two metrics, a stacked vertical bar chart, and a lightning table. Each of these components is sourced by a report in the same Salesforce system, showing data that is stored in the system. In the top right corner of each component, there is a four-arrows icon you can use to expand that one component for a closer look. At the bottom left corner of each component, there is a link to view the underlying source report.

Figure 6-2. Dashboard Example

If you hover over a dashboard component, on its right side or along the bottom, you might see gray scroll bars appear allowing you to reveal more information.

Overview of the Dashboards Tab

Much like the Reports tab, the Dashboards tab is organized to support the storage, easy access, and search of your system's dashboards. When you click into the tab's embedded navigation (shown in Figure 6-3), it'll show you a list of your favorite and most recently used dashboards. The dashboards under My Favorites will be anything that you've marked as a favorite for easy access. The dashboards under "Recent records" will show the five dashboards you've looked at most recently.

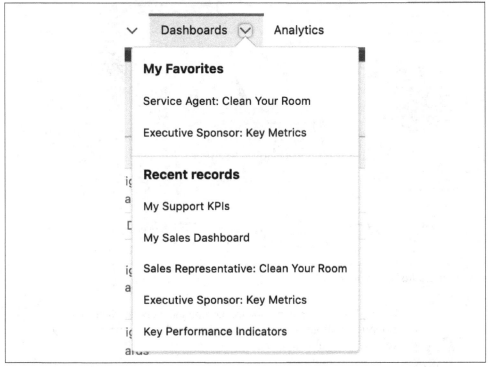

Figure 6-3. Dashboard tab embedded navigation

Dashboard Tab Categories

As you see in Figure 6-4, on the lefthand side of the tab there is a set of links to fixed categories of dashboards: Recent, Created by Me, Private Dashboards, and All Dashboards. Below that you can see a set of categories related to folders: All Folders, Created by Me, and Shared with Me. Finally, there is a category for seeing the list of all your favorited dashboards. When you select a category, the number of items in that category is listed at the top. Private Dashboards are ones that only you can see, which you have saved into the Private Dashboards folder.

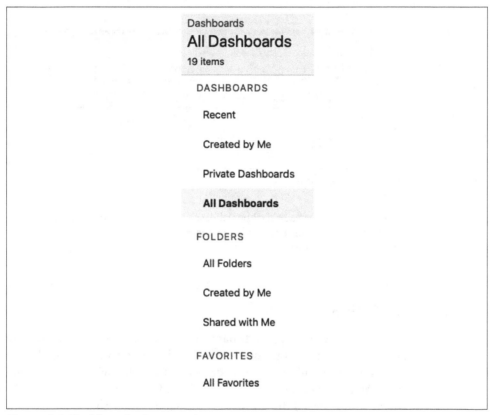

Figure 6-4. Dashboard tab categories

Keep in mind when first logging in to a system that you haven't run any dashboards yet, so you won't see anything under the Recent list. Similarly, because the search context is based on the category selected, your search will also yield nothing. Your best bet when searching is to click on All Dashboards or All Folders first, to see or search for dashboards.

If you've selected one of the dashboard categories, such as Recent in Figure 6-5, you will see a list of dashboards and their relevant details organized into columns. The Description field, though optional, is perfect for providing your users with an explanation of the purpose and intended audience for each dashboard. Folders control who gets to see and edit dashboards, and so it is important to store each dashboard in a place where your intended users can get access. The Subscribed column displays a checkmark for any dashboards that you subscribe to. The gear in the top right corner lets you select fields to display, allowing you to expose the Last Modified By and Last Modified Date values, and also remove and reorder the columns.

Figure 6-5. Dashboard tab columns

A best practice for each dashboard description is to try to describe its purpose and contents. Who is the intended audience? What decisions does it support?

Dashboard Actions

You can view a dashboard by clicking on its name, or as you can see in Figure 6-6, by choosing the View action from the pull-down menu to the right using the small black triangle. Users with View permissions on a dashboard's folder will see View and Favorite as options. With a higher level of folder permissions, when you click on the pull-down menu you'll see View, Edit, Subscribe, Delete, Favorite, and Move. Definitions for each dashboard action are listed in Table 6-1.

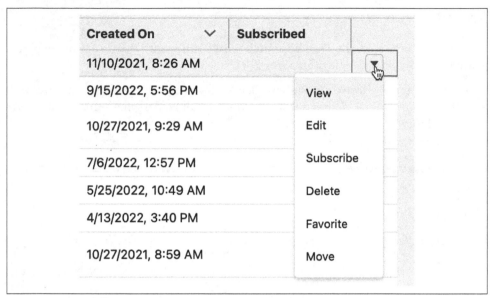

Figure 6-6. Dashboard action menu choices

Table 6-1. Dashboard actions

Action	Definition
View	This opens the dashboard.
Edit	If you have the appropriate profile permissions, and the dashboard is in a folder where you've been granted Edit permission, you will see the Edit option.
Subscribe	This will open the Subscription page, which lets you subscribe or unsubscribe to this dashboard.
Delete	If you have the relevant permission(s), you can delete the dashboard.
Favorite	This allows you to easily mark a dashboard as one of your favorites, or to unfavorite it.
Move	If you have permission on the folder, you can update the dashboard to change the folder where it is stored.

 When granted the appropriate permission, each user can subscribe to up to 7 dashboards (15 in Unlimited Edition). An easy way to manage your subscriptions is to sort the Subscribe column on the Dashboard tab by clicking on it twice to show the list of your subscribed dashboards descending. You'll quickly be able to see what dashboards you're already subscribed to, if any.

Search

The search feature on the Dashboard tab works differently than Salesforce's global search capability in a couple of important ways.

First, the category selected on the left dictates the scope of the search feature built into the Dashboards tab. For example, if you select All Folders, the search context will include all folders, as shown by the arrows in Figure 6-7.

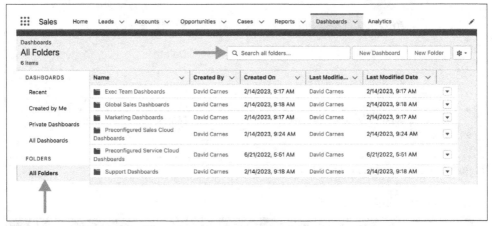

Figure 6-7. Dashboard tab category impact on search context

Second, as you type in the dashboard search window, it will compare your search term to the start of each word in the dashboard names listed for that category, and highlight your search term within any matching dashboard names below. Figure 6-8 shows a search on the Recent category in action. You can search for a dashboard with as few as two characters!

Figure 6-8. Dashboard search results

You have a few options for exporting the full list of dashboards in your Salesforce instance. You can create a report on dashboards by first creating a custom report type on the Dashboard object. A system administrator can also use the Data Loader, Workbench, or other API-based data tool to export a list.

Folders

Dashboards are stored within folders, and it is through folders that we grant access to users within our system. Unlike visibility of individual records, such as accounts or opportunities, your access to folders and their contents is not inherited by the people above you. Explicitly granting folder access is an important way to keep your leadership team from being overwhelmed by what is on the Dashboards tab. You should only show them what they need to see.

 Contrary to popular belief, your CEO does not need access to all dashboards in your system. You should try to ensure they have access to specific dashboards needed for their role, without exposing them to additional clutter.

By clicking on the All Folders category on the Dashboard tab, as in Figure 6-9, you can see a list of all the top-level folders for which you have access. Dashboard folders can be nested up to four levels deep, so it is important to note that the All Folders category isn't showing you all folders, but instead just the top-level folders. When looking at folders, we have no idea whether there are zero, one, or many sublevel folders potentially storing more dashboards.

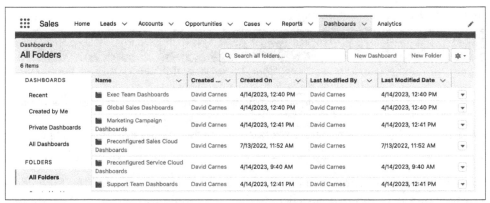

Figure 6-9. All dashboard folders

System administrators and users who have been granted special permission via their profile or a permission set can see all folders except for other users' private folders. Users without these special permissions rely upon a folder-sharing mechanism to gain visibility to folders. Table 6-2 lists out the special profile permissions that allow managing and viewing all dashboard folders.

Table 6-2. Dashboard folder permissions

Permission Name	Description
Create Dashboard Folders	Create folders that contain dashboards.
Manage Dashboards in Public Folders	Create, edit, delete dashboards, and manage their sharing in all public folders.
View Dashboards in Public Folders	View and access dashboards in public folders, which does not include others' personal folders.

 System administrators cannot see the contents of users' private folders directly. However, there is a way they can log in as any other user and thus access private folders. This requires the feature Log In as Another User be enabled in their Salesforce instance.

As with reports, the sharing of dashboard folders is always controlled at the topmost level, with all child folders inheriting the top-level folder permissions. You control access to folders by sharing the folders, using one of the three permission levels as defined in Table 6-3: View, Edit, and Manage. These permissions are given by a user with the Manage permission on that folder or with the Manage Dashboard in Public Folders permission on their profile. If a user in your system isn't granted one of these permissions, they will not see the folder or its contents.

Table 6-3. Dashboard folder sharing

Folder Sharing Level	Description
View	Assigned users can see individual dashboards and view the list of dashboards in this folder. They can also see who else has access to the folder.
Edit	Assigned users can see, create, and edit dashboards in this folder. They can rename dashboards and delete them.
Manage	Assigned users can control permissions for others users in this folder. They also can relabel and delete the folder.

You can share a folder in a couple different ways. If you have selected the All Folders category on the Dashboard tab, click on the action pull-down menu to the right of a folder and select Share. Alternatively, you can open a folder and click on the action pull-down within the folder and select Share. Either method will open up the Share Folder screen.

As you can see in Figure 6-10, the top half of the Share Folder screen allows you to identify who you want to share with and at what access level. You can share a folder with individual users, public groups, roles, roles and subordinates, territories, or a combination thereof. After you've selected who you'd like to share the folder with and at what level, click the Share button in the middle of the screen to finalize the sharing.

The bottom half of the Share Folder screen lists out who can currently access the folder.

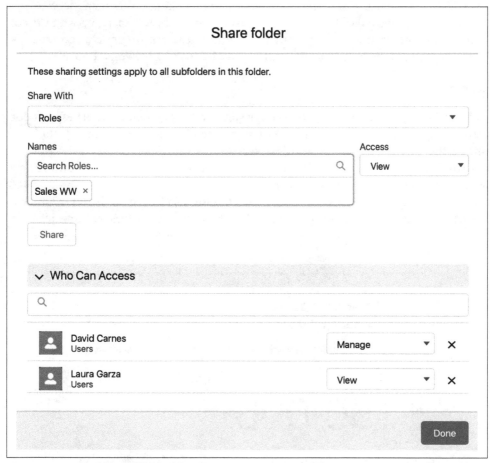

Figure 6-10. Dashboard folder sharing

Since sharing is controlled only at the top-level folder of each folder hierarchy, instead of a Share button at the lower-level folders, users can select View to see the folder permissions.

 By sharing your folder with no one, the folder is essentially hidden from other users in your system, except system administrators and users with the View/Manage Public Dashboard permissions. This can be useful when developing new dashboards, before revealing your work to your colleagues. An example of a hidden folder is an Old Dashboard Archive where you might temporarily store old dashboards before deletion.

Running a Dashboard

In Salesforce, the act of selecting a dashboard and clicking on its name to view it is known as "running a dashboard." Once a dashboard has been run, along with the colorful components there are a number of other features to understand, such as Refresh, the running user, dynamic dashboards, filters, and Download As.

Refresh

When looking at a dashboard, you can see some important details in the top left corner just below the dashboard title. As you can see in Figure 6-11, the "As of" date shows the date the dashboard was last refreshed; a very important concept in dashboards is that they are not updated just because you viewed the dashboard. In fact, you could look at the same dashboard many times without its data being updated. Two ways to update a dashboard are to click the Refresh button at the top right or to have a subscription set up for the dashboard, which runs it at a time you specify.

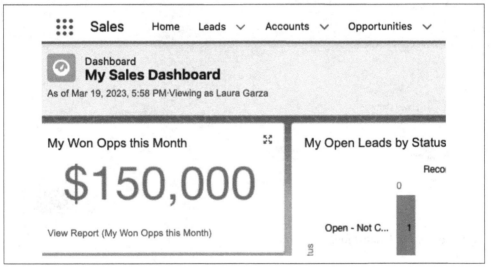

Figure 6-11. Dashboard running user

 You can refresh a dashboard only once per minute using the Refresh button.

Running User

Also in Figure 6-11, just below the title, is the running user, next to the words "Viewing as." Each dashboard has a running user, which is the person in your company whose security permissions determine the data displayed on the dashboard. The running user is set by the dashboard creator, and their goal should be to choose the person whose data permissions best reflect the goal of the dashboard. For example, if you have a dashboard showing the Eastern Sales Team's data, then it is likely the VP of the Eastern Sales team would be the running user.

 While the running user is often someone higher up in your organization to ensure enough visibility to the data on a dashboard, there may be times when you need to set the running user to a person lower in your organization. For example, in order to ensure your CEO will see the appropriate data on the European Support Team's dashboard, the dashboard creator will likely choose the manager or director of that group to be the running user.

Dynamic Dashboards

Some dashboards are set up to allow certain users the ability to change the running user directly on the dashboard. This is called a dynamic dashboard, and it greatly expands the range of use for the dashboard. In Figure 6-12, you can see the current running user and the word "Change" to the right. Clicking on it pulls up a simple window that allows you to choose another running user for that dashboard.

Figure 6-12. Dynamic dashboard Change link

 A common mistake when first working with dynamic dashboards is to not consider the likely running users your users will choose for each dashboard. The running user chosen needs to have at least view access to the folders the dashboard and its supporting reports are in, or else you'll see error messages or no data.

Filters

Dashboard filters are an often overlooked feature by dashboard creators. Each filter allows you to apply additional criteria across the dashboard, against all components with similar data. A dashboard allows for up to three filters (five in Unlimited Edition) to further refine the data displayed. In Figure 6-13, you can see a dashboard in which the filter "China" is being applied on the Account Billing Country field. This will run all of the dashboard components with access to the Account Billing Country again with this added filter applied to show data related to accounts in China. In this example, you could also use the Industry field filter to further refine your search to that country and an industry.

Figure 6-13. Dashboard filters

Each dashboard filter can display up to 50 choices. Filters can be added on a variety of field data types, including date fields such as Opportunity Close Date. If you add a filter on a date field, you can specify dynamic date ranges, such as This Quarter or Last Year. Only someone with the ability to create or edit a dashboard can add or adjust the filters on that dashboard. Anyone who can see a dashboard can use the filters on that dashboard.

Downloads

If you ever need to use a copy of dashboard content in another application, such as a presentation, Salesforce provides two easy ways to download your dashboards.

The first is built into the action pull-down menu at the top right of each dashboard. In Figure 6-14, you can see Download selected in the action menu. When clicked, the entire image of the dashboard is converted into a .png file, with the name of the dashboard as the file name.

Figure 6-14. Dashboard download

The second option for downloading dashboards is to download each component individually. After clicking the icon in the top right of any component to expand it, you will then see a download icon in the top right corner, as shown by the arrow in Figure 6-15. Like in the full dashboard download, the component download is saved as a .png file with the component name as the file name.

 While looking at any dashboard component in its expanded view, you can use the arrows on the left or right (see Figure 6-15) to toggle through all the components on that dashboard.

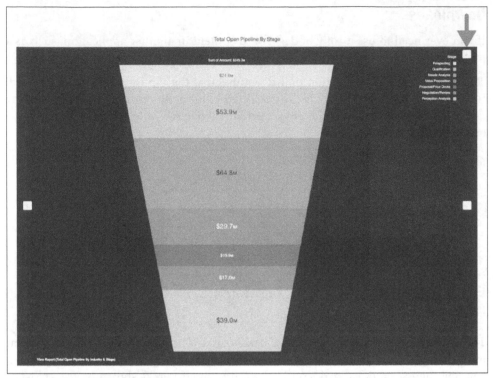

Figure 6-15. Dashboard component download

Subscriptions

Once granted permission via their profile or a permission set, each user in Salesforce can subscribe to up to seven dashboards, to have them delivered via email on set days and at set times. This is a great way to engage users by helping them prepare for regular meetings or spot issues directly from within their inbox. The email that is sent includes an HTML rendition of each component, one on top of the other. You can click on a particular component in those emails and be brought directly to that report in your system.

> Salesforce's Unlimited Edition allows users to subscribe to up to 15 dashboards each.

Figure 6-16 shows how to subscribe to a dashboard while looking at the dashboard. You can do this by clicking on the Subscribe button. Incidentally, that same button is how you unsubscribe from a dashboard.

Figure 6-16. Subscribe to a dashboard

Alternatively, you can subscribe to a dashboard while looking at a list of dashboards on the Dashboards tab, selecting the action menu next to the one you want, and choosing Subscribe.

In Figure 6-17, you can see the Edit Subscription screen. Here you can choose to receive the email daily, weekly, or monthly and at a particular time of day. The default behavior is that subscriptions generate an email, but if you uncheck the Recipients checkbox, the dashboard will just be refreshed at that time. A key thing to note is that like report subscriptions, dashboard subscriptions can be sent to multiple recipients. You can subscribe users, roles, roles and subordinates, and public groups as recipients. Setting more recipients than just yourself requires that you be a system administrator or have additional profile permissions. It is not possible to define a subscription recipient who is not a user in your system.

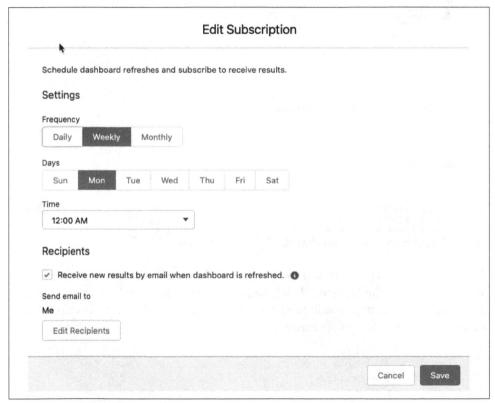

Figure 6-17. Edit Subscription screen

Keep in mind that subscriptions have no end date, meaning that they will keep showing up in your inbox until you unsubscribe.

Unsubscribing from a subscription is as simple as repeating the steps to subscribe, then at the bottom left of the Edit Subscription screen, clicking the Unsubscribe button. This button is pointed out by the arrow in Figure 6-18.

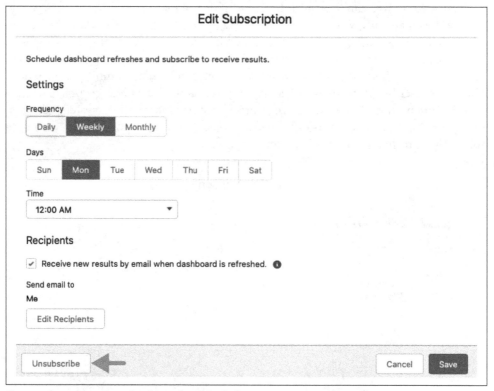

Figure 6-18. Unsubscribe from the Edit Subscription screen

To more easily manage your own subscriptions, add the Subscribed column to the list of dashboards on the Dashboards tab and click twice on the column header to sort the column descending. You'll quickly be able to see and update your current subscriptions, as you can see in Figure 6-19.

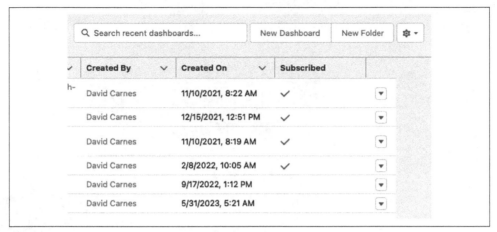

Figure 6-19. Subscribed column on a list of dashboards

Conclusion

Dashboards are a powerful way to visualize data in your system. They are used by people at all levels in an organization to monitor processes and support decision making in their jobs. Salesforce's dashboards come with a rich set of features to support your needs, such as the ability to change the running user, download all or part of a dashboard, and subscribe to receive updated dashboards by email. Dashboards are made up of components, each sourced by a single report in your system.

You access dashboards via the Dashboards tab. They are organized into folders, each of which has its own sharing permissions to ensure that your colleagues see only the dashboards that they need to see.

In the next chapter, you'll learn how to create dashboards.

CHAPTER 7

Building Dashboards

One of the more creative and fun activities in Salesforce is building dashboards. You combine your understanding of the underlying data in your system with visualization tools to support decision making. Key to your success will be knowing the strengths and uses for each type of element that can be put on a dashboard.

As you learned earlier, while everyone can create reports, most users do not start with permission to build or edit dashboards in Salesforce. Your system administrators have these permissions and also the ability to grant others these permissions. Many organizations identify Salesforce users who have the interest, business understanding, and technical skills and make them report and dashboard super users, allowing them to create and modify dashboards. If you are interested in creating or editing dashboards, you can ask your system administrator to grant you the appropriate permissions.

In this chapter, you'll start by learning about what you need to create dashboards. Then you'll tour the dashboard editor and look at dashboard settings. Next you'll walk through the 11 types of components (13 in Unlimited Edition) that can be added to dashboards, see descriptions of their properties, and step through use cases for each. We'll close the chapter by discussing ways to optimize your dashboards.

Getting Started

The first step in building a new dashboard is creating or identifying one or more supporting reports that will feed data to the components on the dashboard. Source reports for dashboards are typically of type summary, matrix, or joined reports; each of these require that the data be grouped by one or more columns on the report. For example, Opportunity reports are often grouped by sales stage, allowing you to see sums and counts by stage. These might be added to a dashboard using a funnel chart to emphasize opportunity progression through the sales cycle.

To keep things organized and provide relevant information to users, dashboards are created with specific users or levels of users in mind. Marketing managers might each have their own dashboard detailing the progress and outcomes of their campaigns, while the chief marketing officer has an overarching dashboard depicting progress toward their departmental goals.

Each dashboard can display up to 20 components of various types and sizes. This means that a single dashboard can have up to 20 supporting reports that feed it. It also means that dashboards can quickly become quite busy to look at. Unlimited Edition refers to dashboard components as "widgets." It supports up to 25 widgets, including a maximum of 20 charts and tables, 2 images, and 25 rich text widgets.

It is best practice to put all the reports that support a single dashboard into the same report folder, using the dashboard name as the folder name with "Reports" included at the end. When creating the folder, at a minimum, be sure to share it with the user who will be set as the running user for the dashboard. If you want the dashboard's users to be able to click through to the underlying reports, share the folder with them as well.

Once you have created and saved your source reports into a dedicated folder, there are three ways to start building a dashboard. The first way is to click the New Dashboard button that appears in the Dashboard tab, as shown in Figure 7-1.

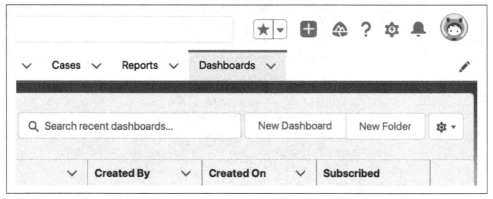

Figure 7-1. New Dashboard button

A second way to start a new dashboard is to use the action pull-down menu to the right of any saved report on the Reports tab. There, you can select the choice to add that report to a dashboard, as shown by the arrows in Figure 7-2. On the next screen, you are given the option to select an existing dashboard or to add it to a new dashboard.

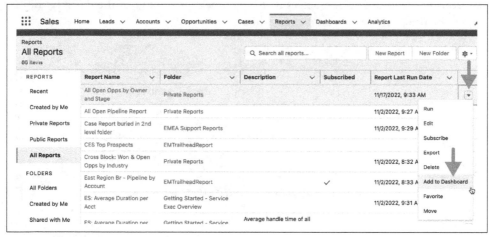

Figure 7-2. Add to Dashboard

The third way to start creating a dashboard is to use the Create button on the Analytics tab. You will learn about the Analytics tab in Chapter 9.

 If you do not see the New Dashboard button on the Dashboards tab, then you currently do not have permission in Salesforce to create dashboards. System administrators can assign these permissions for you.

Each method of adding a new dashboard will bring you to the New Dashboard screen, as seen in Figure 7-3. It asks you to give the new dashboard a name and specify a folder in which to store the dashboard. The default folder is your personal private dashboard folder, which no other users can see. Be sure to select another folder if you would like other users to see your dashboard. Optionally you can provide a description of up to 255 characters that will appear at the top of the dashboard, just below the title, when a user runs the dashboard.

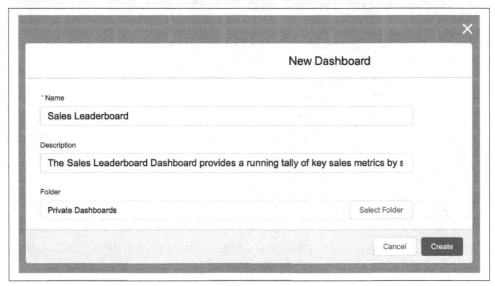

Figure 7-3. New Dashboard screen

Dashboard Editor

Once you click the Create button on the New Dashboard screen, you will be brought to the dashboard editor. This appears as a 12-column grid with a set of controls at the top right. Think of this as a blank canvas where you'll be putting the various components that make up your dashboard. Figure 7-4 shows the editor with buttons for adding components and filters, Undo and Redo buttons, a gear to let you update the dashboard's properties, a Save button, and a Done button. There is a pencil to the right of the dashboard name, which allows you to quickly rename the dashboard. The Save button doubles as a Save As and Delete button by clicking on the small black triangle to the right of the word "Save." The Done button takes you out of the editor and shows you the last saved version of the dashboard.

Figure 7-4. Dashboard editor

In Unlimited Edition the + Component button is replaced by a + Widget button that allows you to add components as before, along with images and text widgets.

Now that you have your dashboard named and stored in a folder, you are ready to start adding components to it. A blank dashboard isn't useful, so let's think about the goals of the people who will be using the dashboard and what information would be most useful to them.

Adding a Component

By clicking on the + Component button, you are brought into the Select Report screen, shown in Figure 7-5. Salesforce asks you to specify the source report for this new dashboard component. Here you can use the categories on the left or the search at the top to find the exact report to feed this new component. By default, Salesforce shows you a list of recent reports you have worked on or run, with the most recent appearing up at the top. If using the search to select a report, note that there is an additional filter you can apply immediately to the right to show only reports or only folders in your results. Once you have found the report you want to use, click on it to highlight it, and then click the Select button.

Select Report

Reports	🔍 Search Reports and Folders... Reports and Folders ▼
Recent	
	Won Opps this Quarter by Owner
Created by Me	David Carnes · Mar 30, 2022, 7:28 PM · O'Reilly
Private Reports	
	All Open Pipeline
Public Reports	David Carnes · Feb 9, 2022, 10:24 AM · Sales Reporting
All Reports	**Cases by Create Month and Current Status**
	David Carnes · Mar 9, 2022, 11:49 AM · System Reports
Folders	
	Case Spike Analysis YoY by Month
Created by Me	David Carnes · May 11, 2022, 10:08 AM · Service Reporting II
Shared with Me	**Net New Logos**
	David Carnes · Apr 20, 2022, 8:37 AM · Sales Reporting II
All Folders	
	Sales Funnel
	David Carnes · Apr 20, 2022, 8:11 AM · Sales Reporting II
	Pipeline Coverage Ratio
	David Carnes · Apr 20, 2022, 7:17 AM · Sales Reporting II
	Win Ratio vs Average Deal Size by Owner
	David Carnes · Mar 31, 2022, 9:54 PM · O'Reilly
	Case Formula Day of the Week Open Mid
	David Carnes · Mar 23, 2022, 9:05 AM · Formulas for Service Reporting
	Case Formula Day of the Week Opened
	David Carnes · Mar 23, 2022, 12:40 AM · Formulas for Service Reporting
	Closed Case Trending by Month YoY

Cancel   Select

Figure 7-5. Select Report

Once you have selected a report, you now see the Add Component screen, as in Figure 7-6. Here you can choose from the 11 types of components to display as and also specify properties for that chosen component type. Next up in this chapter, you will learn about each type of component and its properties. Using these properties, you do have a good amount of control over the appearance of the component. Once you have reviewed and updated the component's properties on the Add Component screen, click the Add button to put this component on the dashboard.

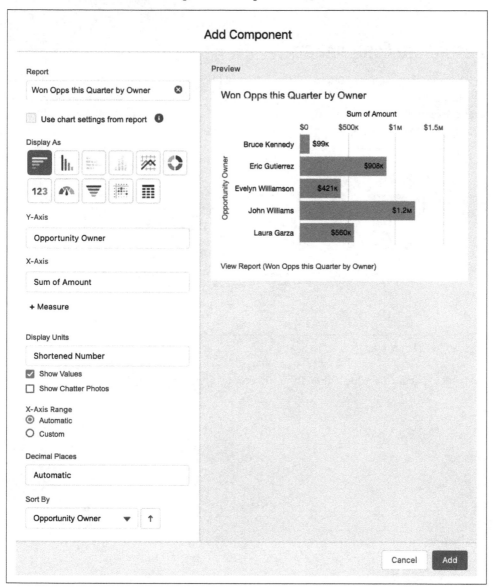

Figure 7-6. Add Component

If your source report is not grouped by a column, then only 1 of the 11 types of components, the lighting table, will be available to select when adding that report to a dashboard.

Dashboard Components

When selecting components to add to your dashboards, it is helpful to know about all of the types, their uses, and unique properties. In Figure 7-7, you can see the icons that correspond to each type of component available. As you select one and adjust its properties, a preview appears off to the right of the icons.

Figure 7-7. Display As

Now let's take a closer look at each of the component display options.

Horizontal Bar Chart

The horizontal bar chart is the default view of newly added components. It shows off subtotals by one or two groups from your source report in the form of horizontal bars. These are excellent for long lists of groupings, such as industries or billing states. Figure 7-8 shows a preview of a horizontal bar chart, showing the number of leads owned by the users listed.

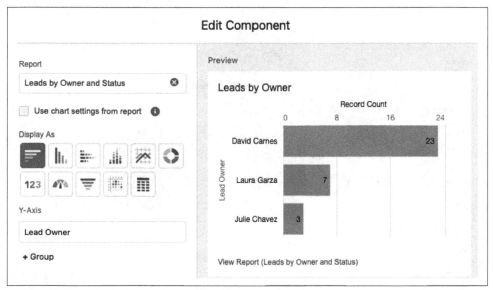

Figure 7-8. Horizontal bar chart

Vertical Bar Chart

The vertical bar chart is similar to a horizontal bar chart and shows subtotals by one or two groups from your source report in the form of vertical bars. These are great for depicting trends over time, such a month-over-month or year-over-year reporting. In Figure 7-9, you can see a vertical bar chart showing the sum of won opportunities by calendar year.

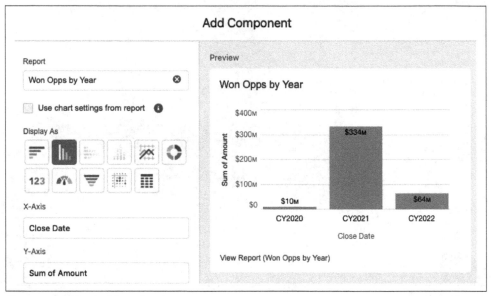

Figure 7-9. Vertical bar chart

One of the special features available in vertical bar charts and stacked vertical bar charts is the ability to use a second measure to plot a line across the bars. You can even display a second axis for it on the right side. Figure 7-10 shows arrows where, when adding a vertical bar chart, you can make each of these additions to add meaning to your chart.

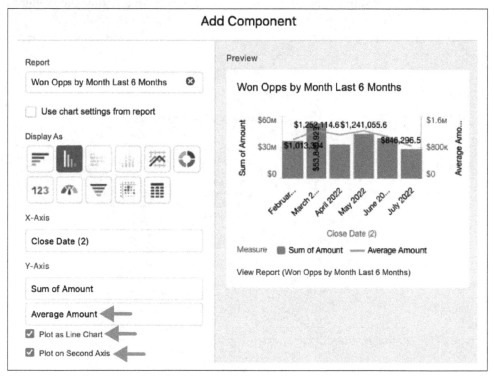

Figure 7-10. Plotting a second measure as a line

Stacked Horizontal Bar Chart

The stacked horizontal bar chart adds a second grouping from the source report as striations on the bars of the chart. Figure 7-11 shows cases by owner and status. This component type will appear as grayed out unless there are two groupings on the source report. Stacked horizontal bar charts have a special property that allows you to "Stack to 100%," revealing the proportions of each grouping to one another.

Figure 7-11. Stacked horizontal bar chart

Stacked Vertical Bar Chart

Much like the horizontal version, the stacked vertical bar chart relies upon a second grouping on the source report to add colorful striations to the chart. These show time series well, such as the one in Figure 7-12. The icon for the stacked vertical bar chart will be grayed out and unselectable unless there are two groupings on the source report.

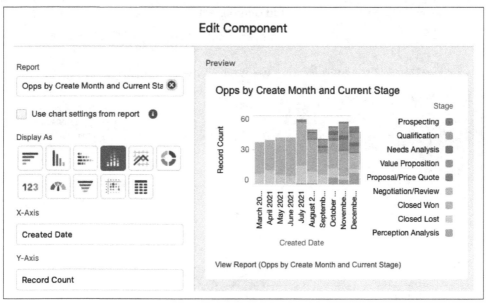

Figure 7-12. Stacked vertical bar chart

Line Chart

Line charts are excellent for showing comparative trends of data over time, but they can be quickly overwhelmed when too many groupings (lines) are included in the source report. In Figure 7-13, you can see the sales performance across six quarters of three regions: North America, APAC, and Rest of World.

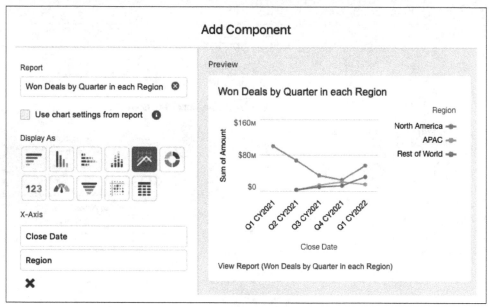

Figure 7-13. Line chart

One of the useful settings on a line chart is the Cumulative checkbox. You can change a line chart that shows actuals per time period to one that keeps a tally going as the time periods pass. Figure 7-14 shows the same line chart as before, with the lines going up as each time period adds to the totals. Down in the bottom left corner is the checkbox that changes the line chart in this way.

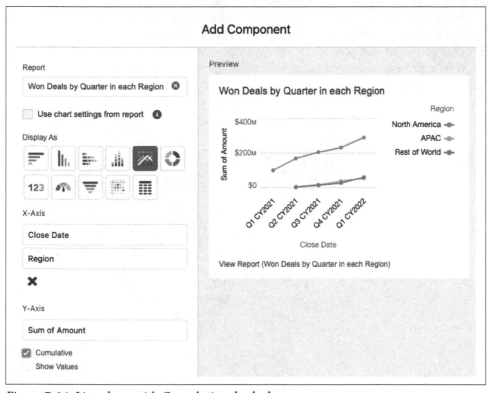

Figure 7-14. Line chart with Cumulative checked

Donut Chart

The donut chart is a type of chart that is divided into slices with a hole in the middle showing the grand total of the report. Donuts depict the proportion of each group compared to the others through its size, with a color assigned to each group. By default it only shows six groups from your report, and combines the rest into an Other category. In Figure 7-15, you can see cases by case origin for this year, and the special properties available to donut charts such as Show Percentages and Combine Small Groups into Others. Show Percentages will add the percentage of the total of each slice onto the slice. The Combine Small Groups into Others will automatically create an Other grouping.

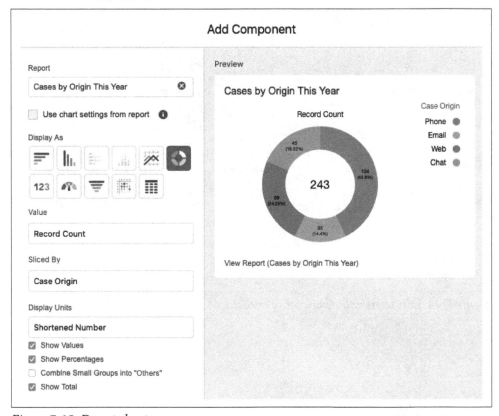

Figure 7-15. Donut chart

 The Max Values Displayed setting is distinct from the Combine Small Groups into Others setting. If you want to show all values, make sure both Max Values Displayed exceeds your number of groupings and Combine Small Groups into Others is unchecked.

Metric Chart

The metric chart shows the grand total of a source report, making these excellent for tracking numeric values such as % Growth, Total Revenue $, Total Number of New Customers, and so on. Within its properties you can apply conditional highlighting on the amount displayed. Figure 7-16 shows the total number of leads created, with conditional highlighting making the number appear yellow since it falls between 33 and 67. By clicking on the red, yellow, or green color blocks immediately to the right of the Ranges showing 33 and 67, you can choose from other standard colors or up to millions of colors, to convey meaning through the highlights.

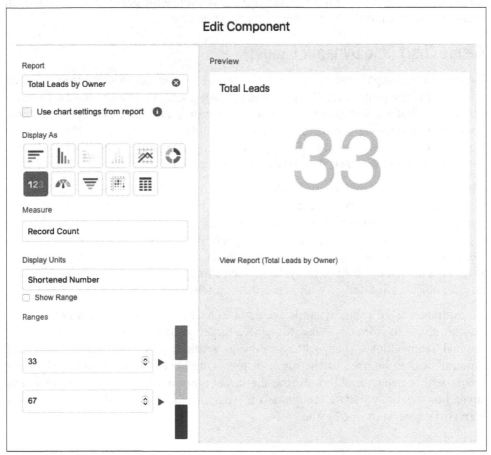

Figure 7-16. Metric chart

If you do not want to leverage conditional highlighting on a metric chart, you can set the number threshold well below the grand total that is typically returned by the report. This will ensure the numbers displayed are always the same color.

You may want to relabel your metric chart component for clarity. While a metric chart requires that the source report be grouped, it disregards the groupings entirely to focus on the grand total of the report. The default label of each new component is the source report name, and those names often reference the groupings in the report, meaning that the metric chart name might be confusing.

Gauge Chart (and Dynamic Gauges)

Gauge charts compare the grand total of a report with target thresholds that are set within the gauge properties. There are two types of gauges that can be used on a dashboard. The first is a standard gauge, as seen in Figure 7-17, which allows you to hardcode the red-yellow-green thresholds directly within the component. For years, the nondynamic nature of standard components has required that dashboard owners manually update the targets defined in the gauges each time the targets change.

The second type is called a dynamic gauge chart, which allows you to pull in the gauge's target value from a record in Salesforce. When adding a gauge chart, toggle from Standard to Dynamic to change from the default standard gauge type. In Figure 7-18, you can see the properties and preview for a dynamic gauge chart, which pulls in the target number from a separate object and allows you to then set percentages of that number for the red-yellow-green thresholds. In this example, there is a custom object called Target, with a record storing the annual quota.

A common way of using dynamic gauges is to have a system administrator create a custom object to store target records, with a target name and an amount, such as the Annual Team Quota. Then, within the gauge settings, you specify that record and amount field to be used in the gauge display. One benefit of using dynamic gauge charts with a separate object storing the target amounts is that you can do a data upload or manually update the quotas on a tab, instead of manually updating every standard gauge chart one by one.

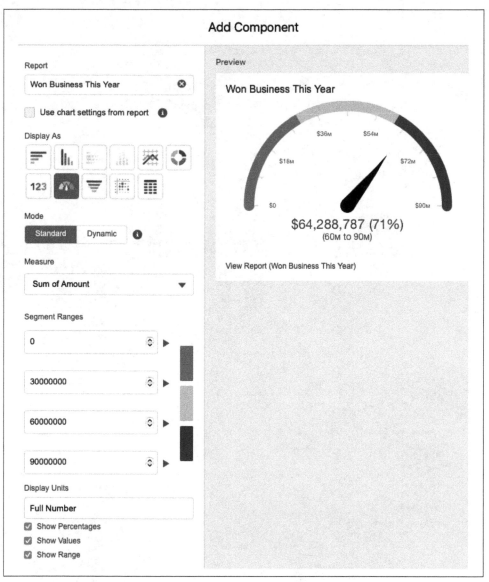

Figure 7-17. Standard gauge chart

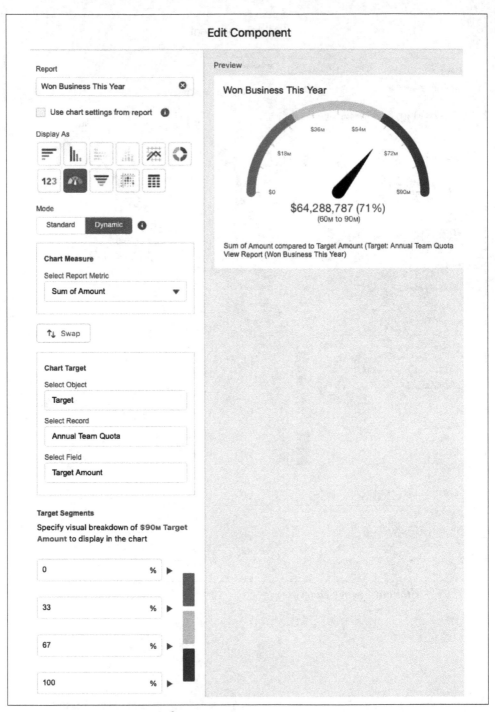

Figure 7-18. Dynamic gauge chart

Funnel Chart

The funnel chart is a favorite among sales leaders wanting to see the proportional amounts by stage visually in the form of a funnel. In Figure 7-19, we can see the open pipeline by stage, where the thickness of each stage corresponds to the amount in the stage. By default, funnel charts only show the first six groupings from your source report and combine other smaller groups into an Other category.

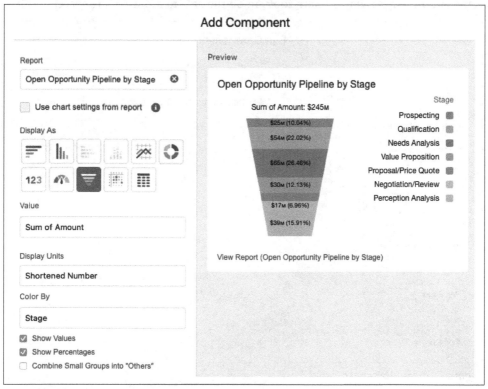

Figure 7-19. Funnel chart

When working with funnel charts for sales, the best bet is to increase the Max Values Displayed to at least the number of stages in your sales pipeline. Also, in most cases you will want to avoid the unwanted groupings of small amount stages into Other.

Scatter Chart

Scatter charts are great for showing correlations within sets of data. They require multiple columns in the source report that are summed to be able to correlate them in the scatter chart. In Figure 7-20, you can see dots representing individual sales team members plotting their average deal size versus their win rate. Dashboard users can hover over any of the dots to see the underlying details. Defining a custom Y-Axis Range in properties allows you to zoom in on the data to reduce white space.

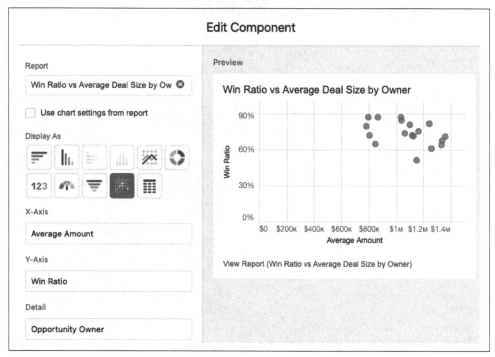

Figure 7-20. Scatter chart

When first trying to add a scatter chart, many people are discouraged by what appears as a diagonal line of circular plots on the graph. By default, the x-axis and y-axis values are the same, yielding the diagonal line. By adjusting one of these values, you will start to see correlations in the data.

Lightning Table

The most powerful of all of the component types is the lightning table. It allows for up to ten columns and up to two hundred rows of information to be displayed. It can show individual records or grouped data, and supports summed totals and conditional formatting. Figure 7-21 shows someone's forecast for the current month, grouped by forecast category and summing the amount and record count with a total row at the bottom. Lightning tables are great for leaderboards and for displaying records with issues that might need attention. They also support conditional highlighting on one numerical column to automatically call out data which has fallen below or risen above set thresholds.

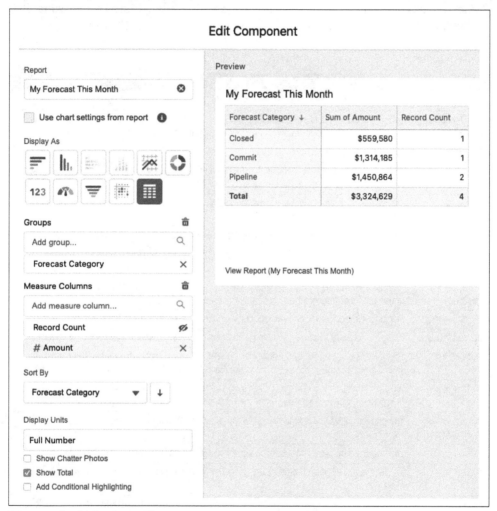

Figure 7-21. Lightning table

Unlike the rest of the component types, lightning tables support ungrouped source reports and also are based more on the source report's underlying report type than the source report itself. One example is even though a source report may only have 10 columns on it, because lightning tables are based on the underlying report type, you can select from any of the columns available on that report type—which could literally be over a thousand fields!

Dashboard Component Properties

Table 7-1 lists out the many properties you can set while adding components. It is through these properties that you can fine-tune the display of each component.

Table 7-1. Dashboard component properties

Property	Definition
Report	You can see and change the source report directly from within the component properties.
Use Chart Settings from Report	This setting allows you to pull a chart that you created on the source report directly through to appear on the dashboard. It is grayed out unless your source report has a chart on it.
Display As	Choose the chart type for the component.
Y-Axis	You can see and change the grouping that appears on the vertical part of the chart. If the source report has more than one grouping, you can add a second y-axis label.
X-Axis	Specify either the record count or a summed column from the report to appear on the horizontal part of the chart.
Display Units	This defaults to Short Number, which is rounded up or down. Other options include Full Number, which shows the exact number, or specific quantities such as thousands or millions.
Show Values	This will display the number on the chart.
Show Chatter Photos	If the data involves users, you can choose to show photos that users have uploaded into Chatter. This is grayed out for nonuser groupings.
X-Axis Range	Salesforce either gives you an automatic range or allows a custom range for the x-axis.
Decimal Places	While the default is Automatic, you can be intentional about displaying zero or up to five decimal places.
Sort By	Salesforce supports sorting by the groups on the report or record count, ascending or descending. A second grouping option appears when a source report has more than one group.
Custom Link	All of your dashboard components include a link to the source report. Use this property to add your own link, perhaps to an external data source. The link appears to the user when the component is expanded.
Max Groups (or Values) Displayed	This property allows you to limit the results appearing on the component based on the count of groups.
Title	The title of a component appears on the top left corner and can be up to 80 characters long.
Subtitle	The subtitle of a dashboard component appears below the title in smaller font and can be up to 40 characters long.
Footer	A component's footer appears at the bottom of the component in small font. While these can be up to 255 characters long, the limit is really the width that you make the component because the text is truncated.
Legend Position	The default legend position is right, though often to preserve real estate on the component, we switch it to appear on the bottom of the component.
Component Theme	While a dashboard theme can be either light or dark, so can an individual component. This can be used to emphasize the component.

As you are first learning to build dashboards, a habit that will serve you well is to carefully review each of the properties available within any component that you select. There are additional unique properties; for example, lightning tables also have groups and columns, and scatter plots also provide detail and color by options.

Widgets Replace Components in Unlimited Edition

The Unlimited Edition of Salesforce introduces two additional items that can be added to your dashboards—Text and Image. When creating or editing a dashboard in the Unlimited Edition, you'll notice that Salesforce renamed Components to Widgets, and see that dashboards now support up to 25 widgets, including a maximum of 20 charts and tables, 2 images, and 25 rich text widgets. Figure 7-22 shows the + Widget button, which replaces the + Component button. When clicked, it offers the 11 components reviewed earlier in this chapter by selecting Chart or Table, and adds the two new choices Text and Image.

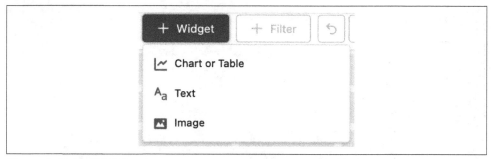

Figure 7-22. Add Widget button

Text

Selecting the Text widget opens a rich text editor that allows the entry of up to 500 characters. This can be a helpful way to provide an explanation for other dashboard items, announce the winner of a contest, or just share relevant information in text form. Figure 7-23 shows the editor that appears, which supports changes to font size, font color, text alignment, bold, italics, underline, and strikethrough. It also provides a tool to embed links into the text and another that strips text of all formatting. Once the Add button is clicked the Text widget will appear on the dashboard.

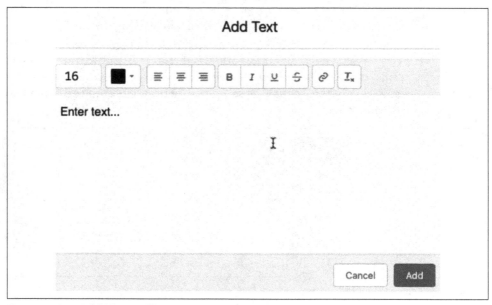

Figure 7-23. Add Text widget

Image

Images add a new range to content you can put on your dashboards. You might use them to post a photo of your monthly sales winner or to embed graphics that are relevant to the data being analyzed. Figure 7-24 shows that when adding an Image widget to a dashboard, you are immediately prompted to drag an image onto the screen or browse files for one on the Upload tab. Each time you upload an image to a dashboard it is added to the Gallery tab, allowing you the option of selecting a list of past images to choose from.

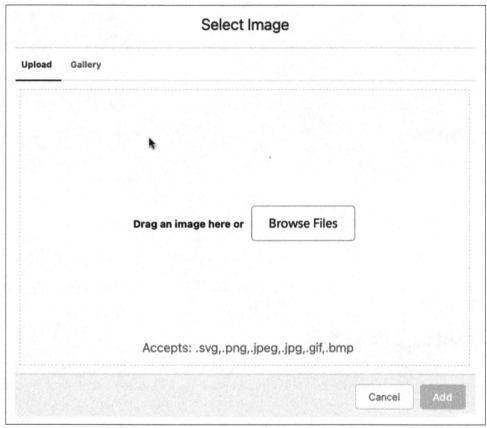

Figure 7-24. Add Image widget first screen

Once added, additional image settings appear on the Select Image screen, as shown in Figure 7-25. You select the image's scale from a pull-down list, which includes Original, Stretch, Tile, Fit Width, or Fit Height. There are controls to set the horizontal and vertical alignment, and the option to add a Tooltip and define Alternate Text. Once done you can click the Add button to add the image to your dashboard.

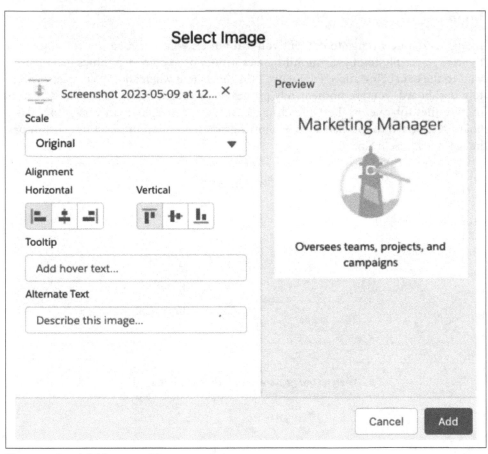

Figure 7-25. Add Image widget second screen

Dashboard Properties

While working on your dashboard, it is worthwhile to review and update the dashboard properties. These control not only colors, name, and location, but also who the dashboard is viewed as. To see the properties while editing a dashboard, click on the gear icon near the top right corner. Figure 7-26 shows the full set of dashboard properties, each of which you will step through. At the top, you can see and change the dashboard title, description, and folder.

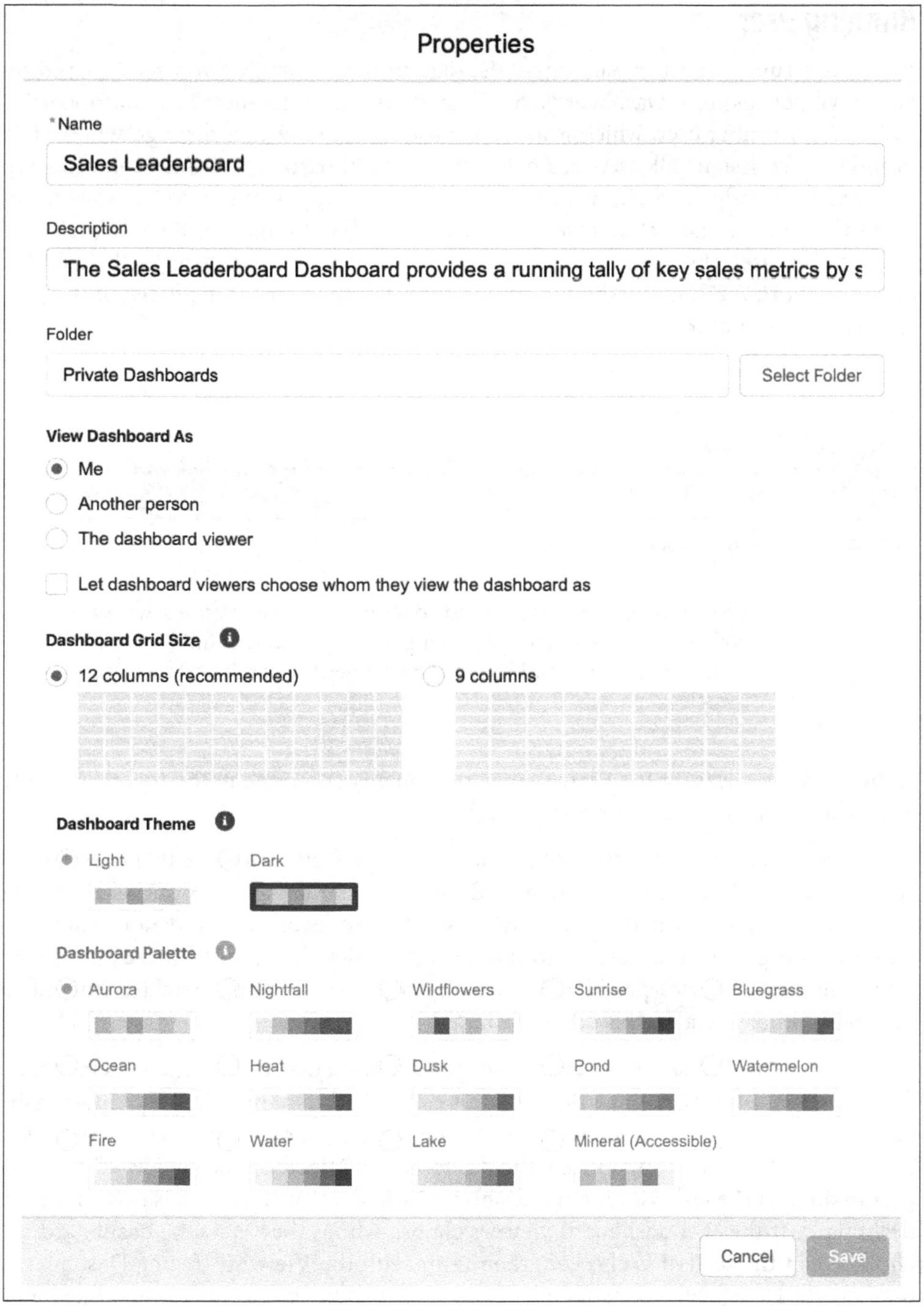

Properties

* Name

Sales Leaderboard

Description

The Sales Leaderboard Dashboard provides a running tally of key sales metrics by s

Folder

Private Dashboards   Select Folder

View Dashboard As

● Me

○ Another person

○ The dashboard viewer

☐ Let dashboard viewers choose whom they view the dashboard as

Dashboard Grid Size ⓘ

● 12 columns (recommended)   ○ 9 columns

Dashboard Theme ⓘ

● Light   ○ Dark

Dashboard Palette ⓘ

● Aurora   ○ Nightfall   ○ Wildflowers   ○ Sunrise   ○ Bluegrass

○ Ocean   ○ Heat   ○ Dusk   ○ Pond   ○ Watermelon

○ Fire   ○ Water   ○ Lake   ○ Mineral (Accessible)

Cancel   Save

Figure 7-26. Dashboard properties

Running User

When you run a report in Salesforce, the data in the report that you see is based on your own permissions. Dashboards, however, do things differently. Each dashboard is assigned a running user, which is an active user in your system through whose data visibility permissions all users see data on this dashboard. For example, a sales rep may normally only see their own leads, accounts, and opportunities in Salesforce. But when they look at their chief revenue officer's (CRO) dashboard, if the CRO is set as the running user, the sales rep sees the data on the dashboard through their CRO's eyes. In Figure 7-27 next to the words "Viewing as," you can see the name of the person who is the running user of this dashboard.

Figure 7-27. Running user

 The running user's override of data visibility permissions works both ways! If a dashboard's running user is a sales rep, and the head of sales looks at the dashboard, they will see the dashboard through the sales rep's eyes.

If the sales rep clicks on the View Report link on any component, the report will only show them data through their own permissions.

The View Dashboard As section of the dashboard properties defines that dashboard's running user. When you create a new dashboard, the default running user is you, which may be good or bad, depending on what your visibility is to data in your system and the goal of the dashboard. Often, for a sales dashboard, the running user might be set as the vice president of sales, to allow everyone in their department to see the summary data on this dashboard.

While you will often set the running user to be a particular user in the system, Salesforce gives additional options to make this dashboard dynamic. In a dynamic dashboard, the running user is set based on the View Dashboard As properties. As shown in Figure 7-28, by selecting to view the dashboard as "the dashboard viewer," the data permissions of the user viewing the dashboard will control what data is shown on the dashboard. If the "Let dashboard viewers choose whom they view the dashboard as" checkbox in the section is checked, then users with the View My Team's Dashboards or View All Data profile system permissions can change the running user while looking at the dashboard.

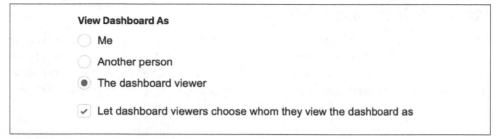

Figure 7-28. Dynamic dashboard settings

Salesforce's Enterprise Edition allows for up to five dynamic dashboards, with the ability to purchase up to five more. The Unlimited Edition allows for up to 10 dynamic dashboards. Use them wisely, such as in instances where instead of creating dashboards for each member on a team, you leverage one dynamic dashboard to support a whole team of individuals. In that scenario, the underlying reports are set up with Show Me filters such as "My opportunities" or "My cases" so that each time a new user looks at the dashboard, the underlying report filters run with them being the running user.

Dashboard Grid Size (12 vs 9)

When Salesforce first made the move from Classic to Lightning, they introduced a nine-column grid, allowing for snap-to-grid sizing of components. In the years since, they changed the default to 12 columns, granting you more control over placement and sizing of components, with the same snap-to-grid sizing. Figure 7-29 shows the toggle on the dashboard properties to set the grid size.

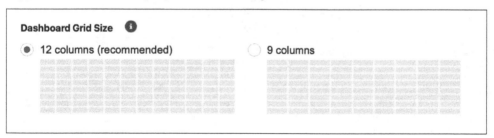

Figure 7-29. Dashboard Grid Size

Best practice is to stick with a 12-column grid size because it affords more precision in sizing and placing components on your dashboard.

Dashboard Theme and Palette

The final dashboard properties are the dashboard theme and palette, as seen in Figure 7-30. Each dashboard's theme can be set to light or dark, which in turn sets the initial theme coloring for each component. Components don't have to have the same theme as the dashboard, allowing you to emphasize one or more components, for example, by setting the dashboard to be dark and those components to be light.

Salesforce provides 14 color palettes to choose from, including an accessible one called Mineral, which can greatly liven up your dashboard. My own favorite combination is a dark-themed dashboard with a Watermelon palette! If you are unable to change the theme or palette on a dashboard, you may need to ask your system administrator to grant you the Change Dashboard Colors permission on your profile or via permission set.

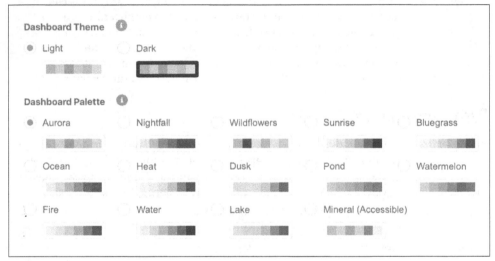

Figure 7-30. Dashboard theme and palette

Some types of components adopt the entire dashboard palette you choose, while others such as metrics and gauges, which both have their own color settings, ignore the palette entirely.

Dashboard Optimization

Once your dashboard has taken shape and you've added all of the components you need, or if you've inherited someone else's dashboard, it's time to optimize the dashboard. There are a handful of additional features and practices to consider. They include component sizing and placement, two-level sorting, and dashboard filters.

 A great way to try out making improvements to an existing dashboard is to clone that dashboard by saving it with a different name and editing the clone instead of the original. You can work on the clone in a private folder, and then swap it out for the original once you are satisfied with your updates.

Component Sizing and Placement

Each component that you add to a dashboard has a default size, not optimized for your dashboard. While some level of uniformity across a dashboard can be helpful for readability, it is worth thinking through the sizing and placement of each component that you add to a dashboard. Adjusting the size is as easy as grabbing a corner of a component and dragging it to make it larger or smaller. Once you have sized the component, you can drag and drop that component into another position on the grid.

As you add each component, determine its smallest acceptable size, watching for subtitles and footers to truncate or disappear, charts to adjust, and gray scroll bars to appear. Once done adding elements to a dashboard, you might then click anywhere on a component to drag them to reorganize them.

 If you are having trouble moving components around, you can always adjust the Display Settings on your computer's desktop to shrink things down. This can be helpful when you are having trouble dragging and dropping components on the grid that are *far away* from each other on the dashboard.

Two-Level Sorting

Bar charts, line charts, scatter charts, and lightning tables each support two-level sorting. This is where you can sort a group ascending or descending, then sort the data within a second group ascending or descending. You can use this feature to help make your charts appear in an expected order or make more logical sense. In Figure 7-31, you can see a stacked horizontal bar chart showing leads by owner and status. The arrows highlight that this component is sorted by Record Count descending, then Lead Status ascending. You can also use this to emphasize leaders or those falling behind.

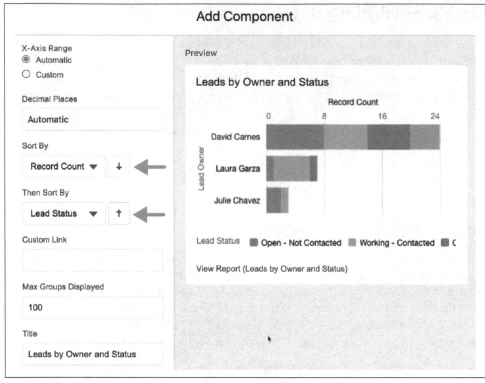

Figure 7-31. Two-level sorting

Additional Measures

Horizontal bar charts, vertical bar charts, and line graphs support adding additional measures to each component. You can have up to four total measures, though they must be of the same data type, and must appear summed on the source report. These can appear as bars or lines, and support having a second axis added to the component. The arrows in Figure 7-32 show a second measure added to a My Won Opps This Year component, adding the average amount of each sale plotted as a line.

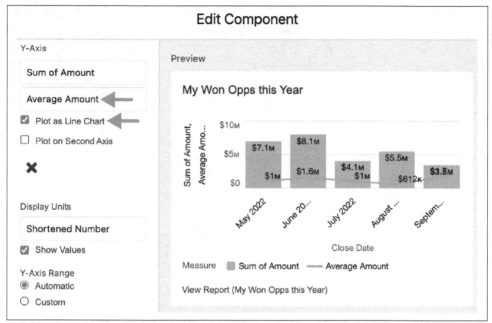

Figure 7-32. Additional measures

 The Undo and Redo buttons in the dashboard editor work while in the same editing session. You can go backward and forward through at least 25 recent edits!

Dashboard Filters

One of the most powerful features you can add to a completed dashboard is a filter. Can you imagine looking at a sales dashboard and running the dashboard filtered by a single industry? Or by using two filters, zeroing in on the agriculture industry within China? Filters allow your users to further refine the data displayed on a dashboard by adjusting one or more picklists at the top of the dashboard. When you use a filter, the next time you run the dashboard the same filter will be remembered and applied again until you clear the filter.

A dashboard can support up to three filters (up to five in Unlimited Edition), each of which allows you to add a list of up to 50 values to further refine data shown in that dashboard. While editing a dashboard, you can click on the + Filter button to start adding a new filter. The next step is to specify a field that drives the filter. You will want to choose one that applies to the data displayed on the dashboard. Figure 7-33 shows the final step in adding a filter on the Account Industry field, with four filter values added to allow a user to choose from the specific industries.

Add Filter

* Field

| Industry | × |

Display Name

| Industry |

Filter Values (4)

1	Agriculture	×
2	Apparel	×
3	Banking	×
4	Biotechnology	×

Add Filter Value

Cancel   Add

Figure 7-33. Add Filter

 Dashboard filters can be a big time saver. They spare whoever creates a dashboard the trouble of having to add individual filters for every report that has a component in the dashboard.

There are a few ways to get more value out of using filters. One way is to combine values separated by commas to allow a series of potential values to be filtered within one value. An example on a country filter would be adding a filter value of "Finance, Banking, Insurance" with the display text of "FBI."

Another option to do more with dashboard filters appears when filtering a dashboard on date fields: you can use dynamic date ranges. For example, when filtering on open opportunity data, you might add a filter on the Close Date field showing opportunities with a close date This Week, This Month, or This Quarter. The arrows in

Figure 7-34 show our ability to select the date type Relative and to use dynamic values such as THIS QUARTER in our dashboard filters.

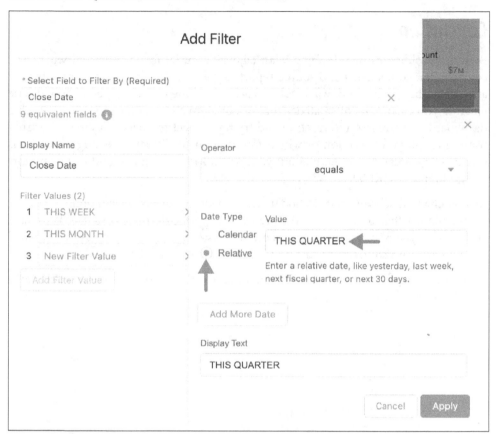

Figure 7-34. Relative Date filter

 There is a document entitled "Relative Date Filter Reference" in Salesforce Help (*https://oreil.ly/wkxEW*) that lists out all of the relative date values you can use in filters. These are useful across Salesforce, be it in dashboard filters, report filters, list views, and so on.

One consideration with dashboard filters is that they are really intended for dashboards with similar data coming in from the dashboard's source reports. Filtering a dashboard on the Opportunity Close Date field that has components showing Lead, Case, Campaign, and Opportunity data just won't work correctly. If the field you filter on is not a field that is part of a component's source report data, the component ignores the filter. Salesforce has a mechanism by which you can reconnect the filter to another field of the same data type, but it doesn't always make sense. Your best bet is to try to use filters when the fields you filter by are common to all of the components on your dashboard.

Conclusion

Building dashboards in Salesforce is an enjoyable outlet for creativity at work. You control what components and source reports appear on the dashboard, how big they are, what they show, and what color palette and theme are applied. You decide whether you create a set of small dashboards, or glom all the components into one big dashboard. You are also interpreting and trying to meet the needs of the dashboard's users through your selection of which information to display. Creating dashboards can also be a great way to learn about your organization, its goals, and its key performance indicators (KPIs).

In this chapter, we saw that dashboards are made up of visual components fed by source reports that are created and stored within your Salesforce instance. We talked about each type of component, their common uses, and things to be aware of when using them. We also covered some best practices for building dashboards.

In the next chapter, you will learn how to organize and share your reports and dashboards using folders.

CHAPTER 8

Report and Dashboard Folders

One of the most important responsibilities for system administrators and report and dashboard super users in Salesforce is organizing reports and dashboards into folders for users to find and access easily. It is not uncommon for companies to have thousands, or even tens of thousands, of reports and hundreds of dashboards! These can be organized into folders that are shared with all or a subset of users.

Folders can be nested up to four levels deep, with each folder containing an unlimited number of items. Without some planning, users can have a hard time sifting through folders, reports, and dashboards to find what they are looking for.

In this chapter, you'll learn how to control access by creating folders, putting reports or dashboards into the folders, and then granting permissions to those folders through sharing. Your goal should be that each user sees exactly what reports and dashboards they need to do their job—no more, no less.

Organizing Reports and Dashboards

Reports are organized into folders on the Reports tab, and dashboards are organized into folders on the Dashboards tab. While the folder mechanisms look identical across the Reports and Dashboards tabs, they are completely separate from one another.

As you can see in Figure 8-1, when you first click on one of the tabs, on the lefthand side there are drill-down categories to use in filtering, such as All Folders. Click on one of these under Folders to see the corresponding list of folders appear to the right. Once selected, the category name is visible at the top as well as the number of top-level folders in that category. In this example, you can see that All Folders has nine folders within it on the Dashboards tab. The Reports tab looks almost identical, with one additional category choice for Public Reports.

Figure 8-1. Folder categories

Once you have selected a category on the left, such as Created by Me, you will see the corresponding list of top-level folders in that category in the main part of the screen. Figure 8-2 shows that there are ten top-level folders that I have created. Note that the search context has also changed to "Search folders created by me."

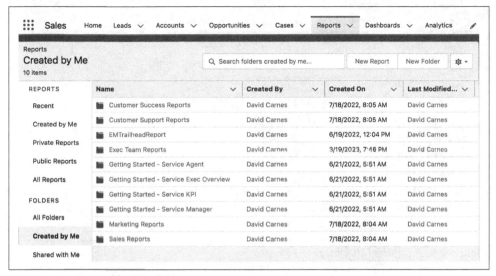

Figure 8-2. Created by Me folders

While clicking on one of the three folder-related categories on the left will only reveal top-level folders, the corresponding search feature for each will dig deeper into nested folders to return results, including nested folders.

Another place to see and manage report and dashboard folders is the Analytics tab, which allows users to interact with, search for, and manage reports, dashboards, folders, and favorites all in one place. Figure 8-3 shows the Analytics tab with the ability to create, manage, and drill into report and dashboard folders. This newer option in Salesforce reporting allows users to find and interact with reports, dashboards, and their folders from the same tab. You'll learn more about the Analytics tab in the next chapter.

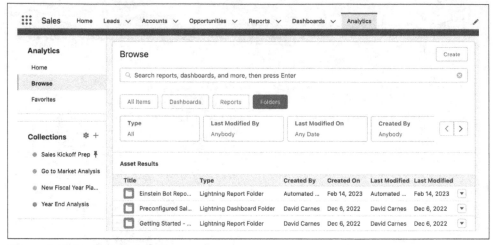

Figure 8-3. Analytics tab folders

Navigating and Nested Folders

For years in Salesforce, we were limited to a single level of folders, which led to a disorganized feel to reports and dashboards. With the Lightning user interface, Salesforce introduced nested folders, which allow you to store folders and their items within other folders, up to four levels deep! When used, nested folders greatly reduce the number of folders appearing at the top level, making the tab feel more organized.

 Establishing a folder-naming scheme can be helpful to you and other users in your system. If your organization is divided into business units or has a focus on geographic regions, you might prepend those in your folder names. For example, within a Global Sales Reports folder might be a folder called European Sales Reports.

As is true in many parts of Salesforce, clicking on a folder name opens that folder. Within each folder you might see reports (or dashboards, on the Dashboards tab) and the next level of any nested folders. Figure 8-4 shows an example of a Global Sales Reports folder and its contents of reports and subfolders. Note the navigation back to All Folders near the top left and the bolded header to indicate which folder you are looking at. Subfolders have a folder icon to the left of their name to differentiate them from reports within the same folder.

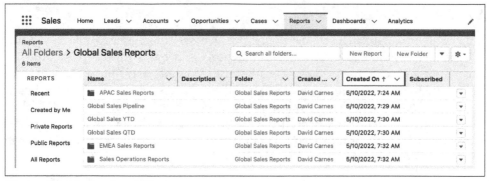

Figure 8-4. Navigating folders

At this time, there is no way to see from the top level how many items or folders are nested within a folder. You can either click on folder names to drill down to see what is in any nested folders or use search if you have a particular report or dashboard you are looking for.

When looking within nested folders, as you can see in Figure 8-5, the name of the current folder appears in bold, in this case it is "Fourth Level Folder." It displays a link to the immediate parent folder, in blue to the left, and an ellipsis to select any of the parent folders above.

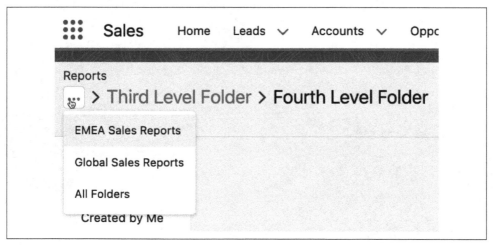

Figure 8-5. Accessing parent folders

System-Generated Folders

On the Reports tab, all users have access to two system-generated folders: Private Reports and Public Reports. The Private Reports folder is great for storing one-off reports for your own use or those you are working on that may not be ready for others to see. To make something available for all other users to see, save it in the Public Reports folders. Figure 8-6 shows the Save Report screen, with the default folder selected being your Private Reports folder. To the right you can see a Select Folder button, which allows you to specify another existing folder or create a new folder in which to store your report.

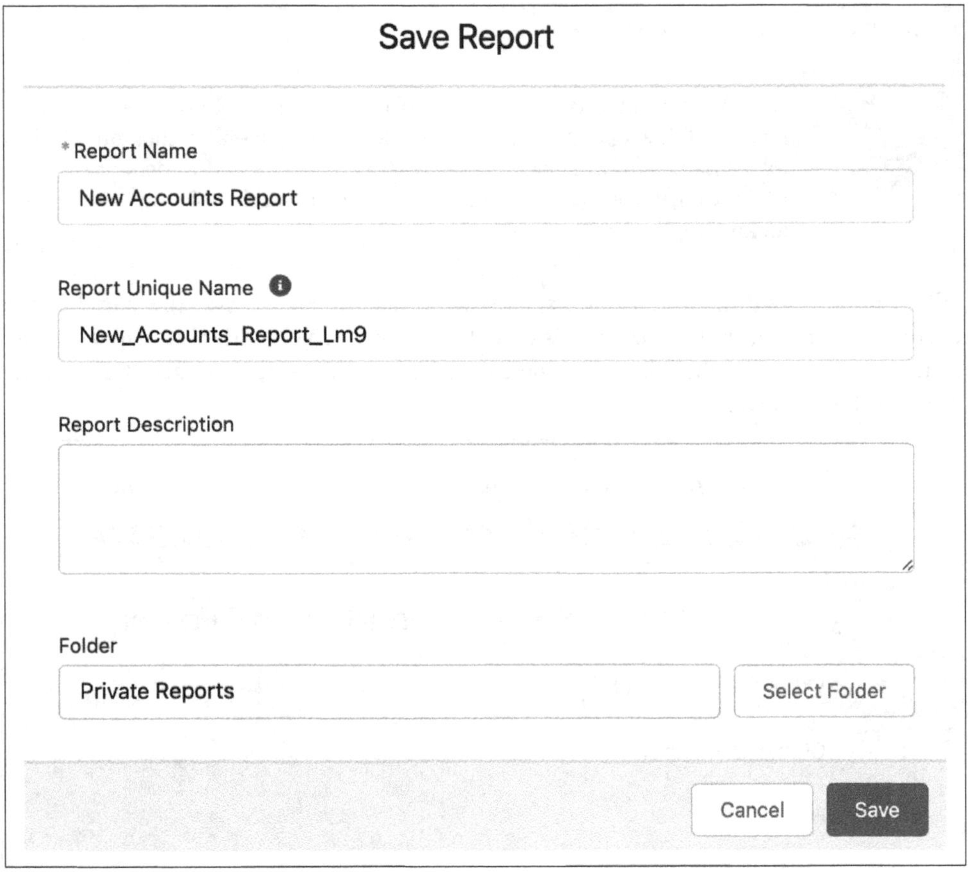

Figure 8-6. Selecting a folder while saving a report

The Dashboards tab differs slightly in that each user has a Private Dashboards folder but there is no common Public folder like there is for reports. All publicly visible dashboards have to be stored in folders that you create and manage. When you create a dashboard, the default storage location is your Private Dashboards folder, and if you want others to see it, you will need to store it in a folder that is visible to those users.

Creating Folders

When creating a new folder, you will want to start from within the place you want the folder stored. For example, to create a top-level folder, you might start from the All Folders list, and to create a third-level nested folder, you would start from inside the corresponding second-level folder. If you have sufficient permissions, you will see the New Folder button appear in the top right corner of the Reports or Dashboards tabs. Figure 8-7 shows this button on the Reports tab.

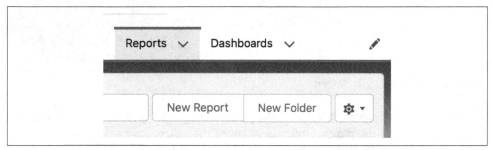

Figure 8-7. New Folder button

If you click on the New Folder button, you will be asked to name your new folder in the Folder Label field, as in Figure 8-8. Rather than typing in a Folder Unique Name, simply click into that field, and Salesforce will autogenerate a unique name based on the label you entered. While you can use the same folder label multiple times in your Salesforce instance, the Folder Unique Name must be just that, unique!

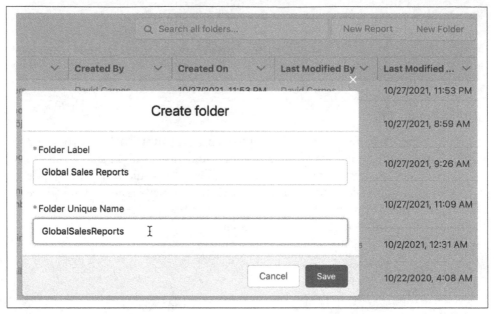

Figure 8-8. Create Folder screen

Note that if you're creating a new folder within an existing one, you will only be allowed to do so if the parent folder is no more than three levels deep. If you're in a folder that is four levels deep, the New Folder button will be grayed out, as seen in Figure 8-9.

Figure 8-9. Grayed-out New Folder button

Folder Access and Permissions

Unlike other aspects of Salesforce, managers do not inherit the folder visibility of their subordinates, and instead need to be granted explicit access to individual top-level folders. Beyond this, if there are nested subfolders, all folder permissions are controlled at the top-level folder.

Folder Permissions

There are three levels of folder permissions in Salesforce. When you create a new folder, no one else can see it and you are set as the manager. Other users must be explicitly granted access, as detailed in Table 8-1, by someone with permission to manage the folder.

Table 8-1. Folder permissions

Permission	Definition
View	Allows you to view the reports or dashboards in a folder.
Edit	Allows you to view and save the reports or dashboards in a folder.
Manage	Allows you to view, share, save, rename, and delete the reports or dashboards in a folder.

 As creator of a folder, you are responsible for sharing it with the appropriate users at the appropriate time. You might, for example, keep the contents of a folder hidden while you are building them, then share it with someone who will validate your work, and then share it more broadly with the target users.

Folders can be shared with other users in two ways. While looking at a list of top-level folders, you can select the folder you want to share, click the action menu to the right, and select Share, as shown in Figure 8-10. The other method is to open the folder you want to share, then click the Action button in the top right. If you are looking at sub-folders, instead of Share you will see View Shares, which lets you view but not control the sharing on that folder.

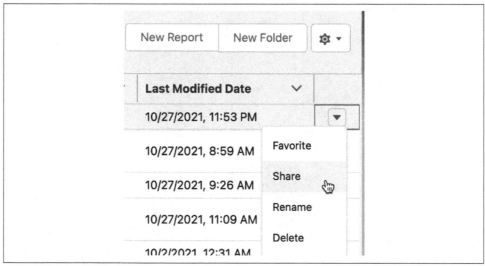

Figure 8-10. Sharing a folder

Figure 8-11 shows the Share Folder screen with its sharing mechanism on top and the current shares listed at the bottom. Folders can be shared with users, roles, roles and subordinates, and public groups. You can mix and match the View, Edit, and Manage permissions, with the highest level permission granted winning out. Here we can see that David has been granted Manage permission, while Julie has Edit rights, and the Sales EMEA Role has View access to the folder's contents. If this was a nested folder, and we clicked on View Shares, we would only see the Who Can Access section.

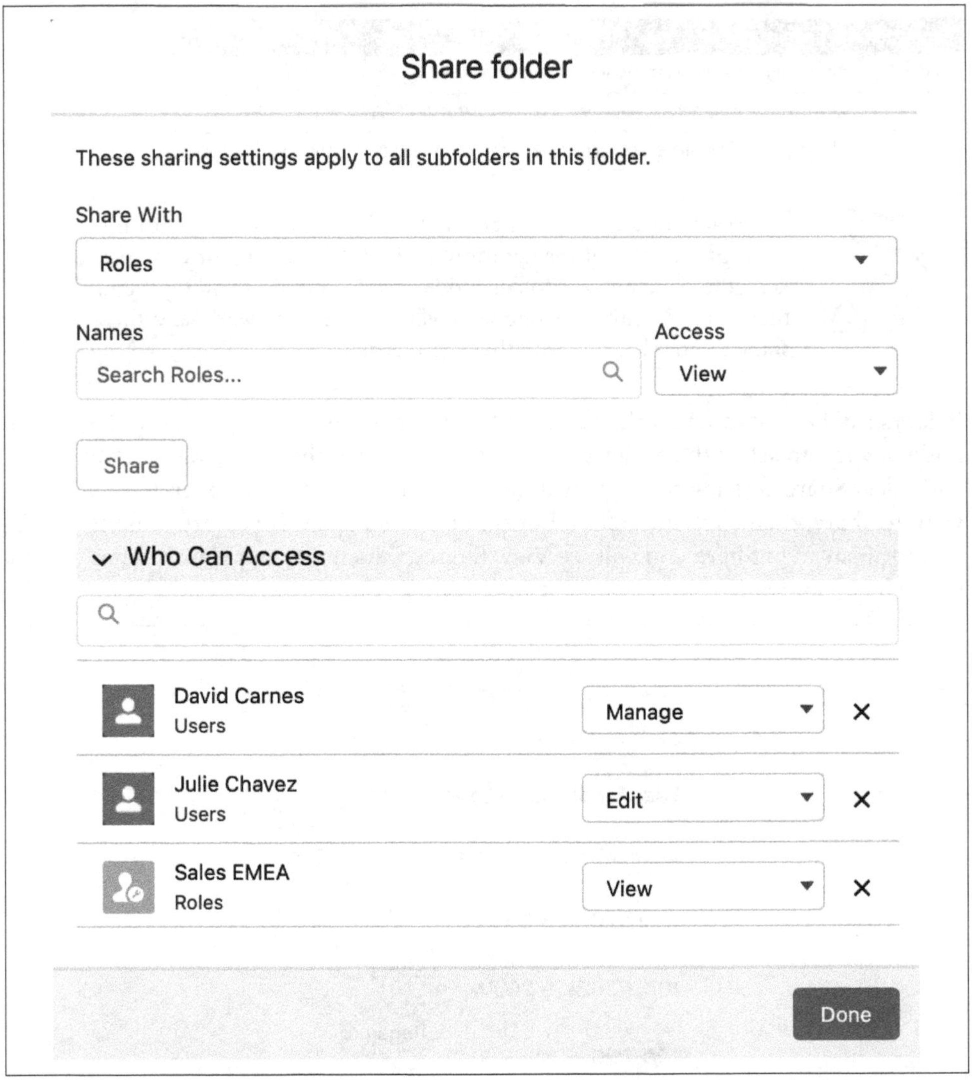

Figure 8-11. Share Folder screen

It is best to be conservative when sharing folders. Unless you know for sure that someone needs to be able to edit the reports or dashboards within that folder, your best bet is to give View permissions. Those with Edit or Manage permissions can inadvertently change and overwrite the contents of the folder.

Managing Folders

System administrators can access all public folders, as can users with the Manage profile permission granted to them for the corresponding Reports or Dashboards tab. There is one Manage permission for each of these tabs, as well as a third permission that allows editing of reports you created, regardless of which folder they are stored in. These three permissions are granted by your system administrator directly on your profile or by using permission sets. Table 8-2 shows the options when editing a profile to allow users to edit and store reports in public folders.

Table 8-2. Profile permissions

Profile Permission	Description
Manage Reports in Public Folders	Create, edit, delete reports, and manage their sharing in all public folders.
Edit My Reports	Edit, move, save, and delete user's own reports in shared folders.
Manage Dashboards in Public Folders	Create, edit, delete dashboards, and manage their sharing in all public folders.

Moving Reports and Dashboards

Moving reports and dashboards from one folder to another is done in one of two ways. On each tab, as shown in Figure 8-12, you click the action menu to the right of each report or dashboard when you're viewing them in a list, then select the Move action. Alternatively, when you have run an existing report or dashboard, you can edit it and within Properties change the folder it is assigned to.

Moving a lot of reports or dashboards can be a time-consuming exercise. In Salesforce Classic we can drag and drop reports or dashboards, one by one, to more easily move them between folders. If you need to move many items, it may be helpful to switch to Classic to do so.

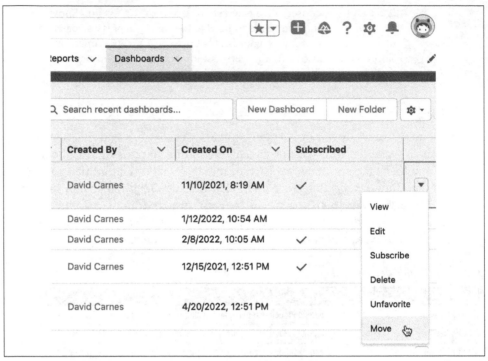

Figure 8-12. Moving reports and dashboards

Conclusion

It is not uncommon for Salesforce systems to have thousands of reports and dashboards. Given these numbers, it is important that you use folders to keep them organized and easy for users to find. Through sharing, folders control the users who can see reports and dashboards. Users can be granted no access, and thus not see the folder at all, or View, Edit, or Manage permissions to allow them increasing degrees of control over the folder.

The Reports and Dashboards tabs each have their own separate list of folders, which can be nested four levels deep. To manage folders, you might need to ask your system administrator for the three additional profile permissions.

Now that you have learned all about reports, dashboards, and their folders, it is time to learn about a newer tab in Salesforce where you can take advantage of all of them. In the next chapter, you'll learn about the powerful Analytics tab.

CHAPTER 9

Analytics Tab

Salesforce recently unveiled a new feature, a tab that it calls the Unified Experience for Analytics Home, or the Analytics tab for short. When enabled, it allows users to do everything that they can currently on the Reports and Dashboards tabs, while on a single tab. This includes accessing, creating, and editing your reports, dashboards, report folders, dashboard folder, and related favorites. It also introduces a more intuitive interface with a more powerful search capability and a new way of organizing your reports and dashboards into something called Collections. If your organization has CRM Analytics licenses, then those assets will appear on the tab as well. It truly intends to be a unified home for analytics in Salesforce.

Given that the Analytics tab can do what the Reports and Dashboards tabs each do individually, your system administrator might even consider phasing out the Reports and Dashboards tabs entirely. This may warrant some retraining for users in your system, but would require one less tab across the top of your system's interface.

Analytics Tab Overview

Your first look at the Analytics tab may make you wonder why it looks so different than any other tab in the system. Salesforce's user interface designers spent time trying to optimize access to your reports and dashboards, their respective folders, and your related favorites. The key to the tab's power is your ability to find the things you are looking for.

For the purpose of this book, you are seeing the Analytics tab without the add-on CRM Analytics functionality enabled. If your Salesforce instance has CRM Analytics enabled, you will see additional features across the Analytics tab. These include additional subtabs on the left, a more powerful search using Salesforce's Ask Data capabilities, and more types of reporting assets that you can view and create.

When you first click into the Analytics tab, as seen in Figure 9-1, you are brought to the Analytics Home page by default. Near the top left corner, you can see the Analytics section with links to Home, Browse, and Favorites. Below that are listed three Collections, which are groupings of reports and dashboards that each user can create and share. In the top center there is a sophisticated search feature. Just below that in the center of the screen are short lists of Recently Updated items, ones Shared with Me, and others Created by Me. Below these are View All buttons to drill into fuller versions of each list. At the bottom under My Analytics are subtabs for lists of Recent items and also Favorited items.

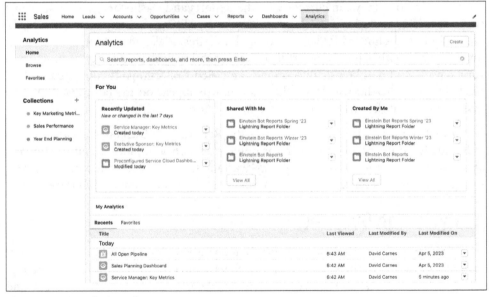

Figure 9-1. Analytics tab

Search

The Analytics tab provides a search mechanism at the top of the Home, Browse, and Favorites categories in the lefthand menu. Much like you saw in the Reports and Dashboards tab searches, the Analytics tab search will look for matches on individual words, or the start of words, in report, dashboard, and folder names. Unlike the

Reports and Dashboards tab searches, the lefthand menu category doesn't define the scope of the search. Figure 9-2 shows the start of a search on the word "sales," which as you type yields three quick results on recent items.

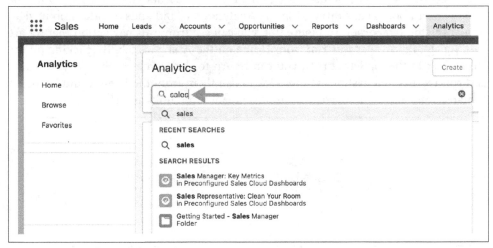

Figure 9-2. Analytics tab search

When you click the Enter key on your keyboard on this search, you are brought to a page called Keyword Results. Figure 9-3 shows the results of the search on "sales," which introduces filters just below to further refine your search, and the list of results below that. Note the breadcrumbs at the top left allowing you to return to the Search page, the number of results returned "6 Items" on the left side, and the icons indicating what asset type each result is next to each result.

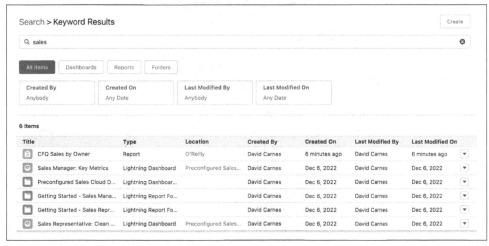

Figure 9-3. Keyword search results

Navigation

One difference between the standard Report and Dashboard tabs and the Analytics tab is revealed when you actually click on a report or dashboard name to run it. The report or dashboard runs directly on the Analytics tab, and adds breadcrumb navigation at the top left corner. In Figure 9-4, you can see from this navigation that we are looking at a report that was run from Home on the Analytics tab. By clicking on the Home link in the top left corner, you can return to the search results. As you search and run reports and dashboards, or click to run them from the Browse and Favorites subtabs, you will see these words appear as breadcrumb links as well.

Figure 9-4. Breadcrumb navigation

Because reports and dashboards are run within the context of the Analytics tab, their URLs are effectively lost. To remedy this, Salesforce added Share buttons to both reports and dashboards. Figure 9-5 shows you this button on a report that has been run on the Analytics tab.

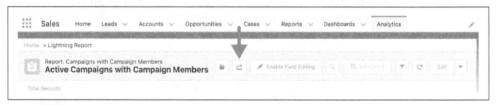

Figure 9-5. Share button

Clicking this button reveals an overlay that allows you to copy and paste the URL. Figure 9-6 shows the report being grayed out and the Get URL window giving you the URL, which you can then copy and paste to share with another user in your system through email or Slack.

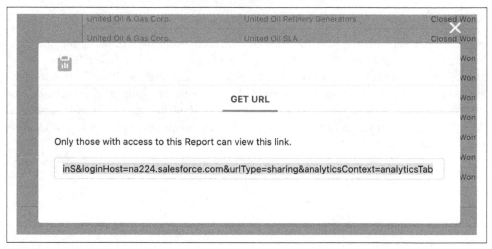

Figure 9-6. *Get URL overlay*

Create Button

Above and to the right of the search on each category there will be a Create button, as shown in Figure 9-7. Based on your profile permissions, you can use it to create new reports, dashboards, and folders. If your Salesforce instance has CRM Analytics licenses, you will see these listed under the word "Lightning" to differentiate what CRM Analytics assets you can create. Creating reports and dashboards using this method differs in that you remain on the Analytics tab to do your work, with the subtle breadcrumb links back to the Analytics Home in the top left corner.

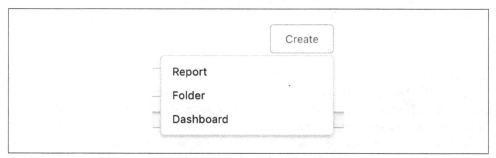

Figure 9-7. *Analytics tab Create button*

As on the Reports and Dashboards tabs, to create a nested folder you need to be looking at the contents of the folder where you want to add the folder, and then click the Create button.

Action Menus

Next to each asset on the Analytics tab there is an action menu offering the ability to Share, Add to Collection, Edit, Delete, and Favorite or Remove Favorite. Figure 9-8 shows this menu for a dashboard in the Recently Updated widget. Your ability to share, edit, and delete a particular item will depend on your profile permissions assigned and the sharing that was set on the folder that the report or dashboard is in. All users can favorite or unfavorite items that they can see, such as reports, dashboards, and folders.

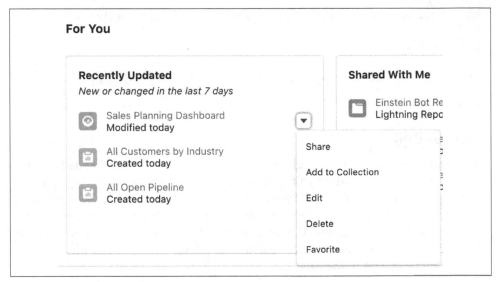

Figure 9-8. Analytics tab action menus

Browse

You can access the Browse page using the link under Analytics in the top left side of the Analytics tab. The page reveals sophisticated drill-down filters that can optionally be combined with a search to find specific reports, dashboards, and folders. The search box at the top center of Figure 9-9 can be used or ignored while browsing. By default you are browsing all items, but using the buttons just below the search box, you can limit your results to just dashboards, reports, or folders. Below that are four additional filters that let you further specify filters for Created By, Created On, Last Modified By, and Last Modified On. When clicking on one, such as Created By, you can change the default open filter of Anybody to a specific user in your system. When Folders is clicked, a fifth option, to limit the search by Type to dashboard folders or reports folders, is also made available.

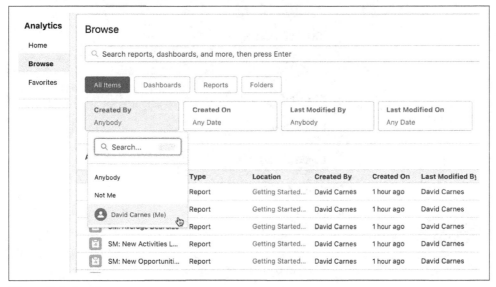

Figure 9-9. Browse

 A clever filter choice available in the Created By and Last Modified By search filters is Not Me. If you are not sure who created a report, dashboard, or folder that you are looking for, but know it wasn't you, this is a nice way to trim down the results.

The Created On and Last Modified On filters allow you to select from preset date ranges or select a Custom Range to enter fixed start and end dates. Figure 9-10 shows the preset ranges for last 7, 30, 90, or 180 days and the Custom Range option.

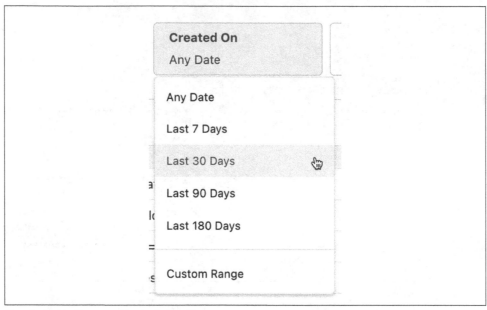

Figure 9-10. Browse Created On filter

It is your ability to combine a search with the useful filters below it that makes the Browse feature on the Analytics tab so powerful. This is especially helpful in larger Salesforce instances where many thousands of reports, dashboards, and their folders are stored.

Favorites

The last option in the Analytics section of the Analytics tab is Favorites, which can be accessed by the link in the left menu. As you know from Chapter 3, each user can have up to two hundred personal favorites in the system, and among them, you can include reports, dashboards, and their folders. The Favorites area on the Analytics tab allows you to search and filter on what you have already favorited. Figure 9-11 shows the Favorites tab with no filters applied. You can see the search, the specific asset buttons, and the list of asset results here.

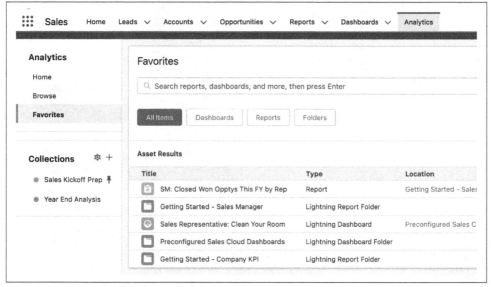

Figure 9-11. Analytics tab Favorites

One subtle difference in wording on the Analytics tab involves the word "Lightning." There are references to "Lightning Dashboard," "Lightning Report Folder," and "Lightning Dashboard Folder" to indicate the type of asset in lists. This is done to clearly differentiate them from CRM Analytics functionality, which unfortunately has similar names.

Collections

A useful tool available to all users of the Analytics tab is the ability to create and share collections of reporting assets. These allow you to curate your own groups of reports, dashboards, and CRM Analytics assets (if you have a license for the CRM Analytics add-on) for your own private use or to share with others. Think of using these to pull together reports and dashboards relevant to an upcoming conference or board meeting, or to keep track of reporting assets you used for your annual planning efforts.

Collections differ from folders, which store and control access to reports and dashboards, in that they are something any user can create to include any reporting asset that is visible to them. Figure 9-12 shows your list of visible collections on the Analytics tab. You can see that the top one, Sales Kickoff Prep, has a pin icon next to it, which ensures it is visible and at the top of the list. The two small icons to the right of the word "Collections" are the gear, which allows you to manage your list of collections, and the plus sign, which lets you create a new collection.

Figure 9-12. Analytics tab Collections

Clicking the gear icon brings you to the Manage Collections overlay screen, as seen in Figure 9-13. Listed on the screen are all of your existing collections. For each you can specify whether to show or hide the collection, and to pin or unpin them. Hiding a collection simply removes it from the lefthand navigation on the Analytics tab. Pinned collections appear at the top of your list of collections and are also shown prominently on the Analytics tab's Home page.

Manage Collections

Title	Show	Pin	
● Sales Kickoff Prep 📌	☑	☑	**Manage your collections like a pro!**
● New Fiscal Year Planning	☐	☐	**Hide Collections** so they no longer appear in our left navigation.
● Year End Analysis	☑	☐	**Pin Collections** so they appear at the top of the list and are featured on our Home for easy access.
			Learn more about collections.

Cancel   Save

Figure 9-13. Manage Collections

Folders control visibility to reports and dashboards. Collections lay on top of that security access, respecting folder sharing controls. This means that if a report or dashboard that you can't see is in a Collection shared with you, you still won't be able to see that item.

From back on the lefthand list of collections, if you click on the plus sign, you are brought to the New Collection screen, as shown in Figure 9-14. Here you can give it a name of up to 40 characters, assign the collection 1 of 13 colors, and give it a description of up to 120 characters.

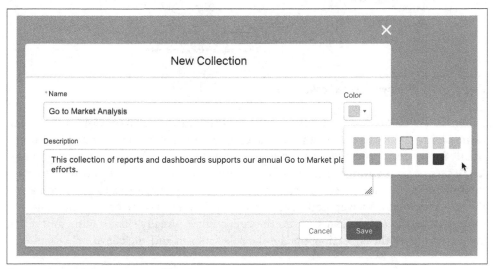

Figure 9-14. Create a new collection

 When creating collections for multiple departments in your organization, consider choosing a color to use for each separate department so that you can easily identify them visually.

Once saved, you are brought in to your collection, as seen in Figure 9-15. Here you can share the collection with other Salesforce users, using the Share button on the right, and add assets to your collection, using the Add button. Tucked under the action menu to the right of the Add button are the options to edit and delete the collection.

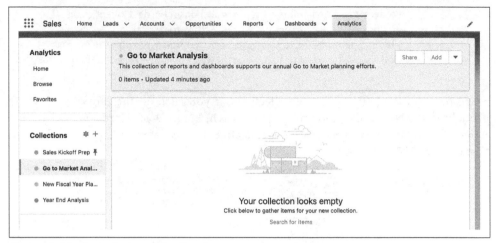

Figure 9-15. A newly created collection

When you click on the Share button, you are brought to the Share Collection screen as in Figure 9-16. Here you can grant access to your collection to individual users, public groups, and roles within your system's role hierarchy. You can also assign blanket access to your entire organization using this mechanism. As we saw with managing folders in Chapter 8, you can assign three levels of permissions to those you share the collection with: Viewer, Editor, and Manager. These roles are defined in Table 9-1. On the same screen you can see who the collection is already shared with, and if you are a manager of the collection, update the role for each and click Save.

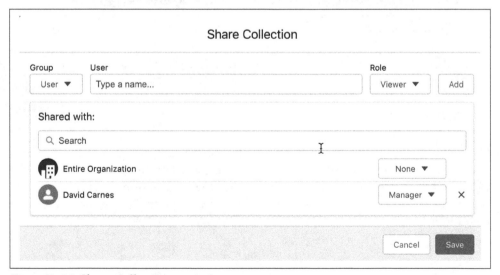

Figure 9-16. Share Collection screen

Table 9-1. Collection roles

Role	Definition
View	Allows you to view the collection.
Edit	Allows you to view the collection, and add and remove reporting assets.
Manage	Allows you to view, share, save, rename, and delete the collection and its contents.

The "Add items to your collection" screen, shown in Figure 9-17, lets you quickly search for reports, dashboards, and CRM Analytics assets (if you have the CRM Analytics add-on) to include in your collection. Here you can see that a search on the word "sales" has revealed three reporting assets, the first of which has been selected using the plus sign to the left of the asset. The last step to include this asset in your collection is to click the Add button.

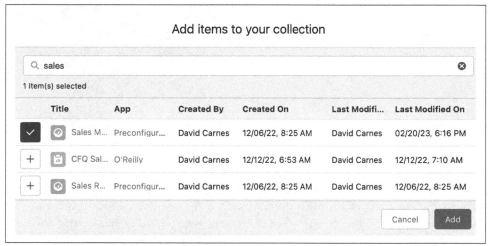

Figure 9-17. Add Items to Your Collection screen

Another option for adding a report to a collection appears when you run a report while on the Analytics tab. There is a small icon at the top of the report, seen in Figure 9-18, that lets you add the report to an existing collection or create a new collection, using a simple screen.

Figure 9-18. Add Report to Collection When Run screen

The Add to Collection screen that appears when you click the Collections icon at the top of a report is shown in Figure 9-19. Here you can see that this report will be added to two existing collections, Sales Kickoff Prep and New Fiscal Year Planning, when the Save button is clicked. This screen also provides a Create Collection link to start a new collection from the report.

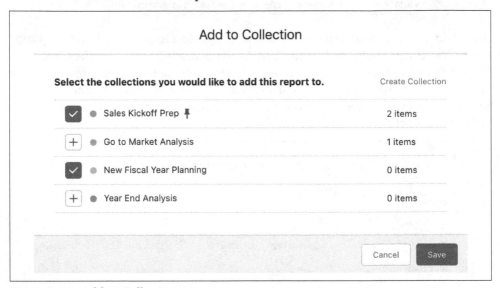

Figure 9-19. Add to Collection screen

Once you have added an item to a collection, you can use the action menu on the item to further interact with this item, as seen in Figure 9-20. From this menu you can share the asset, remove it from the collection, add it to other collections, and edit, delete, and favorite the asset.

Figure 9-20. Action menu on asset in collection

Preview thumbnails in collections

Preview thumbnails add color and meaning to the list of reporting assets within a collection. Once enabled by your system administrator, when reports and dashboards are edited, a thumbnail is recorded and will be shown when that asset is part of a collection. In Figure 9-21, you can see thumbnails for three reports and the top row of one dashboard in the Sales Planning collection. Two of the reports have charts and one shows grouped individual records. Clicking anywhere on the thumbnail image will run the report or dashboard. The report or dashboard's name and folder location also are visible as clickable links at the bottom of each thumbnail.

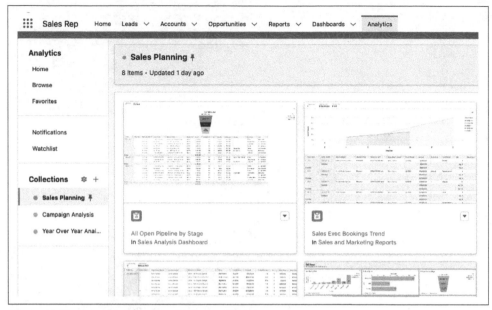

Figure 9-21. Preview thumbnails in a collection

If no thumbnail has been generated for a report or dashboard in a collection, then a light green clipboard icon will appear for reports and a pink gauge will appear for dashboards.

Enabling the Analytics Tab

Your system administrator may need to enable the Analytics tab in your system. There are two related checkboxes on the Reports and Dashboards Settings page in Setup, as shown in Figure 9-22. Tick the bottom checkbox to "Enable the Unified Experience for Analytics Home" in your system. This makes the Analytics tab available to all users in your system. When ready, you may also want to ask your system administrator to add the tab to specific apps so that users can more easily see the tab. Mark the top checkbox to "Show preview thumbnails for Lightning reports and dashboards" while using the Analytics tab. This will show a screenshot of each report and dashboard that appears within a Collection on the Analytics tab, usually within a short time after editing the report or dashboard.

Figure 9-22. Unified Analytics Home settings

Separately, your system administrator may need to update your profile or reporting permission set to make the Analytics tab visible to you, and add the tab to appropriate apps within your system. You can see the Analytics tab to the right of the Reports and Dashboards tabs in the Reporting app in Figure 9-23.

Figure 9-23. Analytics tab added to an app

To see the newly enabled tab, you may need to search within the app launcher, as shown in Figure 9-24. The first step is to click on the nine-dot app launcher, which allows you to search for a specific app or a tab. The second step shows the typing of the first letters of the word "analytics," which reveals the new Analytics tab under Items, as shown by step three.

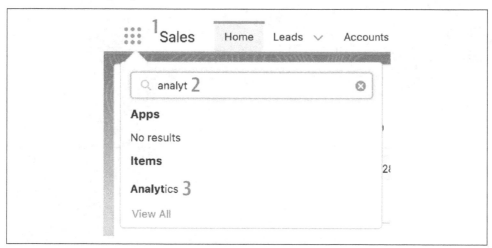

Figure 9-24. Accessing the Analytics tab

Conclusion

Salesforce is positioning the Analytics tab as the future home for all your reports, dashboards, and their folders. They are doing this to simplify reporting and to make it easier for companies that also use the add-on CRM Analytics functionality to see standard reporting in the same place. One great reason to try out the tab is the more powerful search feature and its additional filters. This is especially valuable if you have a large Salesforce instance with thousands of reports and dashboards.

A powerful feature introduced on the Analytics tab is Collections. These allow you to curate and share reporting assets as you see fit.

It's time to switch gears again. Now that you have the basics of reports and dashboards, it's time to explore some more advanced topics to enhance your reporting experience. In the next chapter, you'll learn about the powerful data foundations for reports called custom report types.

CHAPTER 10

Custom Report Types

Report types provide the data foundation for all reporting in Salesforce. You saw in Chapter 4 that when creating a report, you have to select a report type to get started and that there are about 75 standard report types to choose from in your system. This first choice in report building defines the scope of which records and columns will be available in your report. It determines which objects are included and how they are joined together. The odds are good that you will end up needing more options than the initial 75 report types, and this is where custom report types play an important role.

The list of use cases for custom report types spans across all departments in your organization, and grows with the custom functionality you build out in your system. You can use them to create the foundations for account-based marketing (ABM) reporting, such as accounts with or without opportunities, and accounts with or without activities. You can use them for support, to show all cases and their comments, whether or not there are any comments. Administrators may also want to create a list of all dashboards and their components.

Custom report types allow us control over which objects are available in reports and how the objects are joined. You can also use them to reveal fields from other related objects that are not normally visible when using standard report types.

In this chapter, you'll learn how to create, use, and manage custom report types and understand why custom report types are a powerful tool for solving reporting challenges. You'll see that they allow us to report on data that you can't report on otherwise, provide for nonstandard data combinations, and give us control over the appearance and selection of fields available to be added to reports. Once created, a custom report type can be used over and over by users in your system to build new reports. Custom report types extend your reach as a report writer!

Permissions Required to Create and Manage Report Types

Before you get started creating custom report types, it is important to be aware of required permissions. In most cases, system administrators are the ones tasked with creating and managing custom report types. There is, however, the profile permission Manage Custom Report Types, which can grant this power to nonsystem administrators. A system administrator can give you this permission by updating your profile or assigning you a permission set that has the permission checked. Figure 10-1 shows this permission selected in a profile.

Figure 10-1. Manage Custom Report Types selected

Creating Custom Report Types

Let's start with an overview of how to create custom report types. Then you'll see it all put together with an example of a support organization wanting to report on cases and their comments.

To create a custom report type, while in Setup on the Report Types page, click the New Custom Report Type button. The New Custom Report Type screen, shown in Figure 10-2, is the first step in a two-step wizard. It asks you to choose a primary object, which is the data object in Salesforce that will drive the report. You'll see that the list of objects you can choose from is long, including many objects you've never heard of that live within your Salesforce instance. Next, you are asked to specify a report type label, which is what users will see and use to choose this new report type when creating reports. The description field is required and allows you to write a sentence or two describing the report type.

New Custom Report Type

Step 1. Define the Custom Report Type

Report Type Focus

Specify what type of records (rows) will be the focus of reports generated by this report type.

Example: If reporting on "Contacts with Opportunities with Partners," select "Contacts" as the primary object.

Primary Object   --Select--

Identification

Report Type Label

Report Type Name

Note: Description will be visible to users who create reports.

Description

Store in Category   --Select--

Deployment

A report type with deployed status is available for use in the report wizard. While in development, report types are visible only to authorized administrators and their delegates.

Deployment Status   ○ In Development

○ Deployed

Figure 10-2. New Custom Report Type

The list of data objects in Salesforce that can only be reported on if someone first creates a custom report type is longer than the list available in standard report types! This is one huge reason to know and understand custom report types.

When you create a custom report type, you are asked to select a category in which to store the report type. These categories are defined by Salesforce and are not changeable. They largely align around key objects in the system, though customer support and system administrators have their own categories. Other Reports is the default category for report types based on custom objects. Best practice is to align the category you select to the primary object of your custom report type. Figure 10-3 shows the set of categories available.

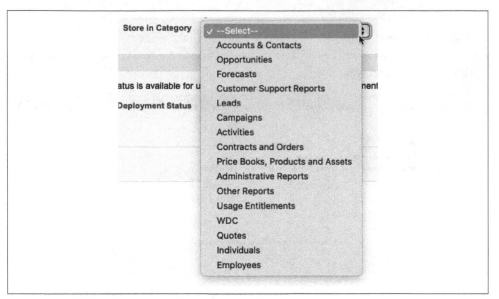

Store in Category	✓ --Select--
	Accounts & Contacts
	Opportunities
	Forecasts
atus is available for u	Customer Support Reports	nent
Deployment Status	Leads
	Campaigns
	Activities
	Contracts and Orders
	Price Books, Products and Assets
	Administrative Reports
	Other Reports
	Usage Entitlements
	WDC
	Quotes
	Individuals
	Employees

Figure 10-3. Report type categories

Before creating a new custom report type, check to see if it already exists with a name that isn't obvious.

An important decision when creating a custom report type is choosing whether its deployment status is In Development or Deployed. A deployed custom report type will be available immediately for all users in your system to build reports on. A report type that is in development will allow system administrators, or those with the Manage Custom Report Types permission, to create reports using the report type, but no one else will be able to use them.

The default deployment status when creating a new custom report type is In Development. You will want to change this to Deployed for others to be able to create reports based on it.

An example of a custom report type that a support team might look to create is Cases With or Without Case Comments. This report type will return a set of case records, and their corresponding case comments, whether or not there are any comments. In database terms, this is known as a left outer join, where two database tables are included in the results set: all records from the left table, and any related records from the right table, will be returned. To get started, you can create a new custom report type and fill in the relevant details, as seen in Figure 10-4.

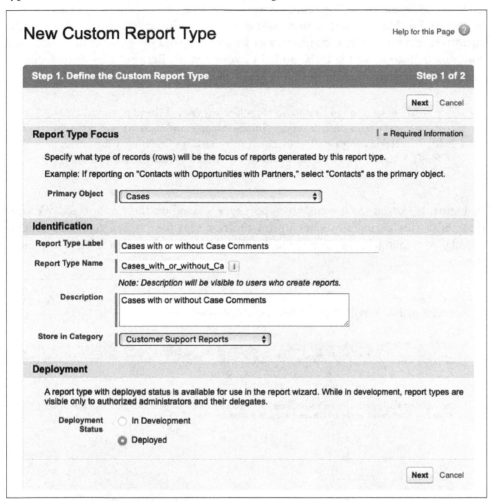

Figure 10-4. Step 1: Define the custom report type

 The label you give a custom report type can be up to 50 characters long. If you enter a longer label, both the label and name will be truncated.

Once you have filled in the fields on the initial screen, click the Next button. On the next screen, you'll further define the report records set you want to see when using this custom report type. Here, you have the option to indicate which related records from other objects are returned in report results by choosing to relate another object. There are more than 15 objects that have a relationship pointing up to cases that are available to be added to this report type. Depending on the child object you select, you might be able to include a third and even potentially up to a fourth object in the custom report type. With each object you add, you expand the number of records and columns that are available to be added to your report. Best bet here is to focus on including the objects that support your reporting goals.

 Keep in mind that there are other ways to get the objects and fields you want onto a report. Joined reports and cross-object formula fields can extend your reach in reporting. Updating your custom report type by adding fields via related lookup is another useful tool that you'll learn about in this chapter.

In Figure 10-5, you see the custom report type started on the Case object. We continue with this example by clicking on the box that has "(Click to relate another object)," and then selecting one of the list of child objects that has a relationship up to the Case object.

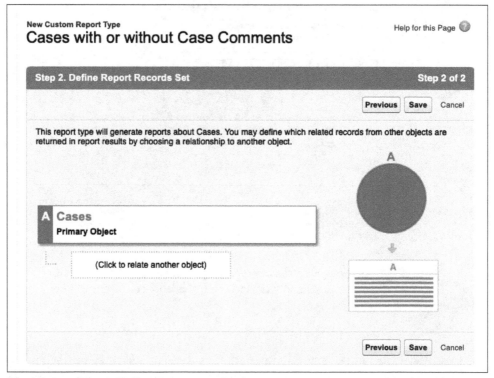

Figure 10-5. Step 2: Define report records set

By selecting Case Comments, we see that the default connection between the two objects is an inner join, meaning that for a case to appear in the report, it will have to have a comment, and for a comment to appear, it will have to be associated with a case. You can see the impact of the inner-join relationship in the Venn diagram on the right side of Figure 10-6.

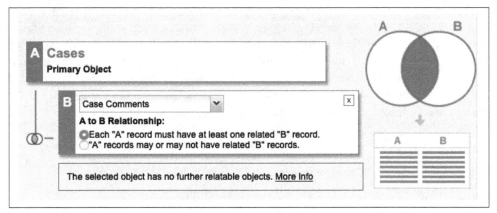

Figure 10-6. A to B relationship with an inner join

In order for your report to show cases with or without case comments, you'll choose Case Comments as a child object to the primary cases object, and you'll want to select the second A to B choice, which states: "A records may or may not have related B records." This defines the left outer join, where all cases will appear, and if they have comments, the comments will appear, but cases without comments will appear too. Figure 10-7 shows this choice selected and its impact on the Venn diagram to the right. In this case, since Case Comments doesn't have any objects related to it, there are no further objects to add to this report type.

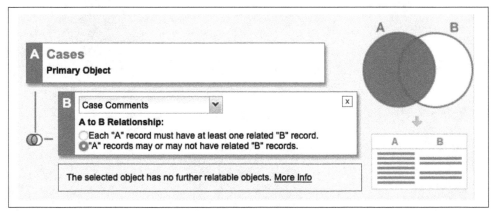

Figure 10-7. A to B relationship with a left outer join

Customer success teams may benefit from a custom report type showing accounts with or without cases. This allows them to see a list of their customer accounts, with associated child cases, whether or not there are child cases.

Once you have created a custom report type and clicked Save in the Step 2 window, you are brought to the Report Type Definition screen, as shown in Figure 10-8. It lists out the properties of the report type and shows the final Venn diagram of which objects are included and how they are joined. This screen also shows how many fields are included for each object in the custom report type. In the section Fields Available for Reports, you can see that there are currently 49 fields from the Case object and 7 from Case Comments, and we are presented with Edit Layout and Preview Layout buttons.

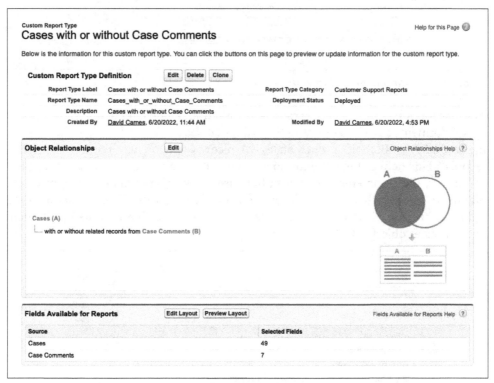

Figure 10-8. Custom Report Type Definition screen

Preview Layout Button

Clicking the Preview Layout button shows you what fields users in your system will be able to add to a report when using this custom report type. Figure 10-9 shows what is one of the oldest screens in Salesforce, a preview of what report building looked like in Salesforce's early years. All these years later, its main use is to show us what fields can be added as columns on reports, and what sections they are stored in.

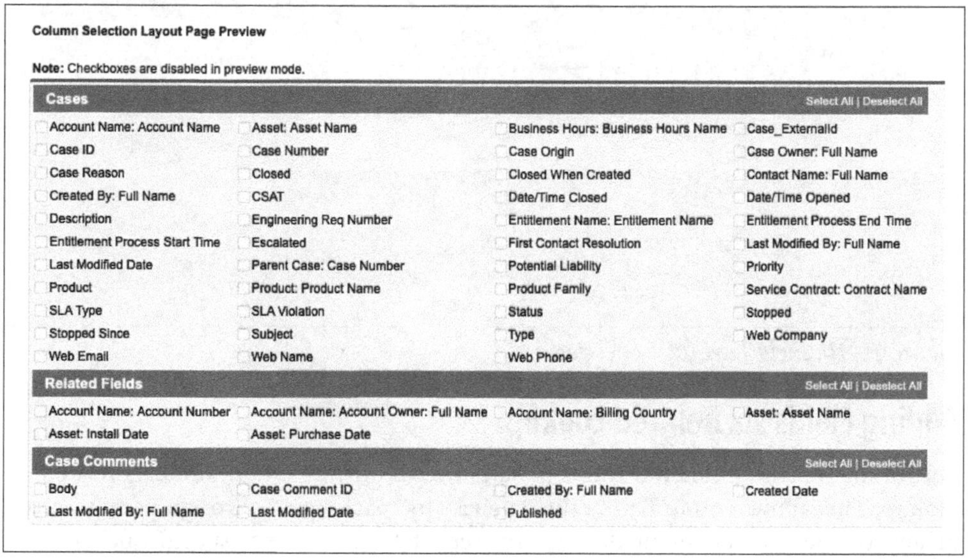

Figure 10-9. Preview Layout button

Edit Layout Button

While not required to get started using the custom report type, clicking the Edit Layout button provides you with some interesting additional customization options. It brings you to the Field Layout Properties screen, where you can add or hide fields from the primary and any secondary objects that make up the report type. You can also relabel columns and specify any columns that you wish to see appear added as defaults when creating reports using the report type.

Continuing with the Cases With or Without Case Comments custom report type example, in Figure 10-10 we can see a page layout control where we can drag and drop fields to control their placement. The Case Number field is set to be added as a default column in new reports based on this report type, and we can see that by clicking on the Business Hours field, we can relabel and also check the field to appear by default. The Field Layout Properties screen also supports adding, relabeling, and removing page sections.

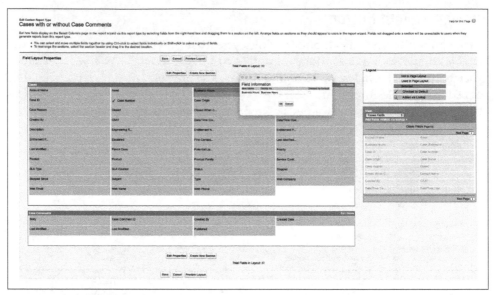

Figure 10-10. Field Layout Properties

Adding Fields via Related Lookup

One of the most significant features in Salesforce reporting is adding fields related via lookup. This allows you to flatten the database by reaching up through parent objects of any of the objects set in the custom report type to select specific fields to be included in the custom report type. For example, if creating a custom report type on opportunities, you can use this to include fields from associated accounts, contracts, opportunity owner's user record, the associated price book, and more.

Using the Add Fields via Related Lookup feature is especially powerful on lower-level objects in your system. An example would be if your system had custom objects to track expense reports and their child expense report line items. If you create a custom report type on the lowest-level object, which in this case is the expense report line items object, then you can use the Add Fields via Related Lookup mechanism to add fields from objects above it. In this case, you might be able to traverse the parent expense report object up to an associated account, opportunity, contract, or project record to pull down fields to use in a report based on this custom report type.

Continuing with the same Cases With or Without Case Comments example, click on the link off to the right called "Add fields related via lookup," as shown in Figure 10-11. This will allow us to pull in fields from related parent objects up above Cases.

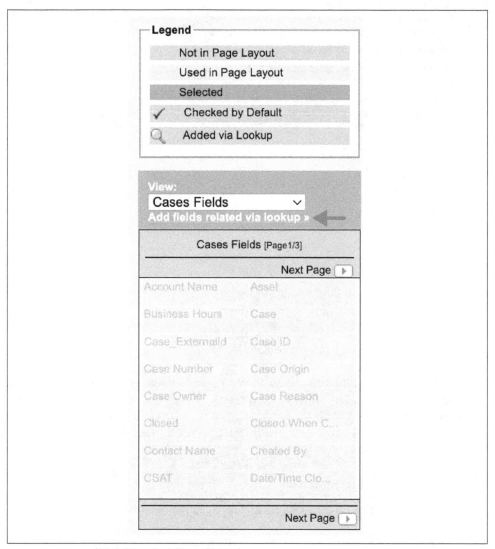

Figure 10-11. Add fields related via lookup

You can traverse lookup and master-detail relationships across objects in Salesforce to find individual fields to include in this report type. A single custom report type can support up to 1,000 additional fields from up to 60 related objects. These can span up to four levels of lookups and master–detail relationships. Figure 10-12 shows the next screen in our example, where we can select objects that the Case object looks up to, such as Accounts or Contacts, to allow us to include fields from those objects.

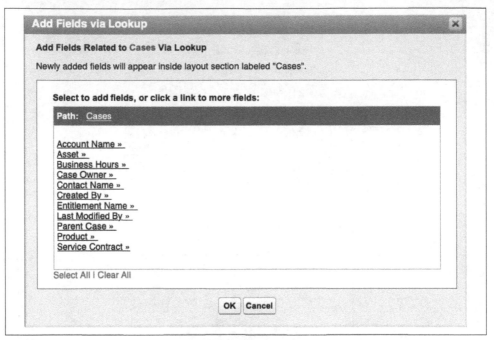

Figure 10-12. Add fields to cases via related lookup

Fields added via related lookup appear with a magnifying glass icon at the bottom of the primary object's section of the custom report type layout. Figure 10-13 shows six fields from our example, with three added from the related account and three from the related asset, moved into a new layout section labeled Related Fields.

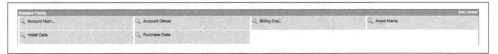

Figure 10-13. Related Fields on a custom report type

 Fields added via related lookup often have very long labels, referencing each object they pass through. Best practice is to relabel each one, and also to put them in new sections with appropriate labels.

One way to think about adding fields via related lookup is that they allow you to flatten the database, pulling fields from many other places down to the same level as your primary object to use in your reports. This could be the best kept secret in Salesforce reporting, greatly expanding the reach of reporting and display of information.

Using Custom Report Types

Using custom report types is just like using standard ones. Upon clicking the New Report button, you are presented with a choice of which report type to build your new report on. Custom report types usually appear below the standard ones in each category in the Report Type selection screen and are identified by the word "Custom" to the right of the name. For example, in Figure 10-14, you see a custom report type called "Accounts with or without Contacts" at the bottom of the list. To create a new report using it, select it from the list and click the Start Report button or click the Start Report option from its action menu. Note that it is labeled as a custom report type in the Category column and in the Details sidebar when the report type is selected.

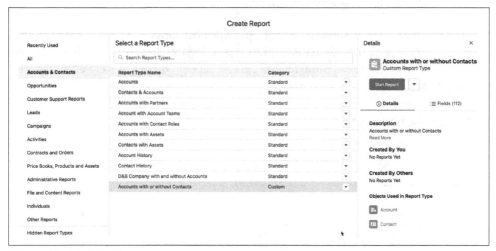

Figure 10-14. Selecting a custom report type

Now that you've learned about creating and using custom report types, it is time to discuss managing them going forward.

Managing Custom Report Types

System administrators and users with the Manage Custom Report Types permission manage custom report types through Setup. By clicking on Setup, Feature Settings, Analytics, Reports & Dashboards, then Report Types, you can see the current list of custom report types in your system. Figure 10-15 shows that each has a label and description, is assigned to a category, and can be set to be deployed. Here you can create, edit, or delete custom report types.

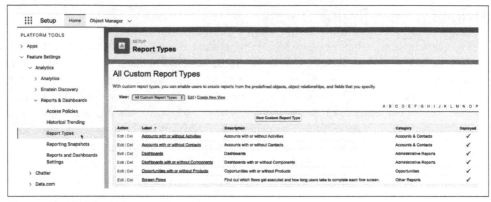

Figure 10-15. Managing custom report types

Similar to other parts of Setup, Salesforce provides list views as a way to manage what could become a long list of custom report types. Figure 10-16 shows a list view created to easily see a list of account-related custom report types. A system administrator can create and share these list views.

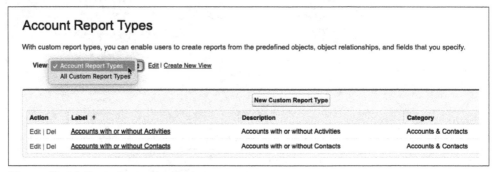

Figure 10-16. Report type list views

Maintaining Custom Report Types

It may be necessary as time goes by to make changes to existing custom report types. This may involve relabeling a field or hiding fields that are no longer in use, but still in your system. You might also want to add fields to an existing custom report type to make them available to a user when they create a report. Be aware that changes you make may impact reports created on the custom report type.

For years, when creating new custom fields in your system, you would have to manually edit each custom report type to ensure those fields were available in reporting. Salesforce now provides a checkbox to the New Custom Field screen so that when a system administrator creates a field, it is added by default to custom report types that have that object defined in its object relationships. This is a significant change, making it easier to maintain custom report types as the years go by. The alternative is a manual editing of each custom report type, dragging fields one by one onto the report type layout. Figure 10-17 shows the checkbox on the New Custom Field screen, which is ticked by default to auto add to custom report type.

Field Label	New Custom Field [i]
	Please enter the maximum length for a text field below.
Length	26
Field Name	New_Custom_Field [i]
Description	
Help Text	[i]
Required	☐ Always require a value in this field in order to save a record
Unique	☐ Do not allow duplicate values
	⦿ Treat "ABC" and "abc" as duplicate values (case insensitive)
	○ Treat "ABC" and "abc" as different values (case sensitive)
External ID	☐ Set this field as the unique record identifier from an external system
Auto add to custom report type	☑ Add this field to existing custom report types that contain this entity [i]

Figure 10-17. New Custom Field auto add to custom report type

Many organizations have older custom report types that are missing custom fields added to related objects after the report type was created. If you are missing many fields, it may be easier to re-create the report type, which adds all of the missing fields, and relabel the old report type with the word Archive included in the label.

Deleting Custom Report Types

While Salesforce makes it enticingly easy to delete a custom report type with the Del link seen in Figure 10-18, doing so may cause a headache you are not expecting. This action deletes all reports created using this custom report type, and if those reports feed dashboards, the dashboards then display broken components when their source reports are missing. Thankfully, before this happens, you will see a warning, such as the one shown here, about the potentially serious consequences of deleting a custom report type. Best practice instead is to relabel the custom report type with the word "Archive" in it.

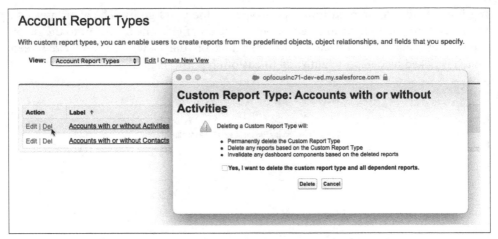

Figure 10-18. Delete a custom report type

Conclusion

Custom report types provide an important mechanism in Salesforce for expanding your reporting options. They do this by allowing you to create custom data foundations using objects that don't come with standard report types, and to leverage left outer joins. Custom report types allow you to relabel columns, remove columns, and have columns appear by default when users use that particular custom report type to build a report. They also allow you to pull in fields from objects connected through lookup and master-detail relationships, which greatly expands the information available in reports. All custom report types that are created and deployed are immediately usable by your users worldwide.

Creating and maintaining custom report types requires that you are a system administrator or have additional permissions granted. As the data model in your systems evolves, you should look to add custom fields to your report types, and retire old custom report types by relabeling them when they are no longer needed.

In the next chapter, you'll learn about embedding report charts and dashboards into page layouts in your system.

CHAPTER 11

Embedded Analytics

A powerful way to leverage your report charts and dashboards is to embed them directly into Lightning pages to provide timely information for your users. For example, your sales reps might log in and see their individual progress toward quota, open pipeline, and recently logged activities appearing visually within a dashboard in their Home tab. Your customer success managers might pull open a key account and can see summary results and activity in the form of report charts visible directly in their accounts.

In this chapter, you will learn how to embed report charts and dashboards as components within Lightning pages. You'll see how to go one step further and have your embedded items appear optionally based on attributes that you specify.

You'll need to be a system administrator or have the help of one to be able to embed items into pages.

Embedded Report Charts

Embedded report charts are great for providing timely information to your users. Figure 11-1 shows an example of two charts embedded in the lefthand sidebar of an account layout in Lightning. The top one shows that customer's cases created by month and their current status, and the bottom one shows the account's won opportunities by quarter.

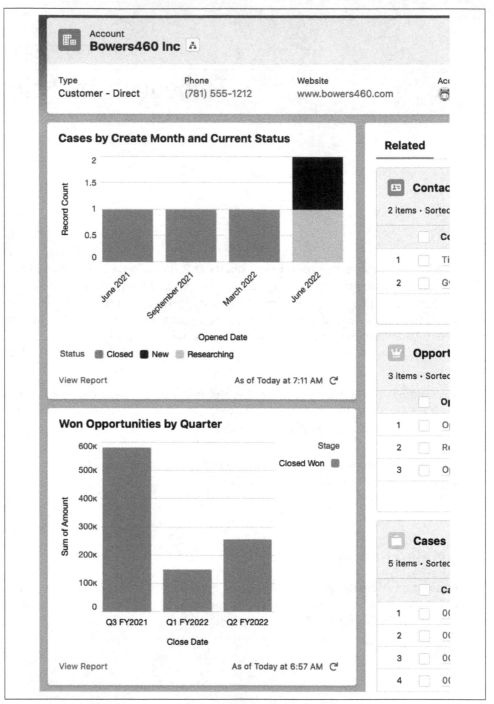

Figure 11-1. Embedded report charts

Adding a report chart to a Lightning page is straightforward, though there are a few things to ensure first. You must select a report that includes the object that the page layout is based on. The report must have a chart and be saved in a folder that is visible to your intended users.

When embedding reports and dashboards into pages, be sure to store them in well-marked, read-only folders. For example, you might create folders called System Reports and System Dashboards and share them with all users you expect to view the pages.

A system administrator can add one or more charts to a page layout by opening the page in the Lightning App Builder. Once they are looking at the page, they can drag the Report Chart component, as seen in Figure 11-2, from the Components list on the left and onto the page template.

Figure 11-2. Report Chart component

Once the Report Chart component is dropped onto the Layout page, the Lightning App Builder will display a sample of the last report chart you looked at. This may not be the one you want to add, so while the newly placed component is still selected, look over to the right pane to see and adjust the source report and other properties for that component. Figure 11-3 shows the handful of attributes we can adjust for report charts. By default the report's name is used as the chart label, but you can set the text to be what you want. The Report field allows you to select another report with a chart from your system to be displayed. The magic happens in the Filter by Field, where you can limit the chart values by choosing the Account ID, the Parent Account ID, or in this case also the Contact Account ID. The system will show a Refresh button on the chart by default, and best practice is to leave it checked. When done making changes to the page layout, click Save to save your changes.

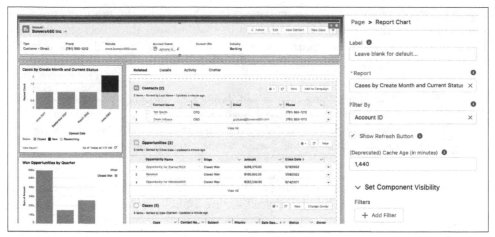

Figure 11-3. Adjusting Report Chart component properties

Based on the sizing of report charts embedded into page layouts and surrounding whitespace, the best fit is often within the narrower sidebar of a Lightning page, such as in the Header with Left Sidebar template.

One time for fun I added 25 report charts to a page layout in Lightning, so the limit is clearly above most of your use cases! Be aware of your page performance if you add more than a few charts, as you wouldn't want to slow down page load times for your users.

Embedded Dashboards

Salesforce allows us to embed entire dashboards into Home pages and App pages, but not Record pages. This means that we can put a sales rep's dashboard on to the Home screen that opens when they first log in, or to a special tab set up to manage their pipeline. We cannot, however, embed a customer-specific dashboard into an Account page. Figure 11-4 shows a sales rep's Home page with their Sales dashboard embedded above a list of Opportunities Closing This Month.

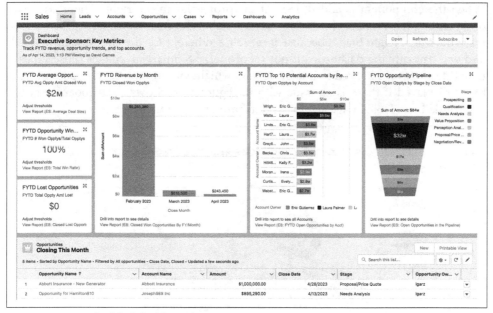

Figure 11-4. Embedded dashboard in Home page

Consider creating an App page to serve as a special tab in your system with relevant dashboards and other content for an executive or midlevel manager. App pages offer more templates than Home pages, allowing you more control over how your dashboards are placed on the pages.

First make sure the dashboard is saved in a folder that your intended users can access. Then, open the Lightning App Builder for the page you want to add the dashboard to. Drag the dashboard component icon, as seen in Figure 11-5, from the lefthand menu and drop it onto the page layout. You can adjust the properties on the right.

```
Components

─────────────

    🔍 Search...                    ⚙ ▾

    📊  CRM Analytics Dashboard

    ◎  Dashboard

    🔷  Einstein Next Best Action
```

Figure 11-5. Dashboard component

When the component is added, look at the properties to the right. There are fewer options than with report charts. We cannot relabel the dashboard. Best practice is to leave the Max Height blank, because it sets a fixed height for the component in pixels and will truncate the dashboard if not set properly. Similarly, it makes sense to leave the Hide on Error checked as it is by default, which will prevent the component from being displayed if there is an issue with it. Figure 11-6 shows a dashboard that has been added to a Home page layout, with its properties on the right.

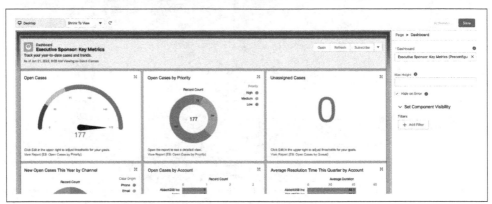

Figure 11-6. Dashboard embedded into a Home page layout

Given their size, best practice is to embed a dashboard in a full-width section at the top of a page layout. On a Home page, this means not using the Standard Home Page template, which doesn't have a full-width layout. Invariably with this template, your dashboard will be squeezed in a way that looks terrible. Figure 11-7 shows the current options for Home Page Layout templates. The other two offer full-width header sections where dashboards fit perfectly.

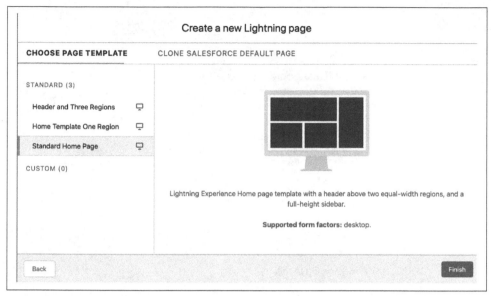

Create a new Lightning page

CHOOSE PAGE TEMPLATE   CLONE SALESFORCE DEFAULT PAGE

STANDARD (3)

Header and Three Regions

Home Template One Region

Standard Home Page

CUSTOM (0)

Lightning Experience Home page template with a header above two equal-width regions, and a full-height sidebar.

Supported form factors: desktop.

Back   Finish

Figure 11-7. Standard Home Page template

A dynamic dashboard, showing a single row of key metrics for the user who is looking at it, can be a great addition to a Home page. Unlike a full dashboard with many rows of components, this allows for other Home page content to be easily viewed along with the dashboard.

Component Visibility

Each time you embed a report chart or a dashboard in a page layout in Lightning, you have the option to set that component's visibility so that it only appears when a filter is true. This allows you, for example, to show a sales performance dashboard only to sales managers, or to reveal a customer case history chart on accounts that are of type Customer.

In the Lightning App Builder, while editing a Record page, click on the component you want to edit, and then the + Add Filter button on the right. Figure 11-8 shows where you can add a filter to set component visibility on a dashboard embedded into a page layout.

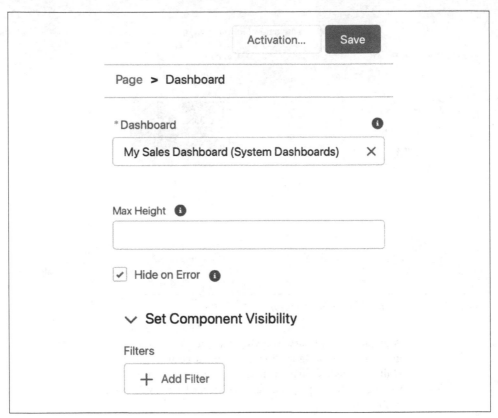

Figure 11-8. Set Component Visibility

Figure 11-9 shows an example of a filter being used to show the report chart when the account is a customer. Since the account Type field is a picklist with two customer-related values, there are two different filters added. If the account is a customer, the chart appears. If not, the chart is not visible to the user.

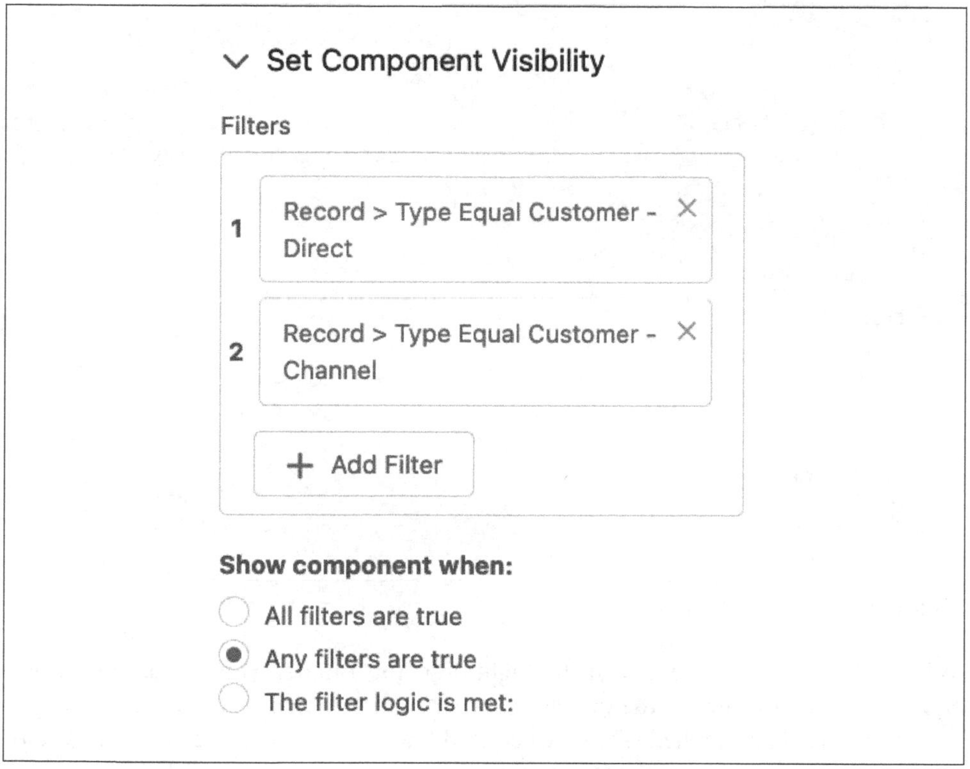

Figure 11-9. Component visible on customers

There are three types of filters that can be applied to a Record page using Component Visibility: Record Field, Device, and Advanced. Record Field filters allow you to display the report chart or dashboard based on the value in one or more fields. While using a Record Field filter is the most obvious use case for many people, applying a Device or Advanced filter can be the most interesting. With a Device filter you can specify the Form Factor where the chart or dashboard will be shown, such as Desktop or Phone. Figure 11-10 shows adding a filter that will only display the chart or dashboard on a desktop device. With an Advanced filter we can identify individual users, profiles, or even users with specific permissions set to display the chart or dashboard.

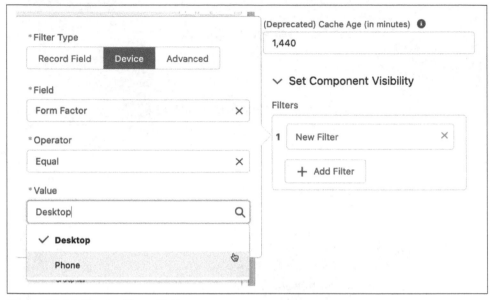

Figure 11-10. Device Form Factor

While editing the page layout in the Lightning App Builder, you can see an orange square with a white eye in the top-right corner of any components that have component visibility filters applied. The chart seen in Figure 11-11 with the orange indicator will now only appear on customer accounts.

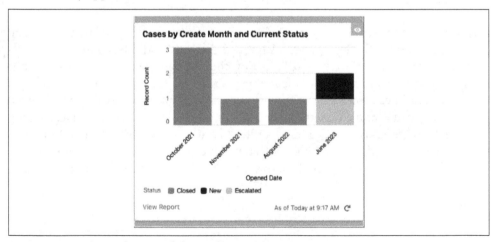

Figure 11-11. Component visibility indicator

In the Lightning App Builder, only Record pages allow this high level of control over component visibility. Home pages and App pages allow setting component visibility solely on user fields and permissions.

Conclusion

Embedding report charts and dashboards into page layouts can add immediate significance and color to your pages in Salesforce. It is a powerful way to highlight what is going on in the business and provides relevant information to appropriate users. Once the reports and dashboards are created and stored in visible folders, system administrators can easily add report chart and dashboard components to page layouts and adjust their properties. Using component visibility on the page layouts adds one more way to control the information being shown based on record fields, user information, or the user's form factor.

In the next chapter, you'll learn about using reports and dashboards on your mobile devices.

CHAPTER 12

Mobile Analytics

Have you ever needed a quick reminder of a number from a key dashboard before starting a meeting? Have you been on the go at the airport or at a conference and thought to check your sales forecast report to better understand what might close before quarter end? Salesforce mobile app allows you to stay on top of your business while you are out and about by making it easy to access your system's reports and dashboards.

As you'll see in this chapter, the Salesforce mobile app allows Android and iOS smartphone and tablet users to run the reports and dashboards that have been created in their Salesforce instance. No setup is needed to start using the app, though your system administrator can control how Salesforce mobile appears to end users. You'll learn about the settings related to reporting that are available, and read best practices to get the most out of the mobile user experience. To learn more about the many other things that the mobile app does and how to administer it, check out Salesforce Mobile App (*https://oreil.ly/LVoZP*) in Salesforce Help.

Installing the App

Salesforce mobile app is a free app that you can install on smartphones and tablets running Android 8.0 or later, or iOS 14.0 or later. You can find the app on your device's App Store or Google Play. Figure 12-1 shows the app's page on the Apple App Store on an iOS device. After installing, you'll need to enter your login and password for Salesforce, and then key in a verification code that will be sent to your email to start using the app.

Figure 12-1. Salesforce mobile app on App Store

Salesforce releases updates to the mobile app periodically, often coinciding with their three major releases each year. It is worth keeping the app up-to-date on your smartphone or tablet to ensure you have the newest features and any bug fixes applied.

Using the App

The Salesforce mobile app can be used to access all editions of Salesforce. It also allows you, as needed, to log in to multiple instances from the same device, such as your sandboxes, developer orgs, or other production environments. One of the first things you'll see when logging in to the Salesforce mobile app is the Menu. As you can see in Figure 12-2, it allows easy access to the App Launcher.

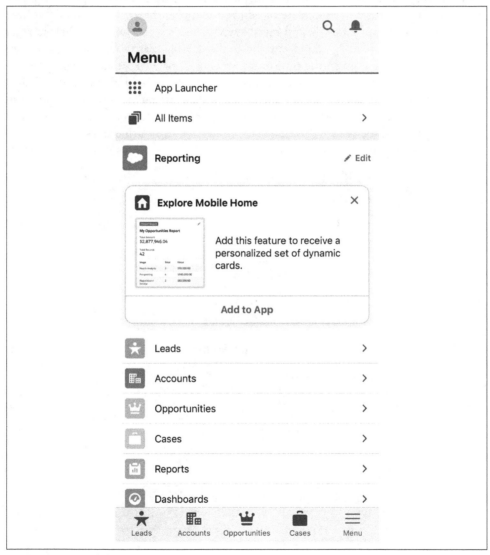

Figure 12-2. Mobile app menu

As in the browser version of Salesforce, you can use the App Launcher to access your apps, such as Sales, Marketing, or Service. You can use it to change apps and, if desired, select the Mobile Only app, which is a special set of tabs that your system administrator can configure to suit your organization's specific mobile needs. You'll learn about Salesforce mobile app administration later in this chapter.

While most reports and dashboards in your Salesforce instance will run as-is, it is good to keep in mind that some features are not available in the mobile app. For instance, you can run but not create or edit reports or dashboards on mobile. Joined reports are not supported at all, and matrix reports are not supported in their normal form, but instead you are given the option to display them as tabular reports as seen in Figure 12-3. When given the option on an Unsupported Format screen, you can click on the View as a Tabular Report link to at least see the underlying detail data from the report. Conditional highlighting and folder sharing are also not supported. Some other features are adjusted or moved to accommodate the smaller screen size on mobile devices, such as reports on smartphones only appearing in portrait mode.

Figure 12-3. Unsupported Format in mobile

Mobile Home

When first accessing the Salesforce mobile app's Menu, you will be offered to Explore Mobile Home, allowing you to click to Add to App, as seen in Figure 12-4. Doing so enables a special version of the Home page for Salesforce mobile, making it easily available by default when using mobile. It is worth trying out because it gives you the ability to pin reports to your view showing their summary data and allowing quick access to run each report. If you instead dismiss this feature by clicking on the X, you can still navigate to find Mobile Home by opening the Mobile Only app, opening All Items, and scrolling to access Mobile, but you are unable to add it again directly to the Mobile Only App.

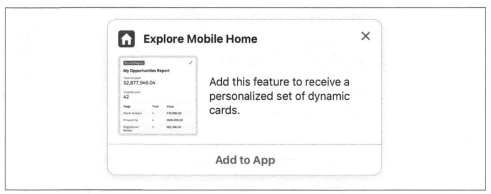

Figure 12-4. Explore Mobile Home

Mobile Home is organized into cards that can be tailored by each user based on their recent activity, preferences, and favorites. By default it includes one pinned report at the top, an example of which you can see in Figure 12-5. By clicking the Edit link at the top right of this screen, you can add more than 10 additional pinned reports to your Mobile Home.

One particularly helpful feature of Mobile Home is that it tells you if the data in a report has changed since you last viewed it. This information appears as gray text below the report name, where the phrase "Since last viewed on mobile 49m ago" and changes can be seen to the right of each summed amount. In this case, the sum of the open pipeline has increased by $5,825,650, the average amount has increased by $30,184.72, and there has been no change to the record count. This feature monitors changes to the report data in between the times you viewed the mobile version of the report and shows you the deltas. You can easily change the pinned report by clicking on the pencil in the top right corner of the card.

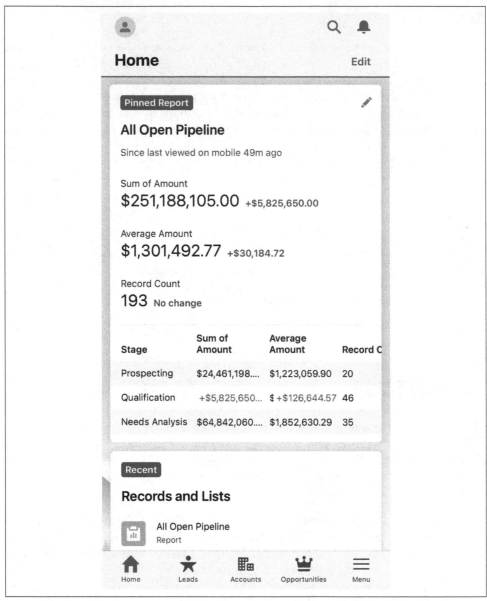

Figure 12-5. Pinned Report

If you've clicked on the pencil on the Pinned Report card seen in Figure 12-5, you are brought to a screen allowing you to select another report to replace that pinned report. Figure 12-6 shows that screen where you can search for a report using keywords such as "pipeline," and by clicking on the report you want, set it as a newly pinned report for Salesforce mobile.

Figure 12-6. Changing the pinned report

If you've clicked the Edit link on the Mobile Home page, you can add more pinned reports to the screen and reorganize the cards that appear. Figure 12-7 shows the controls, which include a button to add a card at the top, "no" symbols to the left of each card to remove the card, and three-line handles to the right of each card to reorder the cards.

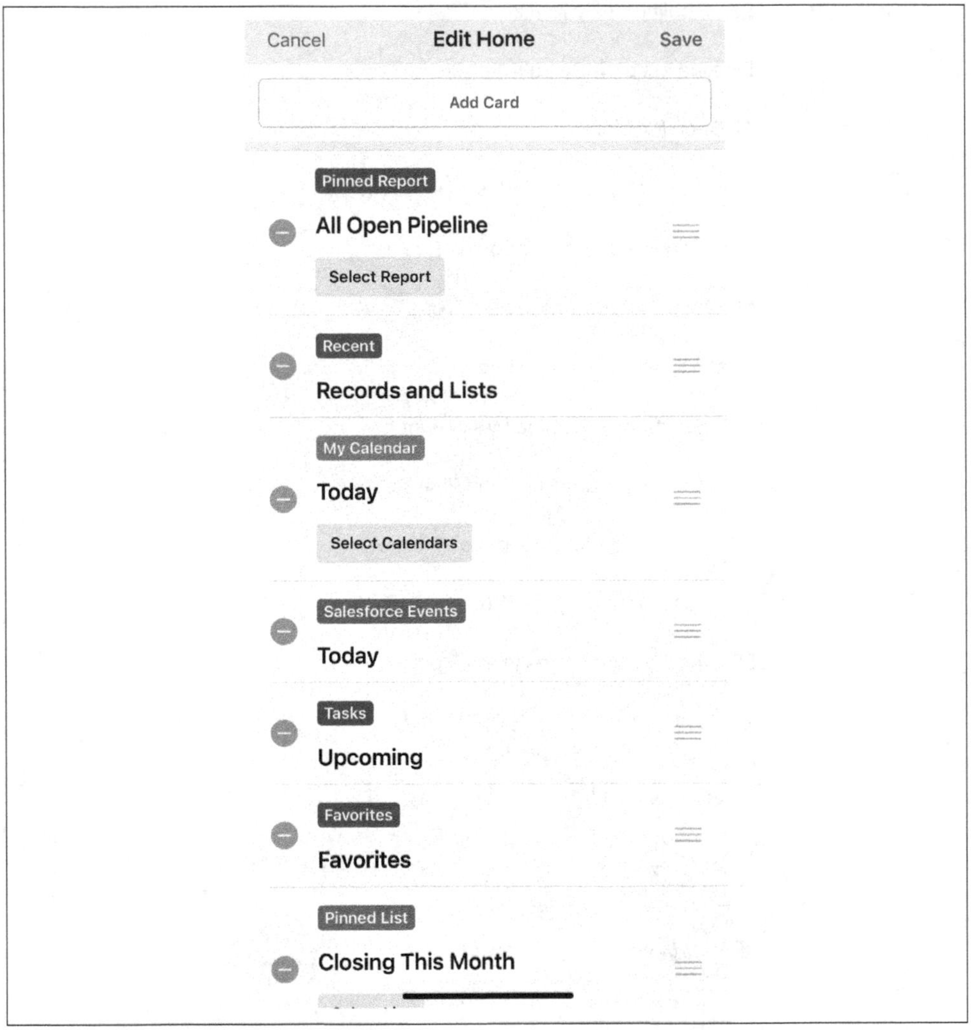

Figure 12-7. Mobile Home Edit screen

Mobile Home also includes lists of Recent Items and Favorites by default, both of which can contain reports and dashboards among other types of records in Salesforce. Figure 12-8 shows the list of your personal favorites set within your Salesforce instance. You would click on one to open that item.

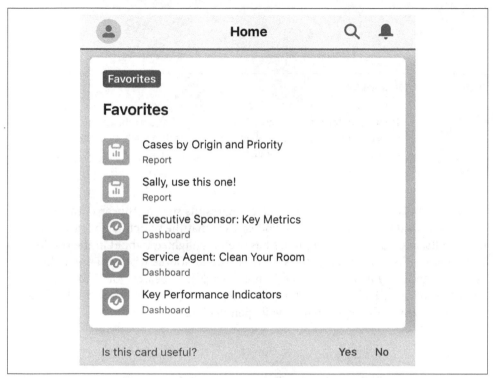

Figure 12-8. Favorites

 Note the "Is this card useful?" question that appears below each card on Mobile Home. While this isn't an editing tool, and clicking No will not remove it from the page, it does provide feedback to Salesforce about which cards are useful or not.

As you've seen, Mobile Home is an excellent way to interact with Salesforce reports. Imagine your executive team, each pinning their top handful of reports and being able, at a glance, to see the summary details and what changed since they last looked! But they'll only use it if you take the time to show them how.

Mobile Search

As with the browser version of Salesforce, the search capability on the Salesforce mobile app offers two ways to enter a search term to return a list of reports or dashboards. The first way is to click on the magnifying glass at the top of any screen in the app, as seen in Figure 12-9. This brings you to a simple global search screen that will look throughout Salesforce to match your search term, including reports and dashboards.

Figure 12-9. Global search

Prior to entering a search term in the global search, the Results screen shows you a list of all recent items, which can include records, reports, or dashboards.

By starting to type a word or phrase, matching results start to appear in the list below the search window. In Figure 12-10, you can see that the search term "case" has yielded results, and that the search phrase has been highlighted in bold in the results. Ten matching results can appear in the screen. If you do not see what you are looking for, and want to look further by object, you can click the "Search for" link for a more robust search that includes tabs for any matching objects, reports, and dashboards. Clicking on any of the report names will open that report.

Figure 12-10. Global search results

A second option for searching is to select the Reports or Dashboards tab from the menu and to do a tab-specific search from there. This search mechanism will yield only reports or dashboards, respectively. Figure 12-11 shows that Salesforce embeds "Search Dashboards" in the search field at the top of the Dashboard tab. By starting to type in a dashboard name, the list will appear below.

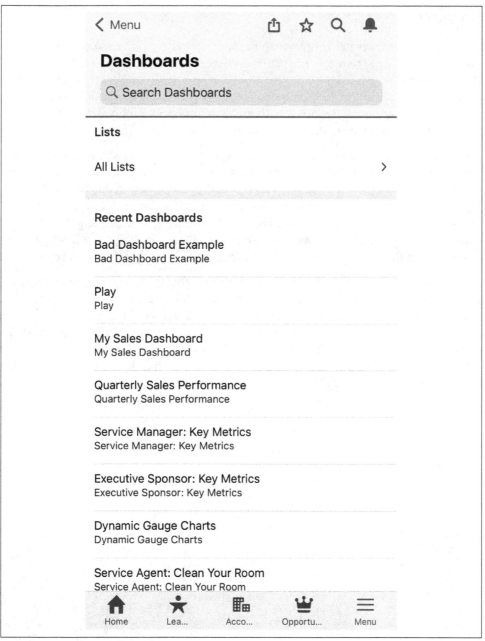

Figure 12-11. Dashboards tab search

Reports

While you cannot create or otherwise modify reports in the Salesforce mobile app, you can run them, favorite, and unfavorite them. You can find reports on your Mobile Home as pinned reports, in Mobile Home lists, such as Recent Items or Favorites, on the Reports and Analytics tabs, or in the results of a search. Report folders are not visible on the Reports tab, though folder permissions are respected, and so any reports you can see are those made visible to you through folder sharing.

To run any report, click on the name of the report. Figure 12-12 shows a report called Cases by Origin and Priority that has been run in the app. This report is grouped twice, by Case Origin and Priority, and shows the record counts for each subgrouping. As the report was saved with its detail rows hidden, the report only shows summary data. Note the icons in the top right corner of the figure. Clicking the filter will show you the filters that have been applied to the report. Clicking the star will favorite or unfavorite the report. Under the ellipsis icon is an option to refresh the report.

When run in mobile, reports with no groupings (tabular reports) appear with summary data at the top, a frozen header row of column names, and row counts fixed in the left-most column down the side. Figure 12-13 shows the top left of a simple report on Cases, which you can easily scroll through on your mobile device by swiping down and to the right. The mobile app allows you to scroll right to left across the other columns in the report that are off the screen, while keeping track of which records you are looking at.

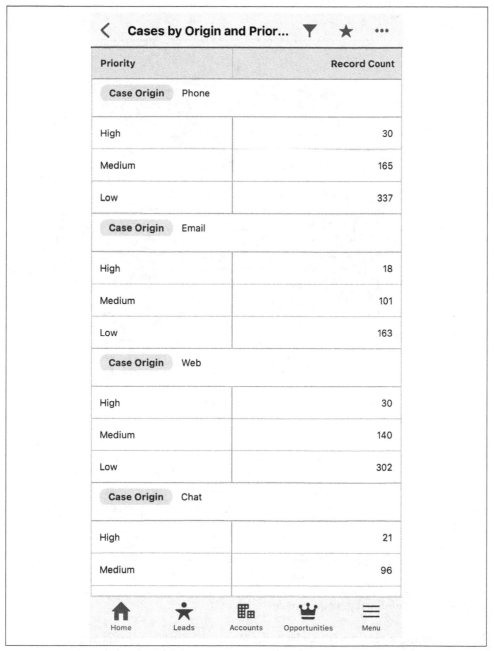

Figure 12-12. Case report

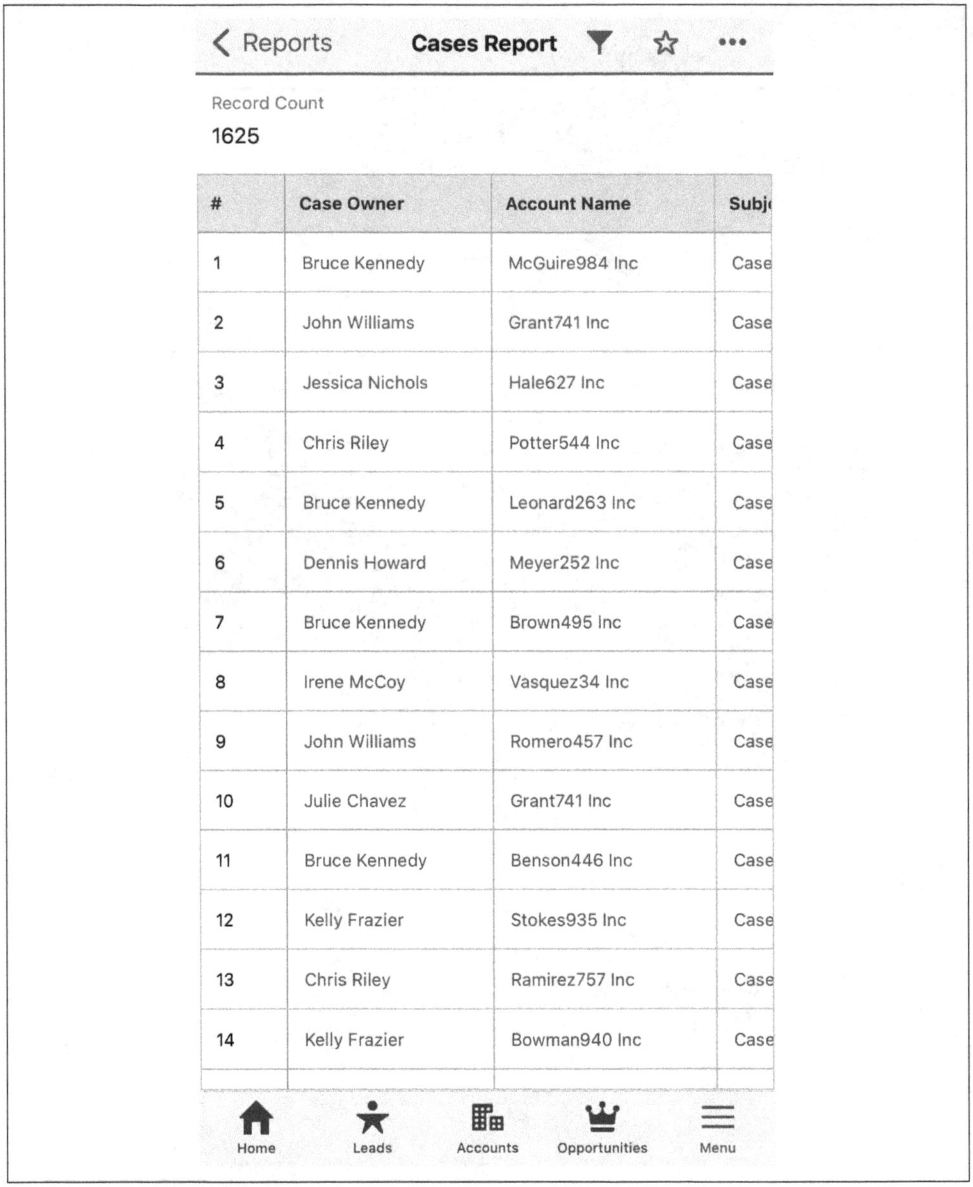
Reports
Cases Report
Record Count
1625
#
Case Owner
Account Name
Subj
1
Bruce Kennedy
McGuire984 Inc
Case
2
John Williams
Grant741 Inc
Case
3
Jessica Nichols
Hale627 Inc
Case
4
Chris Riley
Potter544 Inc
Case
5
Bruce Kennedy
Leonard263 Inc
Case
6
Dennis Howard
Meyer252 Inc
Case
7
Bruce Kennedy
Brown495 Inc
Case
8
Irene McCoy
Vasquez34 Inc
Case
9
John Williams
Romero457 Inc
Case
10
Julie Chavez
Grant741 Inc
Case
11
Bruce Kennedy
Benson446 Inc
Case
12
Kelly Frazier
Stokes935 Inc
Case
13
Chris Riley
Ramirez757 Inc
Case
14
Kelly Frazier
Bowman940 Inc
Case
Home
Leads
Accounts
Opportunities
Menu

Figure 12-13. Tabular report on mobile

When running a report with a chart, the Report Chart tab appears at the bottom of the report, allowing you to show and hide the chart. In Figure 12-14, you can see an arrow pointing to the tab, which is expanded to show the chart. To hide or expand it, click on the tab.

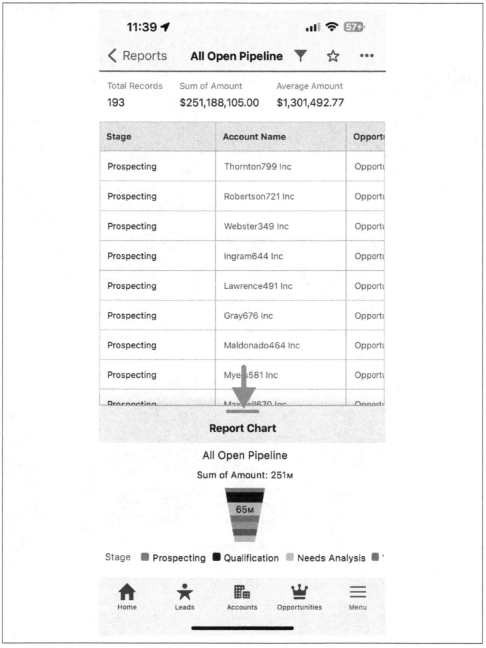

Figure 12-14. Report with chart on mobile

While looking at a report, you can click on any report data shown in blue font to open records directly from the report. You can also click on any column header once to sort it ascending, and a second time to sort it descending. If you click on the ellipsis in the top right corner of the mobile app, a tab appears at the bottom of the screen. You can see the top arrow in Figure 12-15 pointing to the ellipsis, and the bottom arrow pointing to the Report Actions tab. This tab always gives you the option to refresh the report. When opening the Report Actions tab on a report with a chart, you will also see options to Change Chart Type and Hide Chart.

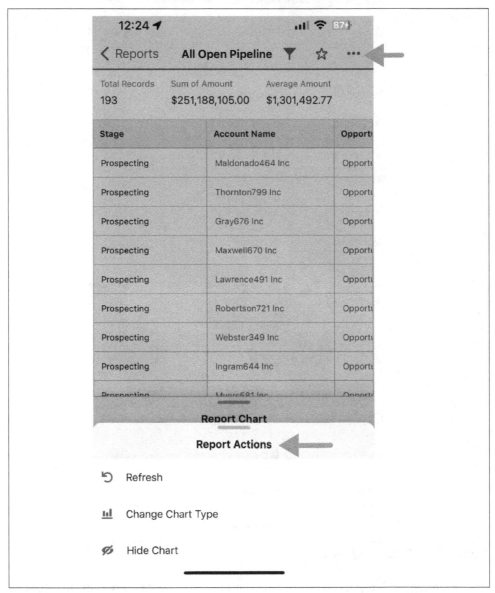

Figure 12-15. Mobile Report Actions

As mentioned earlier, some reporting features are not supported in the mobile app. This includes report editing, joined reports, matrix reports, conditional highlighting, exporting, printing, subscriptions, and historical trend reports. While this might feel limiting, if you consider the app as providing a quick way to check numbers on a report and see what changed since you last ran each report, then the reporting functionality may meet your needs.

Dashboards

To view a dashboard, click on its name in the app, such as on the Dashboards or Analytics tabs, in a search result, or on a list of favorites. One of the first things you'll notice is that dashboards display as a single column of components on smartphones and up to two columns of components on tablets. Figure 12-16 shows the first two components of a sales dashboard, and depending on how many total components there are on the dashboard and their sizes, you may have to keep scrolling to see them all. You can see the last run date and who the running user is set to on the dashboard. There is a Refresh button, which will rerun each source report and redraw each component with updated data. Because this dashboard is dynamic, there is a View As button, which allows the user to specify the running user for the dashboard.

To control the order in which the single column of dashboard components appears in the app, you can create a mobile clone of the dashboard and put all of the components one on top of the next in the order you wish them to appear. You would then mark this dashboard clearly as a mobile dashboard, and perhaps store it in a mobile-specific folder.

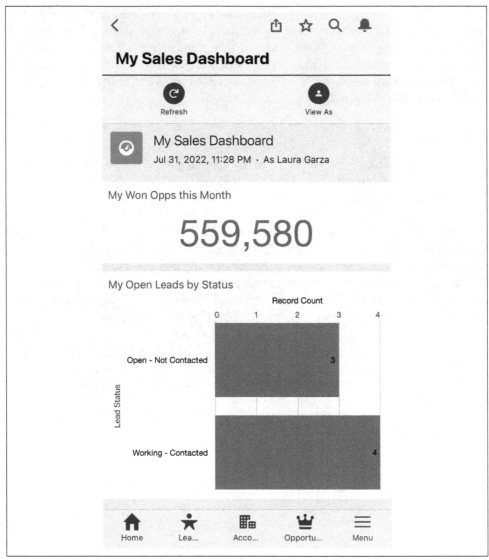

Figure 12-16. My Sales Dashboard on mobile

A useful dashboard feature that is available in the app is filters. If you run a dashboard that has at least one filter on it, you will see a filter icon appear at the top of the dashboard. In Figure 12-17, you can see the icon to the left of the Refresh icon.

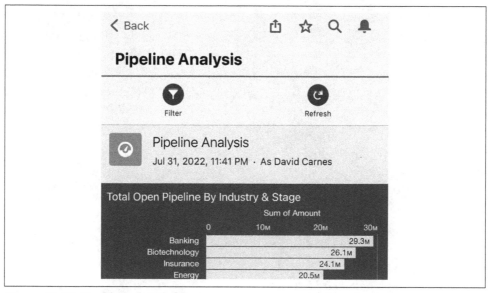

Figure 12-17. Dashboard with filters

Clicking on the Filter icon brings you to a simple screen showing the one, two, or three filters that have been added to the dashboard you are looking at. In Figure 12-18, you can see the two filters on this dashboard, one for Country and the other for Industry. By selecting values in one or both of the filters, and clicking Apply, the dashboard will be rerun with the filters applied.

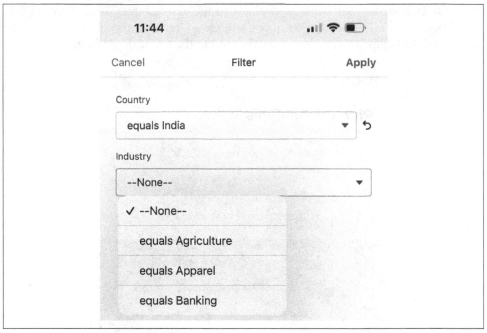

Figure 12-18. Apply dashboard filters

Much like with reports, you cannot create, edit, or delete dashboards from within the Salesforce mobile app. We cannot see their folders on the Dashboards tab or Subscribe to Dashboards. Overall, dashboards look great on the mobile app, though the one-column dashboard view may leave you scrolling on those with lots of components!

Managing the Salesforce Mobile App

While you can use the Salesforce mobile app as it is, your system administrator can also tailor it somewhat to your organization's specific needs. For example, you can control which tabs are available and the order in which they appear. You can also decide if you want a cached version of your instance's data to be available on your users' mobile devices. Other mobile admin controls go deeper, and because they aren't related to reporting, are beyond the scope of this book. Check out Salesforce Mobile App (*https://oreil.ly/LVoZP*) in Salesforce Help for more information on setup and configuration of the Salesforce mobile app.

Navigation

All of the apps, and their collections of tabs, that you have access to in the browser-based version of Salesforce are available to you in the mobile app. In addition, Salesforce provides an app called Mobile Only that all users can choose while using the Salesforce mobile app. To customize the tabs appearing on the Mobile Only app, your system administrator can log in to the browser-based version and adjust a few settings in Setup. By navigating in Setup under Mobile Apps to Salesforce Navigation, as shown by the arrows in Figure 12-19, your administrator can hide unwanted tabs and reorder the rest. They might, for example, make it easier for your end users to access reports and dashboards in the Salesforce mobile app by making Reports and Dashboards tabs appear higher in the list. Since the Mobile Home tab provides a card-based view for users, which includes reports, it is often a good choice for the top of the list.

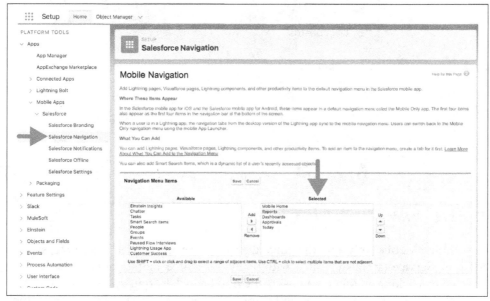

Figure 12-19. Mobile Navigation

The resulting navigation in the Mobile Only app has the first four tabs appear in the tab list, as well as across the bottom of the app. In Figure 12-20, you can see the first three are Home, Reports, and Dashboards.

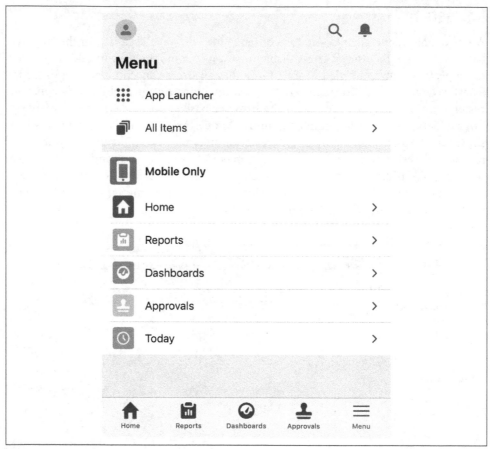

Figure 12-20. Adjusted mobile navigation

Beyond the Mobile Only app, the other apps you have access to in Salesforce, such as Sales or Service, are also visible within the Salesforce mobile app. These can be selected by clicking on Menu and using the App Launcher. Your system administrator controls which apps you're allowed to use, what tabs they each contain, and which user profiles they are assigned to. In this sense, apps are just collections of tabs, so if the Reports and Dashboards tabs are part of an app, they will appear when the app is selected in mobile.

Analytics Tab

One other option for your system administrator to consider when using the Salesforce mobile app for reporting is to show the Analytics tab instead of the two separate Reports and Dashboards tabs. The Analytics tab can be added to any apps, except for the Mobile Only app. As you learned in Chapter 9, the Analytics tab provides access to reports, dashboards, and their folders, along with favorites and collections. Figure 12-21 shows that you can use it to browse through these items and see lists of favorites and recents.

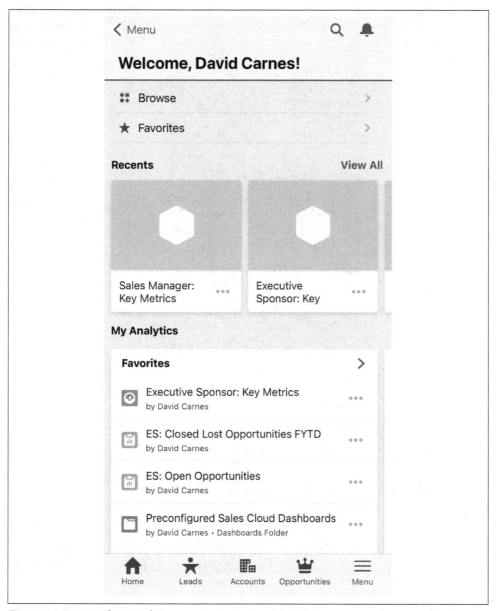

Figure 12-21. Analytics tab

By clicking on Browse at the top of the Analytics tab, you are brought to an All Items screen, as shown in Figure 12-22. There you can search all reporting items, or drill down into subtabs for reports, dashboards, and folders. By next selecting the Filter icon shown by the arrow, the Browse menu appears below, allowing you to further refine the list from All Items to Recents, Favorites, Shared with Me, or Created by Me.

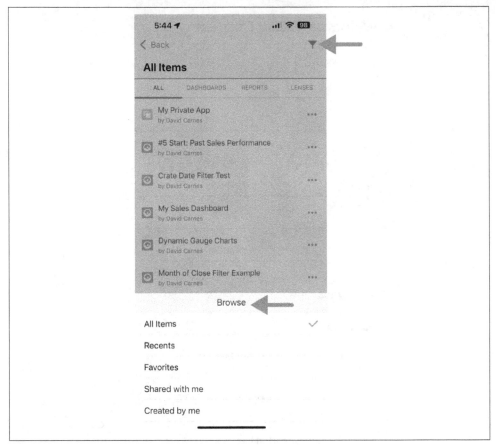

Figure 12-22. Browse filter on analytics tab

Offline

By default, caching is enabled for the Salesforce mobile app, allowing you to use the app while disconnected from cellular and WiFi. Reports are not available while using the app offline, but dashboards can be used to look at cached data.

By logging in to Salesforce via web browser and going into Setup/Mobile Apps/Salesforce/Salesforce Offline, a system administrator can control whether caching is enabled for Salesforce mobile. Figure 12-23 shows the two offline settings available. The top one, if unchecked, disables offline use entirely.

Figure 12-23. Mobile Offline Settings

Conclusion

As you saw in this chapter, the convenience of the Salesforce mobile app outweighs the slightly lesser functionality compared with the browser version of Salesforce. It requires just a few steps to install and start using and provides a quick way to find reports and dashboards, and an intuitive interface for interacting with them. A special Mobile Home page with useful cards for reporting can be enabled by each user with the click of a button. Beyond that, your system administrator can customize and leverage a Mobile Only app to make it easy to access reports and dashboards. The Analytics tab is also a good choice for use within mobile, because it consolidates reporting functionality onto one tab and expands the mobile capabilities slightly.

The next chapter is all about trending, something your leadership team needs but doesn't always ask for. As you'll see, Salesforce provides a number of ways to trend your data within reports and dashboards.

CHAPTER 13

Trending

One of the most powerful techniques in reporting is trending. It provides instant context to numbers that may otherwise not yield a lot of meaning on their own. Trended information is made up of the same data points shown over a timeline. Whether shown directly on a report, or passed through to a dashboard component, data displayed within a trend line helps leaders monitor the health of the organization and make better decisions.

Salesforce provides several tools to support tracking of changes to data over time. Some are available at any time to all users, such as a number of history-related standard report types. Others require varying levels of system administrator support to enable, including Field History Tracking, Historical Trending, and Reporting Snapshots. In this chapter, you'll learn use cases and instructions for each type of trending tool.

Basic Trending

You can use created date fields or other significant date fields to do basic trending on reports in Salesforce. To do this you can select a report type such as Cases, adjust the filters to meet your desired timeline, and then group the report by the Opened Date field. Once grouped, you can adjust the Group Date By to the desired time period, such as Calendar Month, which counts up all the cases created within each month. Figure 13-1 shows the setup of a report on Cases grouped by Opened Date. Immediately to the right of the Opened Date column, you can see the arrow pointing to an open action menu. A second arrow highlights the Group Date By option, and the third arrow shows the last step of selecting the Calendar Month. You can do this kind of basic trending on meaningful date fields, such as Created Dates, Close Dates, Contract Dates, and so on.

Figure 13-1. New records by Create Month

Once the report is grouped by the desired date field, you might add a chart to the report. Figure 13-2 shows a column chart added to the report detailing the record count of cases created by month.

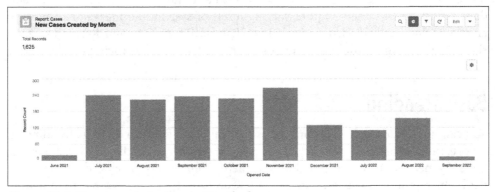

Figure 13-2. New records by Create Month chart

With standard permissions in Salesforce out of the box, most users can delete records. This ability makes the foundation for trend reporting very unsteady. Ideally, when trending, your security on the underlying objects is set up in such a way to severely limit who can delete records.

Depending on your reporting needs, you might consider going a step further by adding a second grouping to the report. This will allow you to use a stacked column chart. In Figure 13-3, you can see the same trend of cases by the month they were created, with the additional information of striations on the columns indicating their current status.

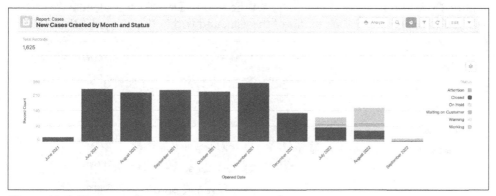

Figure 13-3. New cases by month and current status

 When trending on activity data, keep in mind that Salesforce archives events and closed tasks older than a year by default and that archived activities are not included in reports. Open tasks aren't archived.

You can take this type of simple trending example even one step further by doing year-over-year comparisons by month. This type of analysis highlights seasonality in the business, especially when you look at three or more years of data. Figure 13-4 shows what the output can look like, in this case showing the data across two years.

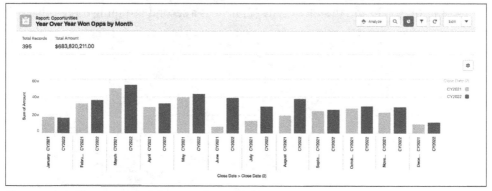

Figure 13-4. Year-over-year by month trending

Start with a report showing won opportunities of all time, or the time period you are interested in. Group the report twice, first by the Close Date field and then by the Close Date (2) field. This special field, which copies whatever date is set as the Close Date, was introduced to Salesforce reporting before the advent of formulas. On the first grouping, set the Group Date By to Calendar Month in Year, as shown in Figure 13-5. On the second grouping, set the Group Date By to Calendar Year. This will group the report by the months of the year, and within that the years themselves.

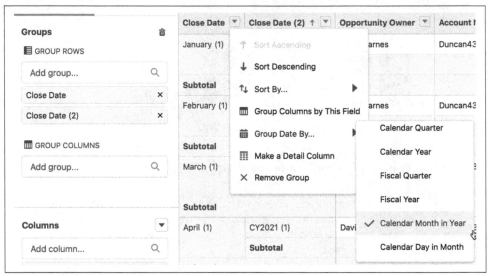

Figure 13-5. Calendar Month in Year grouping

There is one final step when adding the chart to get the years to appear side by side within each month grouping. In Figure 13-6, you can see the top arrow indicating this will be a Column chart, and the bottom arrow where you've clicked the "+ Group" button to add the Close Date (2) field as a second grouping on the chart.

Figure 13-6. Display second grouping on chart

 One reality when trend reporting in Salesforce is that the absence of records in a particular time period will skip that time period on reports. The group name doesn't appear with a zero next to it, but is omitted entirely. This is more likely when your groupings are more granular, such as weekly.

Special Report Types

There are a number of special report types available out of the box that support the trending of information. These include Opportunity Trends, Opportunity History, and Case Lifecycle. There is no setup required to use these; Salesforce does the necessary logging of values behind the scenes. Figure 13-7 shows the two Opportunity report types with arrows.

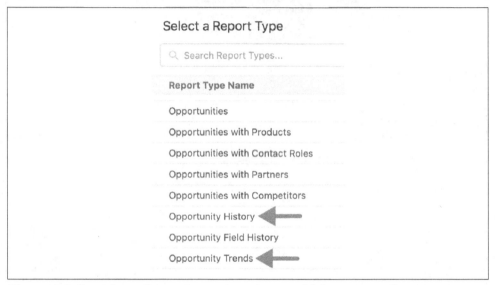

Figure 13-7. Special trending report types on opportunities

Opportunity History

Salesforce automatically tracks all changes to the following Opportunity object fields: Amount, Probability, Stage, Forecast Category, and Close Date. This data is stored forever and is available to report on via the Opportunity History report type. This standard report type introduces a set of fields that can be displayed or filtered on, as seen in Figure 13-8. Note the appearance of the useful true/false field Stage Change, which indicates whether the stage changed during an update to the opportunity, and the Stage Duration field, which calculates how long the opportunity was in the stage.

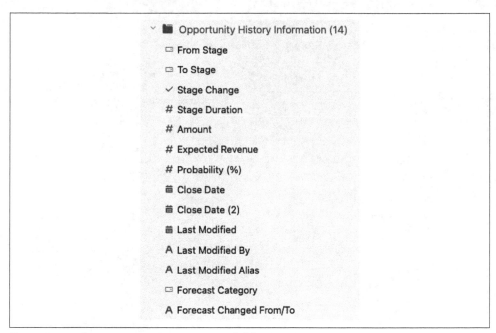

Figure 13-8. Opportunity History report fields

The Opportunity History report type also includes a unique filter that allows you to show only downgraded opportunities. Downgraded opportunities refer to those that have gone from a later stage to an earlier stage. Figure 13-9 shows the Include filter pointed to by the left arrow being adjusted to Downgraded, shown by the right arrow.

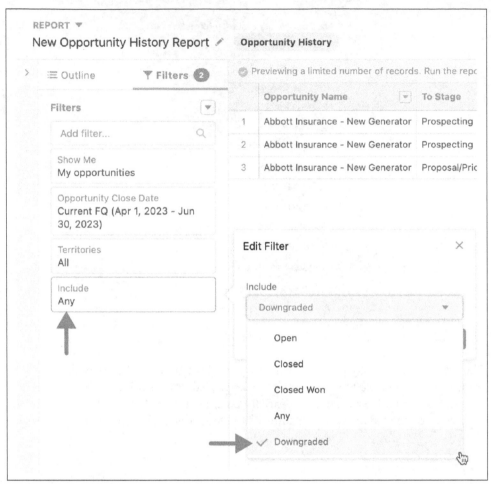

Figure 13-9. Include Downgraded Opportunities filter

Opportunity Trends

Without any setup, Salesforce provides a monthly logging and reporting mechanism on opportunities called Opportunity Trends. On the first day of each month, your system makes a copy of the Amount, Stage, Close Date, and Probability fields for all opportunities. When you create a new report using the Opportunity Trends report type, you are brought to a matrix report showing the sum of the Amount and count of all Opportunities in each stage on the first of each month. Figure 13-10 shows the start of an Opportunity Trends report in the report builder.

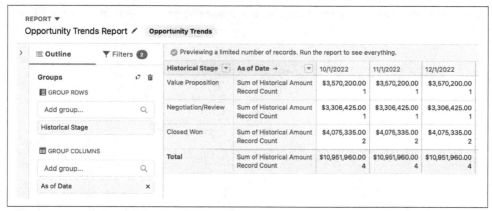

Figure 13-10. Opportunity Trends Report

The Opportunity Trends report type makes a small list of special history fields available to display or filter on, as seen in Figure 13-11. The As of Date field is key to supporting trend reporting and is usually grouped on a report.

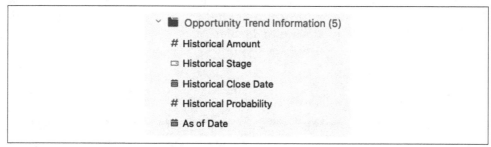

Figure 13-11. Opportunity Trends fields

Where things can get interesting is if you combine filters on these historical values, such as you filter on Historical Stage not equal to won or lost and As of Date equals a particular day. You might use this to list all opportunities that were open on that particular day, and group the report by the current Stage value, to show where the deals are now in the sales process. There are a number of creative ways to use this report type to drill into your opportunity history.

Case Lifecycle

The Case Lifecycle report type does things a little differently than the Opportunity History and Trends report types while providing a way to report on the duration of certain changes made to cases. It enables reporting on a special field called Duration, which measures time. Your system creates a new record for this report for each change of the Case Owner or Case Status field, using the same Case Number and other case information. The Duration field tracks the time that has elapsed since the prior change to either of those fields for each case. Figure 13-12 shows a Case Lifecycle report, which is grouped by Case History Owner and by Case History Status.

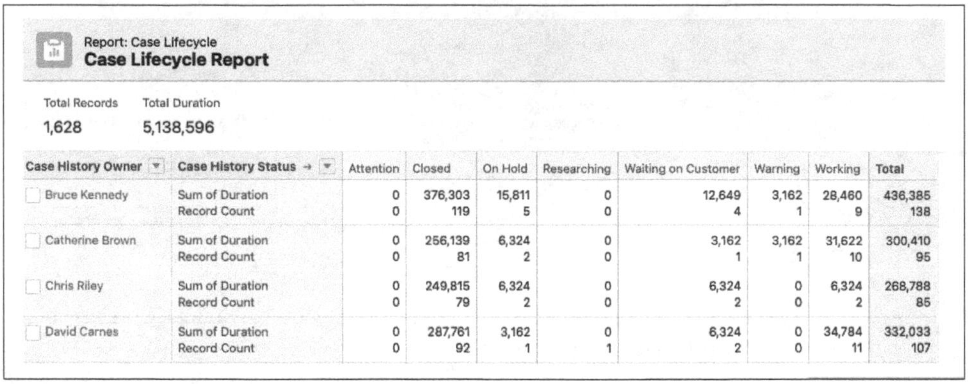
Report: Case Lifecycle
Case Lifecycle Report

Total Records	Total Duration
1,628	5,138,596

Case History Owner	Case History Status →	Attention	Closed	On Hold	Researching	Waiting on Customer	Warning	Working	Total
Bruce Kennedy	Sum of Duration	0	376,303	15,811	0	12,649	3,162	28,460	436,385
	Record Count	0	119	5	0	4	1	9	138
Catherine Brown	Sum of Duration	0	256,139	6,324	0	3,162	3,162	31,622	300,410
	Record Count	0	81	2	0	1	1	10	95
Chris Riley	Sum of Duration	0	249,815	6,324	0	6,324	0	6,324	268,788
	Record Count	0	79	2	0	2	0	2	85
David Carnes	Sum of Duration	0	287,761	3,162	0	6,324	0	34,784	332,033
	Record Count	0	92	1	1	2	0	11	107

Figure 13-12. Case Lifecycle report

The record count value shown on the report isn't the total number of cases, but instead the number of cases plus the number of subsequent changes to the two fields. Figure 13-13 shows the three change records for the first case and two change records for the second case, each with their own duration value.

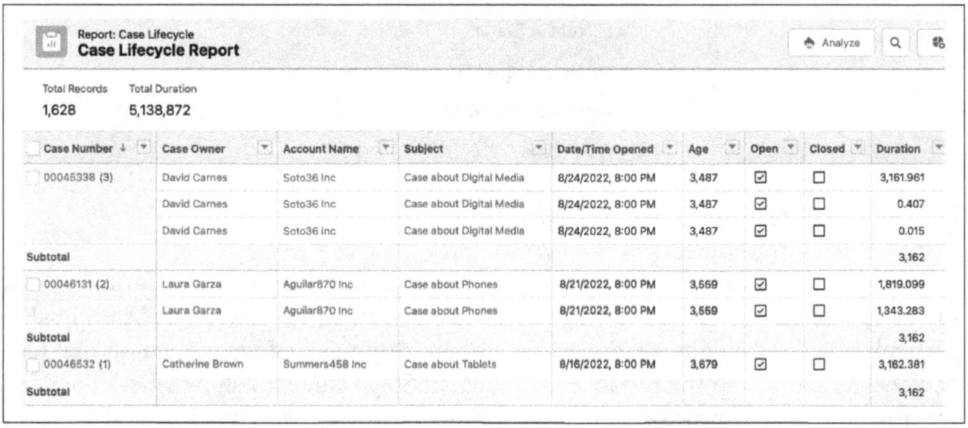
Report: Case Lifecycle
Case Lifecycle Report

Analyze

Total Records	Total Duration
1,628	5,138,872

Case Number ↓	Case Owner	Account Name	Subject	Date/Time Opened	Age	Open	Closed	Duration
00045338 (3)	David Carnes	Soto36 Inc	Case about Digital Media	8/24/2022, 8:00 PM	3,487	☑	☐	3,161.961
	David Carnes	Soto36 Inc	Case about Digital Media	8/24/2022, 8:00 PM	3,487	☑	☐	0.407
	David Carnes	Soto36 Inc	Case about Digital Media	8/24/2022, 8:00 PM	3,487	☑	☐	0.015
Subtotal								3,162
00046131 (2)	Laura Garza	Aguilar870 Inc	Case about Phones	8/21/2022, 8:00 PM	3,559	☑	☐	1,819.099
	Laura Garza	Aguilar870 Inc	Case about Phones	8/21/2022, 8:00 PM	3,559	☑	☐	1,343.283
Subtotal								3,162
00046532 (1)	Catherine Brown	Summers458 Inc	Case about Tablets	8/16/2022, 8:00 PM	3,679	☑	☐	3,162.381
Subtotal								3,162

Figure 13-13. Case Lifecycle report records

The list of special fields available on this report type isn't long, but they can be useful for display or filtering. Figure 13-14 shows the list of fields tracked when changes are made to Case Owner and Case Status. You can use these creatively to support your reporting goals, such as tracking the amount of time your agents spend waiting on customers to respond during cases. If your support process has a status such as Awaiting Customer Action, you can sum the amount of time each case spends in this status using the Case Lifecycle report type.

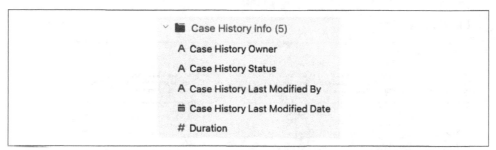

Figure 13-14. Case Lifecycle fields

Reporting on Field History Tracking

Salesforce provides a mechanism for logging changes to standard and custom fields called Field History Tracking. It is available on many standard objects and all custom objects. This feature must first be enabled by a system administrator on a desired object, who then can select up to 20 fields to track changes on. While in Setup, a system administrator can go into Object Manager for a particular object, and then into Fields & Relationships to click the Set History Tracking button, as shown by the arrow in Figure 13-15.

Figure 13-15. Set History Tracking button

On the Field History page, there is a checkbox to enable or disable Field History Tracking for that object. A system administrator will enable it, and then select up to 20 standard or custom fields to log changes for. Figure 13-16 shows that changes to six lead fields are being tracked.

Lead Field History

☑ Enable Lead History

This page allows you to select the fields you want to track on the Lead History related list. Whenever a user modifies any of the fields selected below, the old and new field values are added to the History related list as well as the date, time, nature of the change, and user making the change. Note that multi-select picklist and large text field values are tracked as edited; their old and new field values are not recorded.

[Save] [Cancel]

Deselect all fields

Track old and new values

Address	☐	Annual Revenue	☐
Clean Status	☐	Company	☐
Company D-U-N-S Number	☐	Current Generator(s)	☐
D&B Company	☐	Data.com Key	☐
Do Not Call	☑	Email	☐
Email Bounced Date	☐	Email Bounced Reason	☐
Email Opt Out	☑	Fax	☐
Fax Opt Out	☐	Individual	☐
Industry	☐	Lead Owner	☑
Lead Source	☐	Lead Status	☑
Mobile	☐	Name	☐
No. of Employees	☐	Number of Locations	☐
Phone	☐	Primary	☐
Product Interest	☑	Rating	☑
SIC Code	☐	Title	☐
Unread By Owner	☐	Website	☐

Track changes only

Description	☐

[Save] [Cancel]

Figure 13-16. Set History Tracking

Field History Tracking is most compelling for trend purposes on fields that have occasional or frequent, meaningful changes. On the Lead object, for example, this might mean tracking the history on the Lead Owner, Lead Status, Rating, Do Not Call, Email Opt Out, and Product Interest fields, but not fields that rarely change once set, such as Lead Source or SIC Code.

From that moment on, when data in those fields is changed, the system logs the date, time, nature of the change, and who made the change. The data is visible within a standard report type for that object which has "history" in the name, such as Lead History. Figure 13-17 shows this in action for the Field History Tracking enabled on the Lead object. Opportunity Field History is an exception, as there already was an Opportunity History report type when this functionality was introduced, and so the longer name was used instead.

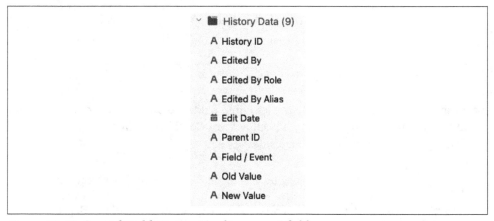

	Lead Owner	Edited By	Field / Event	Old Value	New Value	Edit Date ↓	First Name	Last Name
1	David Carnes	David Carnes	Created.		-	1/16/2023, 11:17 PM	David	Carnes
2	Laura Garza	David Carnes	Lead Status	Open - Not Contacted	Working - Contacted	1/16/2023, 11:15 PM	Higashi	Nakagawa
3	Laura Garza	David Carnes	Rating	-	Hot	1/16/2023, 11:15 PM	Higashi	Nakagawa
4	Laura Garza	David Carnes	Product Interest	-	GC1000 series	1/16/2023, 11:15 PM	Higashi	Nakagawa
5	David Carnes	David Carnes	Lead Status	Working - Contacted	Open - Not Contacted	1/16/2023, 11:14 PM	Bertha	Boxer
6	David Carnes	David Carnes	Rating	Hot	Warm	1/16/2023, 11:14 PM	Bertha	Boxer

Report: Lead History
Lead History Report

Total Records
6

Figure 13-17. Lead History report

Field History Tracking is useful in a number of ways as this information can be reported on to monitor changes to data and identify anomalies. In particular, note that there are a handful of history fields made available as columns and for use in filters. Figure 13-18 shows this list of special history-related fields. One example would be to set report filters to show changes to Field/Event Email Opt Out where the Old Value is false and the New Value is true.

> History Data (9)
> A History ID
> A Edited By
> A Edited By Role
> A Edited By Alias
> Edit Date
> A Parent ID
> A Field / Event
> A Old Value
> A New Value

Figure 13-18. Special Field History Tracking report fields

By default, field history data is retained for up to 18 months for use on reports. Salesforce sells an add-on module called Field Audit Trail that allows field history to be stored indefinitely.

Historical Trending

Have you ever been asked to "just show me what changed since last week"? Historical Trending is a little known and older feature that can answer that request on the Opportunities, Cases, and Forecast Item objects and up to three custom objects. To enable this feature for an object, your system administrator needs to check a box and select which standard and custom fields you want tracked. In Figure 13-19, you can see the left arrow pointing to the location in Setup where you can adjust Historical Trending settings, and the right arrow pointing to the checkbox to tick and then click the Save button to enable the feature. You can select to track changes on up to one hundred fields per object of the following data types: Number, Currency, Date, Picklist, and Lookup.

Figure 13-19. Enabling Historical Trending

From that moment on, changes to the specified fields are tracked for up to three prior months plus the current month. This allows you to show or filter on the historical value and the current value of those fields.

 Salesforce begins logging Historical Trending on an object the moment you enable it. This means that the soonest you can see change data using its corresponding report type is the next day. If you are looking to compare today's values with the values from seven days ago, you will need at least seven days to pass since your system administrator enabled the feature to be able to see this comparison data.

When you first create a report using a Historical Trending report type, you will notice a few features that are unique to Historical Trending reports. Figure 13-20 shows the

Snapshot Dates list displayed on the report. Currently you can see that this report is comparing "7 Days Ago" versus the current values. There is a small plus sign that allows you to add up to four more Snapshot dates. These can be a variety of values such as "2 Days Ago," "1 Month Ago," "First Day Last Month," and so on. The default value "Yesterday" may be most valuable in an organization that has a lot of transactions, whereas other organizations may see the most benefit using "7 Days Ago" or even "1 Month Ago" as their snapshot date.

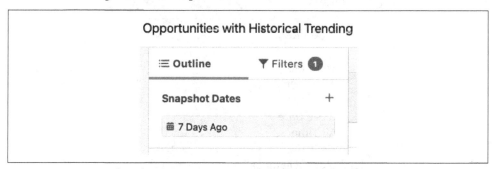

Figure 13-20. Snapshot dates

 Best bet when using Historical Trending is to start with just one snapshot date, such as "7 Days Ago," which compares the values from seven days ago with the current values.

A key reporting feature in Historical Trending is the availability of Historical twin fields for every field your system administrator specified be tracked for that object. Figure 13-21 shows the default fields tracked on Opportunities with Historical Trending. When first starting a new report, the Historical fields are way off to the right in the column order. Ideally these fields are moved to appear immediately to the left of each corresponding current value field.

Figure 13-21. Historical fields

The Historical fields can also be used in filtering the report. You might use this to show all the opportunities that were open last week, to see where they currently are now. In Figure 13-22, the arrow shows that the filter is set to Historical Stage not equal to won or lost. In effect, this returns only the deals open during our snapshot date seven days ago. Each Historical Trend report supports up to four historical filters.

Figure 13-22. Historical filters

The power of Historical Trend reporting is that you can see at a glance which records have changed, through either red or green colors or an extra column that shows the amount changed. Before showing this in action, there are two adjustments that you will want to make on the report. The first is to show changes to the Close Date field that push the date out as red instead of green; as in most sales situations, it is bad when opportunity close dates slip into the future. Figure 13-23 shows the top arrow pointing to the action menu for the Close Date column in the report builder. The middle arrow shows selecting the Format Change option, and the bottom arrow shows changing the formatting from green to red.

Figure 13-23. Format Change

The second change that you might want to make on the report is to show how much the Amount field changed. Figure 13-24 shows a top arrow pointing to the action pull-down menu to the right of the Amount column. The second arrow points to the Show Change menu option. When this is selected, you can choose Value to show the amount changed from the historical value to the current value. Rather than having to do the math in their heads, users viewing the report will be able to see the specific change to the amount.

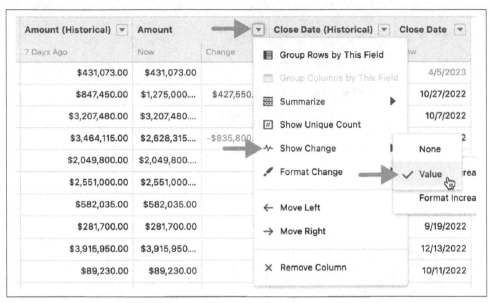

Amount (Historical) ▼	Amount		▼	Close Date (Historical) ▼	Close Date ▼
7 Days Ago	Now	Change			
$431,073.00	$431,073.00		🗐 Group Rows by This Field		4/5/2023
$847,450.00	$1,275,000....	$427,550.	🏛 Group Columns by This Field		10/27/2022
$3,207,480.00	$3,207,480....		🧮 Summarize ▶		10/7/2022
$3,464,115.00	$2,628,315....	-$835,800	# Show Unique Count		2
$2,049,800.00	$2,049,800....		∿ Show Change	None	
$2,551,000.00	$2,551,000....		✎ Format Change	✓ Value rea	
$582,035.00	$582,035.00		← Move Left	Format Increa	
$281,700.00	$281,700.00		→ Move Right		9/19/2022
$3,915,950.00	$3,915,950....				12/13/2022
$89,230.00	$89,230.00		✕ Remove Column		10/11/2022

Figure 13-24. Show Change

One quirk to keep in mind is that changes to picklist values in either direction of a sales or support process will appear as green. In real life, an opportunity that moves backward in the sales process should be shown in red.

Pulling it all together, the Historical Trend report is a great way to show what changed since last week, month over month, or even from yesterday to today. For a director of sales operations in charge of a weekly pipeline review meeting, this kind of intel is gold. Figure 13-25 shows clear visual indicators for the changes a report viewer might care most about. Once again, keep in mind that you can be creative with your use of historical and current fields within filters to get at the exact scenario you need to report on.

Report: Opportunities with Historical Trending
Opportunities with Historical Trending

Total Records
201

	Opportunity Name ▼	Stage (Historical) ▼	Stage ▼	Amount (Historical) ▼	Amount		Close Date (Historical) ▼	Close Date ▼
		7 Days Ago	Now	7 Days Ago	Now	Change	7 Days Ago	Now
1	Opportunity for Daniel1888	Value Proposition	Id. Decision Makers	$1,384,600.00	$1,384,600.00	-	9/15/2022	1/17/2023
2	Opportunity for Phillips1889	Value Proposition	Value Proposition	$39,600.00	$50,000.00	$10,400.00	2/2/2023	2/2/2023
3	Opportunity for Hall1897	Perception Analysis	Qualification	$2,925,000.00	$2,551,000.00	-$374,000.00	3/11/2023	3/3/2023
4	Opportunity for Drake768	Perception Analysis	Perception Analysis	$70,368.00	$70,368.00	-	10/17/2022	10/17/2022

Figure 13-25. What changed since last week?

Reporting Snapshots

The most technical of the trending solutions that Salesforce offers is Reporting Snapshots. These require four main ingredients: a source report, a custom object to store your snapshot data, a reporting snapshot, and the essential ingredient of time passing by. You might use a Reporting Snapshot to track the volume of open support cases week to week, or to monitor monthly progress on projects tracked in a custom object.

An ideal use case for Reporting Snapshots comes when thinking of your open sales pipeline from week to week. Most organizations will use a funnel chart to show the current state of the pipeline. It shows an inverted trapezoid with striations corresponding to the sum of the amount in each opportunity stage. Figure 13-26 shows an open opportunity funnel for the current state of the pipeline.

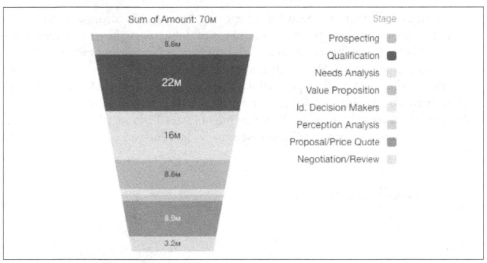

Figure 13-26. Opportunity pipeline by stage

Well, what if you compared this week's open pipeline with the prior 52 weeks of open pipeline, within a more compact stacked column chart on a trend report or dashboard? Figure 13-27 shows just that, retaining the same orientation as the funnel, with earlier stages at the top and closer to contract stages at the bottom. Hand in hand with your sales report for the past year, you can use this to tell a story of your pipeline generation efforts and the effectiveness of your sales process.

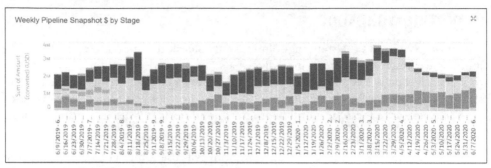

Figure 13-27. Weekly pipeline snapshot by stage

Source Report

The first ingredient that you need for a Reporting Snapshot is a source report. This report should only include the bare minimum of columns required to support the snapshot. Figure 13-28 shows the source report for an opportunity pipeline snapshot that includes Opportunity Name, Owner, Stage, Close Date, Forecast Category, and Amount fields from a tabular report, which has no groups. Since the Reporting Snapshot mechanism will only support snapshotting up to two thousand records at a time, if the number of records surpasses that, you might instead choose to snapshot a grouped report, where you are passing the summary data instead of individual record data.

Report: Opportunities
Open Pipeline Snapshot Source Report
This report feeds our open pipeline snapshot object to support our trending. Please do not modify.

Total Records	Total Amount
191	$245,513,755.00

	Opportunity Owner	Opportunity Name	Stage	Close Date	Forecast Category	Amount
1	John Williams	Opportunity for Daniel1888	Id. Decision Makers	1/17/2023	Pipeline	$1,384,600.00
2	Harold Campbell	Opportunity for Phillips1889	Value Proposition	2/2/2023	Pipeline	$50,000.00
3	Nicolas Weaver	Opportunity for Hall1897	Qualification	3/3/2023	Pipeline	$2,551,000.00
4	Chris Riley	Opportunity for Drake768	Perception Analysis	10/17/2022	Best Case	$70,368.00
5	Laura Palmer	Opportunity for Robbins1143	Qualification	2/17/2023	Pipeline	$365,072.00

Figure 13-28. Source report

When you create your source report for a Reporting Snapshot, be sure to store it in a read-only folder that is clearly labeled something like System Reports so that no one inadvertently changes items within it. If someone changes your report by, for example, removing columns or changing the filters, this could break your Reporting Snapshot.

Custom Snapshot Object

The next step is to ask a system administrator to create a custom object for you. They will want to clearly label the object with the word "snapshot" in it, such as Open Pipeline Snapshot, as in Figure 13-29. They should ensure that the Enable Reports setting is checked on the custom object. Then they will create one custom field for each column in the source report, with matching (or very similar) data types. Finally, they will create a date field called Date to store the date that the snapshot runs.

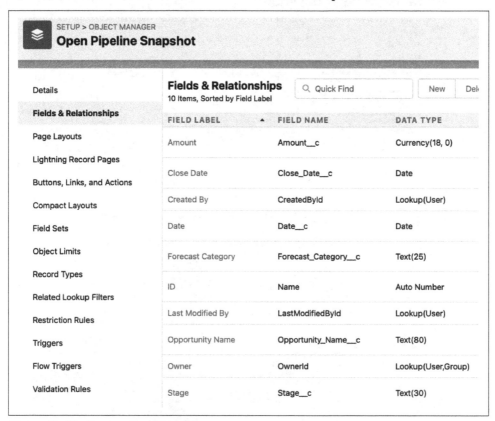

FIELD LABEL ▲	FIELD NAME	DATA TYPE
Amount	Amount__c	Currency(18, 0)
Close Date	Close_Date__c	Date
Created By	CreatedById	Lookup(User)
Date	Date__c	Date
Forecast Category	Forecast_Category__c	Text(25)
ID	Name	Auto Number
Last Modified By	LastModifiedById	Lookup(User)
Opportunity Name	Opportunity_Name__c	Text(80)
Owner	OwnerId	Lookup(User,Group)
Stage	Stage__c	Text(30)

Figure 13-29. Custom Snapshot object

For source fields that are picklists, such as the Opportunity Stage field or the Case Status field, you can create a simple custom text field to store the snapshot value. This prevents future failure of the snapshot if the picklist values change. Be sure to set the field length to exceed the longest picklist value in the field.

The Snapshot Itself

Once the source report and snapshot object are created and in place, it is time for a system administrator, or someone with the Manage Reporting Snapshots permission, to create the snapshot in Setup. Figure 13-30 shows the first screen when creating a new snapshot.

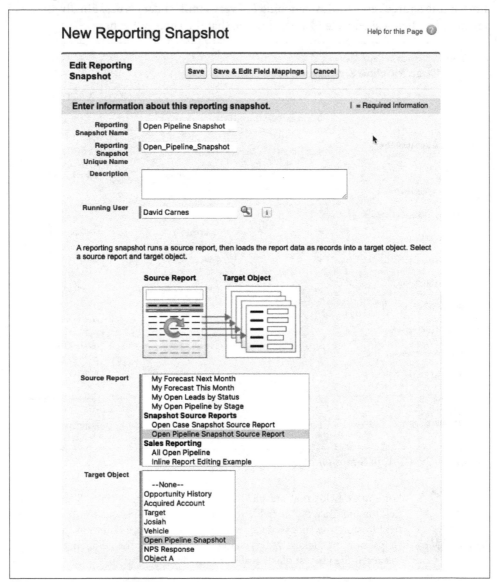

Figure 13-30. New Reporting Snapshot

After giving the snapshot a name, you will need to select the source report and custom object you created for it. You will also need to indicate a running user, which is the person through whose permissions the report will be run to feed the snapshot. Once the report and object are set, you will want to click the Save & Edit Field Mappings button to define the field mappings.

The next screen is where you map the columns from your report to each custom field on the custom object. Figure 13-31 depicts a pull-down menu of possible source fields for every custom field on your target object. You will want to go through the list one by one, and be sure to map Execution Time to the Date field. Once done, click the Save button.

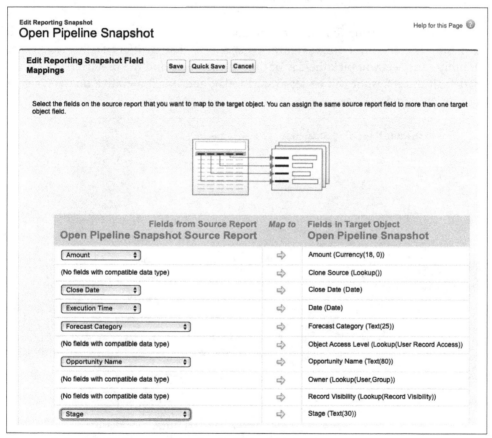

Figure 13-31. Edit Reporting Snapshot Field Mappings

The last step is to schedule your Reporting Snapshot. On the Snapshot screen for your newly created snapshot, click the Edit button to the right of Schedule Reporting Snapshot, as shown in Figure 13-32. Note the Run History list directly below the Schedule section. Since it was just created, it currently has nothing to display, but over time it will be filled with weeks, months, and years of this snapshot's history of having been run.

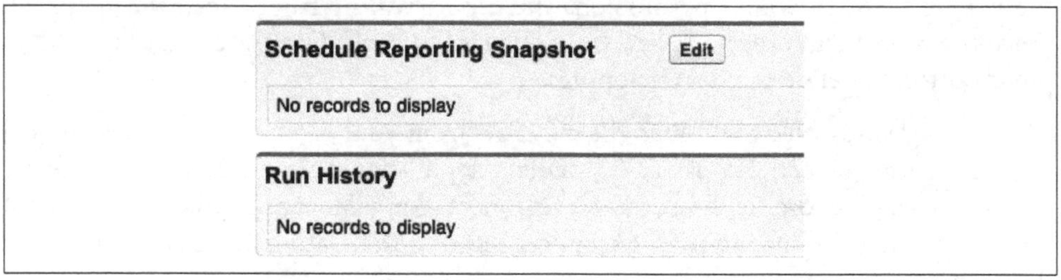

Figure 13-32. Schedule Reporting Snapshot

The Schedule Reporting Snapshot screen allows you or someone else to be emailed each time the snapshot runs. Figure 13-33 shows that it offers Daily, Weekly, or Monthly runs, lets you pick the day or days of the week, and the preferred start time. By default the snapshot will be set to start today, and it is imperative that you set an appropriate end date.

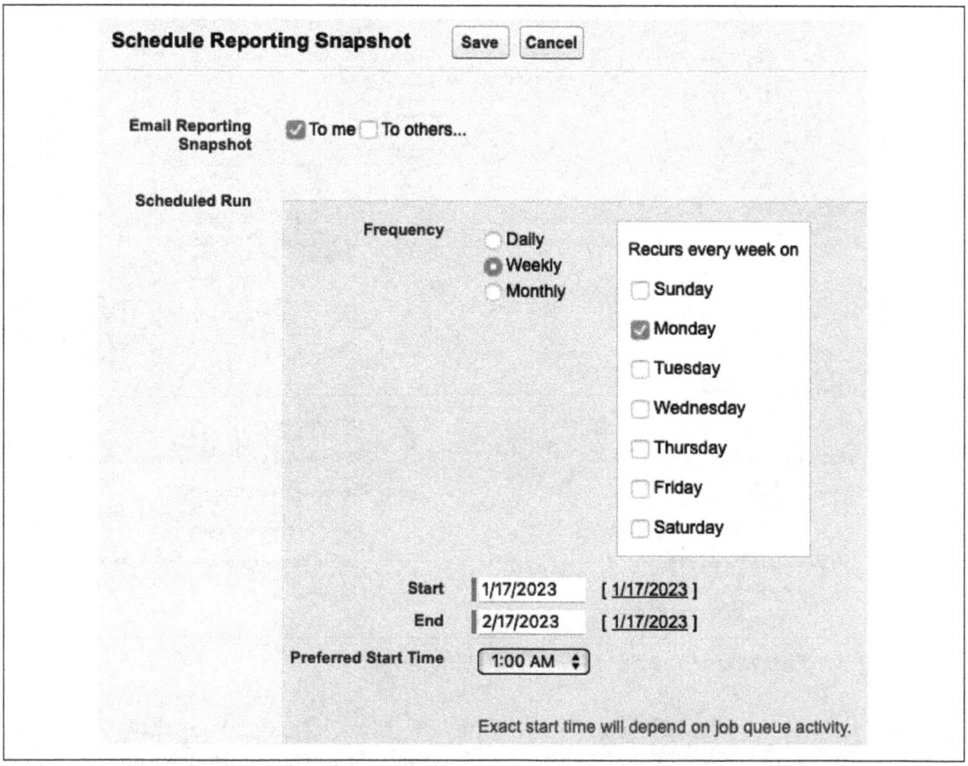

Figure 13-33. Schedule Snapshot screen

The default schedule for every new snapshot is for it to start today and end one month from now. Be sure to put the date way out, even years, into the future to safeguard future snapshot runs.

Time

The final ingredient for trending with a Reporting Snapshot is time. Some time has to go by for the snapshot to run and populate the custom object. Figure 13-34 shows a Reporting Snapshot after it has been set up and run a number of times.

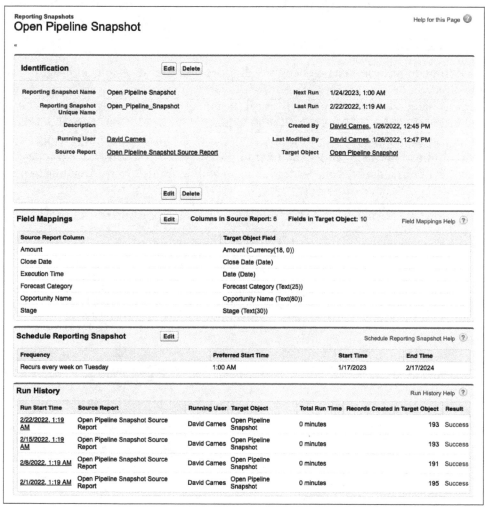

Figure 13-34. Reporting Snapshot settings

Because it is very difficult for anyone to report on an object that has no data, you will either need to wait some time for the snapshot to run or manufacture some data and ask a system administrator to upload it into your custom snapshot object using the data loader. This will allow you to create reports more easily.

Once the pieces are in place and some time has passed, you will be able to create reports and dashboards based on the data within the custom Snapshot object. By grouping on the Date field, which stores the date that the snapshot runs in each record, and the Stage field, and summing the Amount column, you will be able create the trend report shown in Figure 13-27.

Conclusion

Reporting on historical changes and trending are powerful ways to gain insights into the direction of your business. Salesforce provides a number of tools to support this, such as standard report types, Historical Trending, and Reporting snapshots. It is important to understand the benefits and requirements for each one to best put them to use. Some of these tools are available right out of the box, while others require system administrator help, and some time to go by, before you can take advantage of them. Without a doubt, your leadership team will be thrilled to see trending appear on your reports and dashboards.

The next chapter will introduce some final thoughts on reporting in Salesforce.

CHAPTER 14

Final Thoughts

You've covered a lot of ground in this book. Let's recap what you learned. You started with an overview of Salesforce reports and dashboards and their use cases across departments. Then you learned foundational knowledge of Salesforce's data model, permissions, and reporting concepts. From there you stepped into an overview of reports and then on to using the report builder. You even saw how formulas extend your abilities to solve reporting challenges.

Next, you dived into dashboards and saw how to create them. You learned how to organize reports and dashboards into folders and how to use folders to control access to them. Then you saw how the new Analytics tab has introduced a one-stop location for accessing reports and dashboards.

In the final chapters of this book, you saw how report types are the data foundation of reporting in Salesforce and how powerful they can be to create custom report types. You learned about the importance and use cases of embedded analytics and mobile analytics. Finally, you also discovered the power of trending and the many ways you can accomplish it in the system.

You've come to the end of the book, and you're now well equipped to tackle Salesforce reporting. I know you're excited to apply what you've learned, but don't run off just yet. There are a few more things you should know that will help you continue your learning journey and set you up for continued success.

Continue Your Learning Journey

Although you've learned a lot about Salesforce reports and dashboards in this book, things are still changing on the platform. In reality, given the pace of innovation, you really need to keep learning to stay on top of best practices and the regular changes to functionality.

A free resource for learning new skills is Salesforce's Trailhead (*https://trailhead.sales force.com*). There you can earn globally recognized credentials and connect with the Salesforce community around the world.

As a training resource, Trailhead tracks your progress as you complete modules, awarding points, badges, and levels for accurate quiz responses and correctly built reports and dashboards. For example, there's a Lightning Experience Reports and Dashboards super badge you could earn by completing a multihour project building out basic reports and dashboards.

When learning on Trailhead, you'll have access to free Trailhead playgrounds, which are private Salesforce environments ready to go with sample data. This is great if you want to experiment on your own.

Although you can learn a lot on your own, you can also tap into the vast knowledge of the global Salesforce community. There are currently more than one thousand Salesforce user groups worldwide. These groups are organized geographically and by area of interest, and are searchable via Trailblazer Community Groups (*https:// oreil.ly/gkf6f*). The odds are good that there is a Salesforce admin user group or non-profit user group in your area. Either of these types of groups will occasionally offer meetings focused on reporting. These meetings are also places where you are more likely to find others with the same interest in reporting.

The Salesforce community also has more than 30 volunteer-driven events, often with names containing "dreamin," such as Northeast Dreamin'. These events are run annu-ally in their geographies over one or two days and offered at a nominal cost. Speakers from around the world lead sessions at these events on topics they are passionate about. It is common that a few sessions, including hands-on sessions, are focused on report-, dashboard-, and formula-related topics. You can see a list of community-driven events at Community Conferences (*https://oreil.ly/wKyBe*).

Salesforce hosts a number of higher-cost multiday events during the year, such as Dreamforce (*https://www.dreamforce.com*) and TrailblazerDX (*https://oreil.ly/LYpnz*), which offer report and dashboard content. There are also free one-day Salesforce World Tour events in major cities, such as New York, London, Paris, and Sydney, where you will find speakers sharing reporting knowledge. You can find the upcom-ing schedule of global events at Salesforce Events (*https://www.salesforce.com/events*). Salesforce's various teams also provide a variety of useful content virtually on their Salesforce+ (*https://www.salesforce.com/plus*) platform, admin evangelist team pre-sentations, and customer success webinars.

Places to Go for Help

While on Salesforce's Trailhead site, you can also join the Reports and Dashboards group, with over five thousand members worldwide sharing ideas and challenges with each other. To see the list of groups, log in to Trailhead (*https://trailhead.salesforce.com*), expand the Community heading, and click on Groups. While on the Groups page, you can search for the Reports and Dashboards group. Figure 14-1 shows the top of the group, with its Discussion, Members, and Files & Photos subtabs. You can scroll through or search the feed for specific topics that you are interested in. You can also use the "Ask a question" feature to post details and a screenshot about a challenge you are facing to see what group members think. Most posts have multiple responses by people within the Salesforce community who are willing to try to understand your situation and offer helpful tips toward resolution.

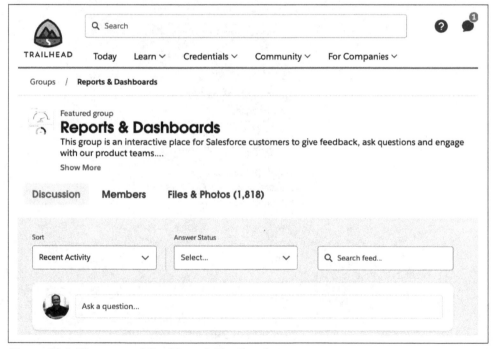

Figure 14-1. Reports and Dashboards Trailhead group

Stay on Top of Releases

Tucked into Salesforce's three releases each year are enhancements and other changes to report and dashboard functionality. You can find the often five- to six-hundred-page notes for each new release within Salesforce's Help documentation or through a simple web search for "Salesforce release notes." There is usually a one- or two-page description for each new feature with a screenshot and indication whether it is in beta or generally available, along with guidance on whether the feature needs to be activated and how. Figure 14-2 lists out enhancements for the Spring '23 release. You will find them in the release notes contents by drilling down into Analytics and then Reports and Dashboards.

Figure 14-2. Release note enhancements

In the two months leading up to each release, Salesforce makes special "prerelease orgs" available, and about a week later publishes the release notes. An org is just the common name for a Salesforce instance, so these provide a temporary instance of Salesforce you can log in to to try out the new features. In the weeks leading up to each release, Salesforce also makes a sandbox preview available with the new features to allow you to test them in your environment before they go into production. Look for "Release Readiness" webinars offered by Salesforce's admin evangelist team at Salesforce Admins Release Resources (*https://oreil.ly/uYgbm*) at the time of each release. There you will see demos of new functionality and other release materials.

Next you'll learn about the power of combining reporting features.

The Power of Combining Features

When working on reporting, it is not unusual to get stuck when you're unsure how to achieve a particular data visualization or reporting goal. In this book, you've learned about a variety of individual features and how to use them. One concept to remember is that it is often through the combination of features that we can reach new heights in reporting.

One example of combining features came when someone shared that they wanted to filter their past sales on a dashboard by the month in which each sale came in. One unusual aspect about the request was that they didn't care which year, but instead wanted to see data in a particular month, across what could be multiple years. Attempting to solve this directly using a dashboard filter doesn't work, as filters don't support using text on dates in that way. With some tinkering, the idea of using a row-level formula on the source report to convert the month of the close date field into text, such as "January," "February," and so on, came to mind. Figure 14-3 shows the simple row-level formula.

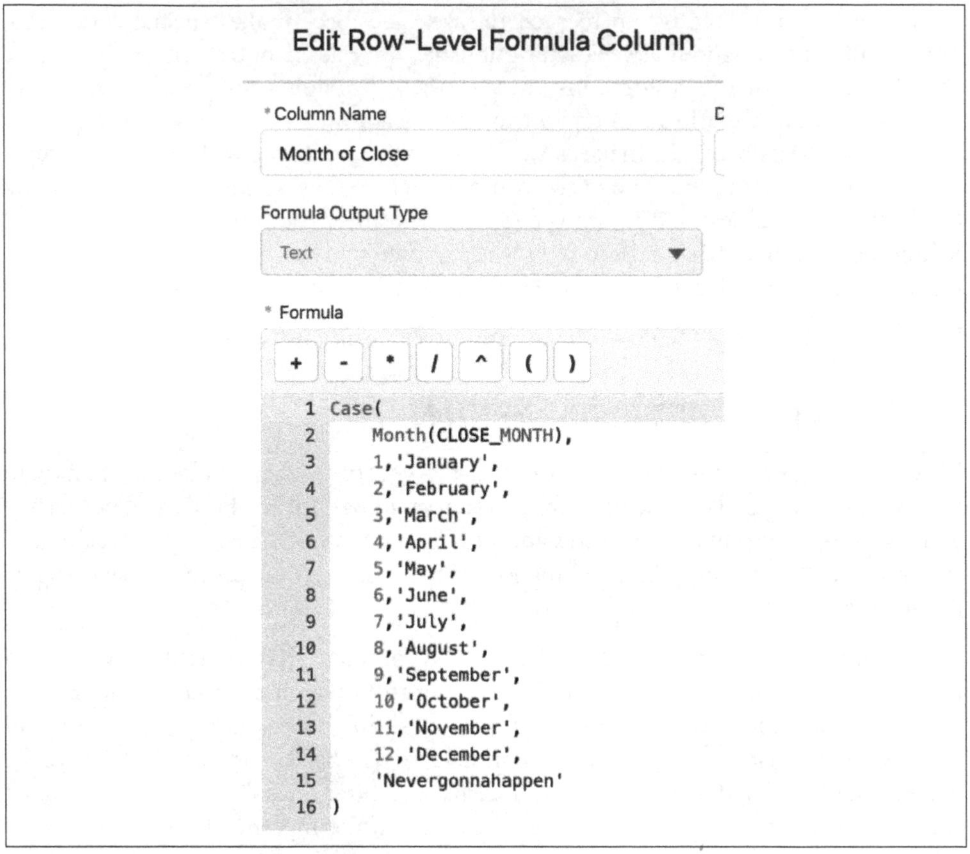

Figure 14-3. Month of Close formula

With the source report updated in that way, a filter could be added to the dashboard using the words for each month to isolate the appropriate opportunities. In Figure 14-4, you can see the dashboard filtered on the Month of Close formula, with March selected. The results show a lightning table with the Month of Close column displayed to confirm the correct results.

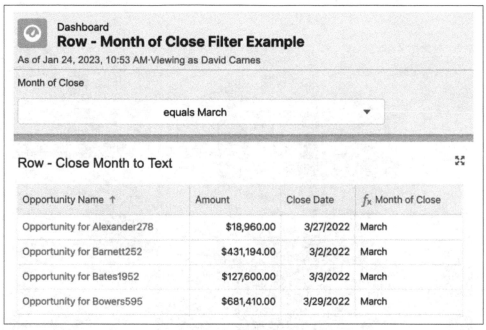

Figure 14-4. Row-level formula feeding dashboard filter

Sometimes it is helpful to take a step back from a challenge you are facing and review the basic tools available for combinations that might give you a chance. Formulas, custom report types, joined reports, lightning tables, and dashboard filters are among the powerful features that yield more options through combinations.

Practice Makes Perfect

Like many things in life, when talking about Salesforce reporting, practice makes perfect. There is likely nothing stopping you from cloning any report or dashboard you can see, and working on ways to improve the copy within your own private folders. Does it meet its business goal or purpose? Are there ways you can present the information more effectively? Could the information be grouped differently? Are there extraneous data points that are noise when considering the goal of the report or dashboard you are looking at?

When adding a component to a dashboard, you can try out a few different chart types and compare them side by side. To emphasize this point, Figure 14-5 shows the top half of an entire dashboard built using the same source report over and over. By engaging in this kind of play, you can start learning what types of components present information best in a given circumstance. You can also realize that it is perfectly normal to use one source report in a few different ways on the same dashboard, as shown by the funnel, gauge, metrics, and bar chart.

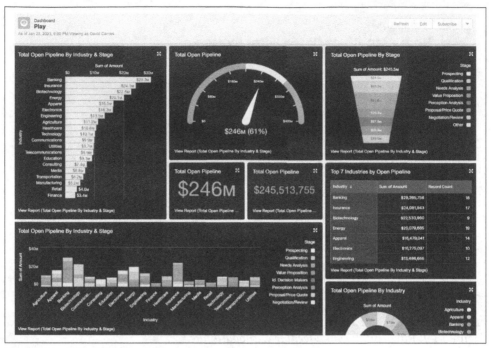

Figure 14-5. Play dashboard

Conclusion

You covered a lot of ground in this book on Salesforce reports and dashboards. Hopefully you've been inspired by the power of the tools to take advantage of them in your own reporting journey. Remember to keep learning, pay attention to releases, and be willing to play to achieve your reporting goals.

Should you wish to find me online, there are a few places you can look. Dashboard Dōjō (*https://www.dashboarddojo.com*) is a group I founded in 2020 to gather people together once or twice a month to study report and dashboard topics together. To learn about me, you can check out my LinkedIn profile (*https://www.linkedin.com/in/davidpcarnes3*). I also try to stay active posting thoughts and observations on Salesforce reporting at my Twitter profile (*https://twitter.com/davidpcarnes3*).

Index